MADELEINE

Helen Trinca has co-written two previous books: *Waterfront: The Battle that Changed Australia* and *Better than Sex: How a Whole Generation Got Hooked on Work*. She has held senior reporting and editing roles in Australian journalism, including a stint as the *Australian*'s London correspondent, and is currently managing editor of the *Australian*.

MADELEINE

A LIFE OF MADELEINE ST JOHN

~~HELEN TRINCA~~

To Im
All with good wishes.
Helen

TEXT PUBLISHING MELBOURNE AUSTRALIA

Photographs supplied by: Felicity Baker: Madeleine and Chris; Madeleine at Swinbrook Road; Madeleine with Puck, by Felicity Baker. Florence Heller: Madeleine in London, by Frank Heller. Nicole Richardson: Feiga and Jean Cargher; Sylvette in Sydney; Ted and Sylvette with John and Margaret Minchin; Ted with baby Madeleine; Madeleine with Sylvette and Ted; Madeleine and Colette 'smiling for the camera'. Deidre Rubenstein: Madeleine with Swami-ji. *Sydney Morning Herald*: 'The Octopus' at *Honi Soit*, by B. Newberry/Fairfax Syndications. Madeleine in 1998, by Jerry Bauer. St John family, by Margaret Michaelis. Cover photo: Madeleine in the snow in Trafalgar Square, 1968, by Daniels McLean.

textpublishing.com.au

The Text Publishing Company
Swann House
22 William Street
Melbourne Victoria 3000
Australia

First published by The Text Publishing Company, 2013.
Reprinted 2013

Cover and page design by W. H. Chong
Index by Nikki Davis
Typeset by J&M Typesetters

Printed and bound in Australia by Griffin Press

National Library of Australia Cataloguing-in-Publication
Author: Trinca, Helen.
Title: Madeleine : a life of Madeleine St. John / by Helen Trinca.
ISBN: 9781921922848 (pbk.)
ISBN: 9781921961137 (eBook)
Subjects: St John, Madeleine, 1941–2006.
Authors, Australian—Biography.
Dewey Number: A823.3

This book is printed on paper certified against the Forest Stewardship Council® Standards. Griffin Press holds FSC chain-of-custody certification SGS-COC-005088. FSC promotes environmentally responsible, socially beneficial and economically viable management of the world's forests.

for Ian Carroll
1946–2011

CONTENTS

A Night to Remember

The Booker Prize dinner in London's Guildhall is a flash affair. The wine flows as hundreds of publishers, authors, agents and critics crowd around their tables to hear which book has won the award for the best novel of the year from the British Commonwealth and Ireland. There is glamour, gossip and apprehension. The Booker brings prize money, but the real value comes from the cachet, which translates to sales and profile. Someone's life will change tonight.

In October 1997, a birdlike woman, Madeleine St John, was perched at one of the Guildhall tables. Her third novel, *The Essence of the Thing*, was on the shortlist. St John had struggled for decades to survive in London—she was financially and physically stretched, already suffering from the emphysema that would claim her life. Scarcely known by the literary critics, she had enjoyed plenty of attention since the nomination, with journalists trooping up the stairs to her Notting Hill council flat for interviews.

At home, a surprised media reclaimed her as the first Australian woman shortlisted for the Booker. St John was furious. She had spent her life reinventing herself and avoiding the Australian tag, even taking British citizenship in 1995. All but one of her novels catalogued the lives of inner London's professional class, not the bush and the beach. The last thing she wanted to be was Australian. But as the Channel 4 cameras panned across the Guildhall and millions of Britons watched the event live, Melvyn Bragg announced St John was from Australia.

The bookmakers had her as the outsider at eight to one, but writer A. S. Byatt told Channel 4 that *The Essence of the Thing* was the novel that excited her above the others. St John was nervous but hopeful of what the night would bring. Winning the Booker would be a vindication of the choices made a lifetime ago, proof to the extended St John clan, whom she loved and loathed, that she had succeeded in spite of them. The sweetest victory of all would be over her father, Edward St John—politician, barrister and pillar of the community. Ted had died in 1994, but his daughter still had scores to settle.

CHAPTER ONE

A War Baby

Madeleine St John was a war baby, conceived after her father signed up for service and born five months after he was shipped out with the AIF to Palestine. Ted St John did not know that his wife was pregnant when he left. Indeed, Sylvette St John appeared to have been unaware she was carrying a child until five months into the pregnancy.[1] She scarcely had time to get used to the idea before her baby was born, two months premature, at 8.40 p.m. on 12 November 1941, at the King George V Memorial Hospital for Mothers and Babies in Sydney's inner-suburban Camperdown. The baby weighed just 4lb 2oz. When news of the birth reached him in the Middle East, Ted knocked on the door of a convent of French nuns in Bethlehem and bought from them a tiny lace collar as a gift for his firstborn.[2]

Back in Sydney, Sylvette, who had come to Australia from Paris just before the war, registered her daughter as Mireille. Mother and baby spent a few days at a specialist Tresillian centre, the custom after a premature birth, before going home to the flat at 22a New South Head Road, Vaucluse, which Sylvette shared with her parents and her teenage sister Josette. It was not quite the perfect start for the baby girl: an absent father and a mother who had been in denial for months before her birth and who seemed unable to decide on the name. Mireille remained on her birth certificate but she was called Madeleine almost from the start.[3]

Yet Madeleine's babyhood was not unusual. Normal life had been on hold since Prime Minister Robert Menzies took Australia into the war against Hitler on 3 September 1939. Children across the country were being reared by their mothers and extended families and friends.

Ted enlisted as soon as he finished his law degree. He was an impatient young man who was desperate for 'some kind of an adventure', but his parents persuaded him to qualify first.[4] By the time he signed up at the Victoria Barracks in Paddington on 25 May 1940, he was working as a judge's associate. Ted was excited about the war but he must have had mixed emotions: he was in love, infatuated even, with the young Frenchwoman he had met through mutual friends in a Sydney restaurant.

Sylvette Cargher was not part of Ted's university crowd. She was more exotic and stylish than the young women he mixed with in the city. She was small, with dark hair and eyes, distinctive rather than beautiful, unlike the robust, fair-haired, sunburnt girls Ted had known in the bush where he had grown up. He was drawn to the young European woman who seemed so worldly with her deep voice and accented English, even though she lacked the formal education of his circle.

The St Johns were from a proud ecclesiastical family with a lineage detailed in those bibles of class stratification, *Debrett's Peerage & Baronetage* and *Burke's Peerage*. Ted's grandfather Henry arrived in Australia from England in 1869 'rather conscious of his family tradition, to make his fortune in NSW'.[5] He did not make his fortune but he left his mark. His eldest son, Frederick de Porte St John, Ted's father, was born in 1879 and grew into an excellent horseman who seemed destined to be a farmer. But a wealthy clergyman cousin in England sent money to Australia and Frederick, along with his younger brother Henry, was enrolled at St John's Theological College in Armidale.[6] The brothers spent their lives as Church of England pastors, with Frederick ministering to bush towns throughout the Liverpool Plains and New England.

Frederick was an imposing and handsome man and he cut a fine figure as he galloped on horseback to tend to his scattered congregation. He married Hannah Phoebe Mabel Pyrke in 1908, and the couple lived first at Boggabri, where Ted, their fifth child, was born, on 15 August 1916. The family moved soon after to Uralla and stayed there for sixteen years before moving to Quirindi in 1932 when Ted was a teenager.

Life was tough. In the 1930s depression, the family often sat down to an evening meal of bread and one boiled egg. Frederick always got the egg and his children took it in turns to get the very top of the egg as he sliced it open.[7] Despite his genial public face, Frederick often beat his children, especially the boys. While Hannah was usually the one who ordered the strapping, she always regretted the way her children were 'thrashed so savagely'. Her life with Frederick was not always easy, and by the time Ted was a young man his parents' relationship had deteriorated.[8]

The poverty of a rural vicarage was alleviated only somewhat by the St Johns' sense of being special, with a heritage stretching back to the sixteenth-century Baron St John of Bletso and a succession of Bolingbroke earls. Australian society accorded clergymen and their families a certain deference, but the St Johns were stuck halfway between the aristocrats of early twentieth-century Australia—the squattocracy—and the wage earners of the country towns.

The St Johns created their own small social group 'without being able to feel a complete identification with any of the other groups' in the country towns where they lived. It was a world in which you hung on tightly to the things that marked you out.[9] In the St Johns' case that was intellect, education and a belief that while they could never afford to visit England they were still entitled to call it home. Ted's older brother, Roland, recalled that the children read their way through the Arthur Mee encyclopaedia in the long, cold winter evenings in the bush. It was their 'window onto the world'.[10] Their parents encouraged them to consider high achievement as their destiny as well as their duty.

Hannah devoured copies of *Grit*, a popular American magazine that focused on building patriotic, religious and family values.[11] She was convinced that Ted would achieve great things. He was a good-looking, bright, lively and confident child, and he had been a brilliant student at Armidale High School. But he almost missed out on university because of a lack of funds. In the end a university grant, known as an exhibition, paid his fees, and a scholarship and bursary covered his living costs at St Paul's College at the University of Sydney.

In his second year of law he met fellow student Gough Whitlam. The two became friends, and remained friends even after they moved into legal firms in the city. Ted loved the legal life. He came to know John Kerr, a young lawyer already demonstrating the intelligence that would take him to the highest level of power in Australia.[12]

The St Johns had a sense of security about their place in Australia. Not so the Carghers, the newcomers who were expected to adopt the customs of the dominant class and culture. Sylvette's parents were Jews from one of Romania's biggest cities, Jassy, in Moldavia, but both left their families as teenagers and travelled alone to newly industrialised Paris, which offered work and a measure of safety.

Sylvette's father Yancu, or Yaakov, was the son of a rabbi, but in France he quickly shed his religion and presented himself as a Frenchman named Jean Meer Cargher. He worked in weapons and aircraft manufacturing during the First World War and learned metalwork. On 30 September 1916, at the age of twenty-four, he married twenty-three-year-old Feica Avram, a machinist in the clothing trade.[13] She was scarcely five feet tall, dark-haired with brown eyes and always elegantly dressed. Feica could barely read or write, but she had a good eye and a sense of style that made her an excellent seamstress.[14]

Sylvette was their first child, born on 19 August 1917. They had a son, Leon, who died from meningitis in 1921 at the age of two, and a second daughter, Josette, born in 1926. Jean was successful in Paris, setting up the Cargher & Leibovitz metalwork shop and producing cots and baby cradles at 7 Passage St-Bernard, close to the Bastille Metro. Madeleine St John was well into her sixties before she discovered that her grandfather was 'no more French than I am'.[15]

Sylvette, almost a decade older than Josette, was spoilt by her parents and was 'made much of by her family in contrast to her younger sister'.[16] But Cargher & Leibovitz struck financial trouble and Jean began to worry about the political tensions in Europe. He convinced his wife, now known as Feiga, that Australia was the answer and that he should head for Sydney, with the rest of the family to follow.

The details of his immigration are unclear. Madeleine always believed that her grandfather and Sylvette arrived in Sydney together in the mid-1930s, and that her grandmother and Josette followed a couple of years later. But the records suggest Jean came to Australia alone in 1929, arriving on the S.S. *Orama* on 29 August.[17] Left alone in Paris with twelve-year-old Sylvette and three-year-old Josette, Feiga worked as a dressmaker.

Sylvette saw her future in Australia. In 1934, not yet seventeen, she went to Marseilles to board the French packet boat, the *Cephee*. She had given her profession as typist and indicated she was going to settle in Victoria, but she did not disembark when the ship arrived in Melbourne on 3 June.[18] In Sydney, five days later, and with a knowledge of English acquired during the two-month journey, Sylvette reunited with the father she had not seen for five years. Feiga went into business in Paris running an *atelier de couture*.

In Sydney, Jean worked as a dealer in second-hand clothes, with a shop in Oxford Street, and father and daughter moved into a two-bedroom flat in Wallaroy Road, Woollahra. Sylvette helped in the shop, found work selling cosmetics for Helena Rubinstein, and gave French lessons. She advertised in the *Sydney Morning Herald*: 'French taught by cultured French young lady. Beginners or advanced pupils.'[19]

Two and a half years later, on 3 December 1936, Jean and Sylvette welcomed Feiga and ten-year-old Josette to Australia, and the Carghers settled into life in pre-war Sydney, where the locals were more indifferent than unkind to the migrants in their midst.

Australia was still a predominantly British society. The Carghers had all but erased their Romanian origins in Paris, but now they had to adjust again. Jews were often regarded with suspicion, but the Carghers had left the synagogue behind and they spent little time practising their faith in Sydney.[20] Feiga was well turned out and vivacious, and her neighbours quickly granted her a special status, calling her Madame. Sylvette had already established a group of friends, some of whom lived in Kings Cross and Potts Point—the bohemian quarter where actors like the young Peter Finch hung out. Perhaps it was due to one of these contacts that Sylvette had a small article published in the *Sydney Morning Herald* on 22 June 1937. Under the byline Sylvette Cargier, she wrote about Romanian students living in the Latin Quarter in Paris. The article suggested first-hand experience: 'A Rumanian girl attending the Paris University explained to me…' she wrote.[21]

Ted and Sylvette met in 1939. Sylvette was the girlfriend of Paul Lawrence, a lawyer a little older than Ted. In August, she and Paul took part in a debate at St Catherine's School in Waverley, where two of Ted's younger sisters, Florence and Pamela, were boarders. Ted was a skilled debater and was friendly with the school's headmistress, Isabel James, who was keen to expand the horizons of her young charges.

Sylvette proved to be the star attraction at the informal dinner party held in the school's new domestic-science room before the debate, which was chaired by Gough Whitlam. Cadet journalist Ria Counsell, who was there that night, recalled: 'Ted was fascinated with Sylvette. She was charming.' Ted's sisters noted her smart clothes and perfect makeup. She was different.[22] But Sylvette seemed cautious and 'was not such a willing participant at that stage'. Ria thought her very conscious of the class difference between them, but Ted won out and soon he and Sylvette were much more than friendly debating rivals.[23] Ted and Gough sometimes swung by the Carghers' flat to collect Sylvette for a drive,[24] and Ted called her his 'sweet Sylvette'.[25] By the early months of 1940, he was insisting he wanted to marry her.

This prospect caused a crisis at the vicarage: Sylvette was not seen as a suitable wife for Ted, and Frederick and Hannah made the 450-kilometre journey down to Sydney to talk their son out of the marriage. But Ted was stubborn and prevailed, and Frederick performed the nuptials in his own parish church of St Alban's at Quirindi. It was 3 August 1940, ten weeks after Ted had enlisted in the AIF. He moved in with his new wife and in-laws to their two-bedroom flat in New South Head Road. The Carghers, regarded as 'enemy aliens' by the authorities, had recently moved there from Wallaroy Road after obtaining permission from the local police station.[26]

Ted was pleased with his new family. He was a man of below average height but he towered over the Carghers—Sylvette was even shorter than her mother, at four feet, ten inches—and was a powerful physical and emotional presence in their lives. He was their bridge to the new world of Australia. Sylvette had married 'in' as well as 'up'.

The Carghers had juggled multiple identities—Romanian, Jewish and French—but the next generation would be part of the new fabric. Madeleine St John would be Australian.

CHAPTER TWO

'Pickled in Love'

W hen she looked back on her childhood, Madeleine claimed she had been 'pickled in love' as a baby.[1] At the flat in New South Head Road, her Cargher grandparents and her teenage aunt doted on the new addition to the household. But her father was largely absent in those early years.

Ted had hung about in Sydney for months after his enlistment and marriage in 1940, waiting for his artillery unit to join the fight in the Middle East. When he was finally shipped out, Sylvette was once again a free agent in a town that quickly adapted to wartime. She was a charmer who loved good perfume, parties and conversation, and her Parisian provenance went down well. In her crowd, it was accepted that even married women would flirt a little. A friend from that time, Lorna Harvey, recalled: 'It was more or less a habit; people paired off. No one worried about it, it was very common.'[2]

But Sylvette resented Ted's absence and she missed Paris. After Madeleine's birth she complained bitterly to Henriette Pile, a young Frenchwoman married to Sydney lawyer Marcel Pile. The two women enjoyed speaking their native language and Sylvette sometimes visited the Piles at Cremorne. Henriette liked Sylvette immensely and, for Sylvette, the friendship was a link with her past.[3]

Around March 1942, when Madeleine was about six months old and Ted was still in the Middle East, Sylvette was ordered by her parents-in-law to decamp from Sydney to the vicarage at Quirindi. War had come to the Pacific and, in February 1942, the Japanese mounted air raids on Darwin. There was panic in Sydney and those who could fled to the bush or the mountains.

Sylvette was unhappy in Quirindi, bored by the routines of the vicarage and the small country town. Ted's sister Margaret was also at the vicarage. She was expecting her first child, and her husband, John Minchin, wrote to her daily. The arrival of the post was a torture for Sylvette, who rarely received a letter from Ted.

Sylvette was unsettled, but Madeleine did not lack attention: Margaret and her younger sister Pam doted on her. After John spent a weekend at Quirindi he told Margaret that he could only hope that 'our baby is as good and happy' as Madeleine.[4]

Life at the vicarage was comfortable but mundane. Sylvette joined other women in aeroplane spotting from a headquarters at the local bowling green.[5] But she resisted outings and seemed sulky and lazy, and she was thin and refused to eat, so much so that Hannah became concerned.[6] When a local Quirindi man came home on leave, Sylvette was so upset by the comparison with Ted's absence that she scarcely spoke. She was always beautifully groomed and made-up in Sydney, but she let herself go in the country, tying her hair up in a scarf, and wearing safety pins for Madeleine's nappies in her dress. She 'gets around all day with no makeup and no stockings and doesn't do her hair', Margaret wrote to John. One day, Margaret threatened to take a photo of Sylvette and send it to Ted. 'The next day you could not see her for the war paint,' Margaret reported to her husband.[7]

By November, when Madeleine celebrated her first birthday,

mother and daughter were back in the city amid the familiar warmth of the Cargher household and her friends. Sylvette was part of a Sydney set dominated by war wives who swapped and stretched their rations. Margaret Whitlam, whose husband Gough was also away, found those war years 'hard and [yet] not hard'.[8] Women with children were far from isolated. Every afternoon, they met and pushed their prams through the local streets. The pram brigades staved off loneliness and built camaraderie among the women.

In Palestine, Ted was restless and frustrated that his anti-aircraft unit had seen no action, and he transferred out of artillery to the Australian Army Legal Corps. On 27 February 1943, he came home on leave and saw his daughter, now fifteen months old, for the first time. The photographs show a delighted Ted and a smiling baby.

Soon Sylvette was pregnant, but she miscarried. And before long she was on her own again: Ted was moved to Queensland to train for an amphibious assault against the Japanese in New Guinea. In August, his unit was shipped to Milne Bay and he joined the invasion force to Finschafen before marching back down to Lae. Ted felt he had got closer to real action in six months in the legal corps in New Guinea than he ever had in the artillery.[9]

Back home, Sylvette was restless. With two-year-old Madeleine she moved out of her parents' flat to Mosman, on the northern shores of the harbour.[10] The accommodation was basic, but Sylvette was free to run her own life. She lived with Alicia Walsh, known as Lic, a forthright kindergarten teacher who had played cricket for Australia and toured England with the women's team in 1937.[11] By February 1944, Ted was back in Australia, but his re-entry into the family was not without drama. Madeleine was wary. One day he pushed her higher and higher in a swing: he laughed when she screamed, and the incident remained lodged in her memory.[12]

Ted was still in the army, working now as a legal officer at the Victoria Barracks in Paddington, but he was home for good, and he and Sylvette looked forward to building the married life that they had never really begun.

It was time to leave Lic's crowded Mosman flat and move back across the bridge. But to where? Residential building was at a standstill during the war and everyone was scrambling for accommodation. Somehow Ted talked his way into rooms at the rambling old artists' colony called Merioola in Woollahra. The house is long gone, but for a time in the 1940s and 1950s it was famous for its avant-garde tenants and its landlady, the redoubtable Chica Lowe. Lowe and her husband did not own the double-storey mansion, but from 1941 they lived in the mews stables out the back and ran Merioola as a rooming house, choosing their tenants carefully from young dancers, painters, writers and people working in the theatre as well as professionals, like Ted, who at least had enough money to pay the rent.

Sylvette, Ted, Madeleine and new baby Colette, born two days before Christmas in 1944, crammed into one room and a closed-in verandah on the ground floor and shared a kitchen and bathroom with others. Sylvette was busy with her young children, but she had the support of Valerie 'Pom' Stillwell, whom she had known for several years when they were single women and who had also moved to Merioola, and Lorna Harvey, who was married to artist Edmund Arthur Harvey.

The young wives burned the milk, spread out their blankets on Merioola's sweeping lawns and had fun. Lorna and Sylvette took turns taking their toddlers to St Mark's kindergarten in nearby Darling Point. Madeleine was very young for the kindy and she did not enjoy her time there but she had extended family close by—two slightly older cousins, Richard and Felicity Baker, were also at St Mark's. They lived with their mother, Marion—Ted's sister—in a rented flat in New South Head Road. Often Marion would do the afternoon run from the kindergarten, collecting all three children, walking them up to the tram stop and delivering Madeleine back to Sylvette at Merioola. Sometimes she would stop for a cup of tea and a gossip with her sister-in-law.[13]

Madeleine, with her thick red curls, was a dazzling child, but Sylvette's focus was on baby Colette—the blue-eyed blonde.[14] Looking back, Madeleine said that her baby sister was far cuter than she was. Even so, she felt secure:

> I am sure that my ego was so well established...I had engulfing adoration from grandparents, especially from my grandmother, and my father at that stage just adored me, thought I was the cat's whiskers. Not that he didn't adore Colette, but really, I was so well pickled in love that I didn't need to feel that my territory was taken up.[15]

Ted paid his eldest daughter a great deal of attention and set about introducing her to the literature he loved, reading to her every night from the greats, including Dickens and Shakespeare. He relished the artistic atmosphere of the boarding house, where the tenants included people like Loudon Sainthill, the theatre designer, and his partner, writer and critic Harry Tatlock Miller. Merioola was always full of visitors. Dancers would pose for sculptor Arthur Fleischmann and photographer Alec Murray; artists painted sets for impromptu theatrical performances.[16]

Ted had missed out on years with his young family, but at least he was alive. His dear friend and Madeleine's godfather, Ian Sly, who had enlisted with him on the same day, was shot by a Japanese sniper in New Guinea in October 1943. Soon Ted was busy with his new life as a civilian: he had returned to his old job as a judge's associate, but eventually he took the gamble and launched himself at the bar.[17] He had no money, but he had connections and enthusiasm.

The war had made Ted more serious in outlook, and Merioola began to seem frivolous and unsuitable. Around the middle of 1946, in a somewhat peremptory fashion and without consulting his wife, Ted moved the family to semi-rural Ryde, about thirty kilometres to the north-west. It was a disastrous decision. Sylvette and the children were isolated. And there was the matter of style. 'It was unspeakable,' Madeleine recalled. 'Ryde, bloody Ryde! My mother would know that one and a half rooms in Woollahra was a better bet than five rooms in Ryde. [It was] a thousand miles from anywhere.'[18] Worse still, Madeleine was bullied at the local state school. Her wild red hair, pale skin and unusual demeanour set her apart. In the end Sylvette kept her at home.

Sylvette had found motherhood a challenge at Merioola, but Ryde threw her into a 'state of the most acute misery'. Two-year-old Colette was 'absolutely impossible' and Sylvette was often 'in an extreme state of irritation and depression'. Ryde proved too much for everyone and within six months the experiment was over. The St Johns moved back across the bridge and into a rented first-floor flat in Watsons Bay. It had a wonderful view of the harbour. 'You have to be by the water, it is part of your consciousness,' Madeleine recalled.[19] The flat was a fifteen-minute walk from the Carghers in New South Head Road. Sylvette was back on familiar turf and the world was back on its axis. The family entered a period of relative happiness. Madeleine and Colette saw their maternal grandparents almost every day and the couple lavished attention and gifts on the little girls. Their futures, growing up in Australia, gave meaning to the Carghers' decision to leave Paris.

But there was already tension between Sylvette and Ted. Now he was focused on the bar and he took a hard line towards the wife he felt was spending too much of his money. He set up an account at David Jones so that Sylvette could shop but he could track her spending. Around this time, Sylvette bought a copy of a Christian Dior 'New Look' suit. She wore it for years and it would take on an almost iconic status for Madeleine.

Ted's control of the purse strings was not the only cause of tension. Sylvette had always been able to tease him out of his tendency to become pompous, but after the war she could not stop herself from mocking this more serious husband. It was a mistake. Ted was not averse to teasing others, but he was prickly. 'You had to take him extremely seriously and admire him,' Felicity Baker recalled.[20]

The Whitlams and the St Johns were still friendly. Gough and Margaret were living temporarily with Margaret's parents in Vaucluse, while their house was being built down south in the newly developing beach suburb of Cronulla. The two young mothers subscribed to American magazines—*House and Garden* and *Ladies Home Journal*—and swapped copies regularly.[21]

Madeleine returned to school. She was enrolled at Edgeworth, a little private school in Vaucluse. Colette, three years younger, so missed Madeleine that she was granted permission to attend the school even though she was only two. In the afternoons, Colette would be put to bed in a dormitory for a nap.[22] The girls played with the Hill sisters, Catherine, Christine and Sue. And their mother Marion and Sylvette became close friends.

Madeleine showed her academic talents early. At the age of seven, according to her report for First Class in November 1948, she excelled in arithmetic, reading, spelling and phonics. Her storytelling was 'very good', her voice 'expressive' and she listened intelligently to the radio. She had also made a good beginning with composition. Headmistress Mary Hall noted that 'Madeleine's work is outstanding. She is thorough in detail but can be beautifully spontaneous in expression. A delightful pupil.'[23] Ted's habit of reading aloud to his daughters every night was paying off. But it was Sylvette who was the centre of Madeleine's existence.

At Merioola, Sylvette had focused on Colette; at Ryde, she had been preoccupied by her isolation. But at Watsons Bay mother and elder daughter were close. Madeleine recalled:

> After we moved to Watsons Bay and she was happier, I can remember outings that we had together and I felt this bond. [One day] we were on the tram and she was telling me about the uniform and she was terribly excited and I was thrilled to bits. She was telling me item by item what I would be getting for the private school, this colossal wardrobe, so I remember that we had—not a conspiracy—that we had a sort of joint enterprise and I felt that we had something together that we shared.[24]

CHAPTER THREE

Sylvette's Despair

Ted St John was proving to be a man of eclectic tastes; he had married an exotic French outsider, and he had hauled his little family to the bohemian Merioola boarding house. With the war over, he made another unexpected decision, buying land at Castlecrag on Sydney's Middle Harbour.

Sixty years ago Castlecrag was revolutionary, a place filled with political and cultural meaning for a certain group of aspirational young Australians. It represented modernity and liberalism and a post-war belief that professionals, artists and academics could forge a truly open community. The suburb was carved out of the bush by architects Walter Burley Griffin and Marion Mahony Griffin in the 1920s, but it had languished in the 1930s and 1940s. But after the war, many of the original planning constraints were lifted and word spread quickly of the land bargains to be had there. Ted's interest was sparked after his sister Margaret and her husband John Minchin bought a block at Castlecrag.

Ted had no funds and, with no money in his family, he turned to his in-laws. Sylvette's parents were not rich but they had recovered from the losses that forced them from Paris before the war, and they agreed to help with the deposit. By the end of 1948, Madeleine, now seven years old, found herself in a new house with a room of her own and, before long, piano lessons and a cocker-spaniel puppy.

Castlecrag was a very different world for Madeleine. Visits to her grandparents were less frequent, and she had a new school, East Lindfield Public, far bigger than the little private school of Edgeworth where she had done so well. East Lindfield meant a bus ride each way and a whole swag of new kids to get to know.

But it was Sylvette who faced the biggest challenge. Socialising in Castlecrag in the 1950s was about cocktail parties on each other's terraces, an obligatory mixing with the neighbours and, for the stay-at-home wives like Sylvette, empty afternoons in empty houses. Still, there were compensations. Some of the St Johns' friends from the eastern suburbs, among them Lorna and Edmund Harvey, also moved to Castlecrag, and Sylvette made new friends. It was a lively community. On weekends, adults partied as the kids ran freely in and out of the unlocked back doors and roamed along the edges of the harbour. Ingrid Relf, the same age as Madeleine, remembered long evenings when adults and kids would gather on the deck of her parents' house 'waiting for the southerly buster to come in, drinking beer and talking politics and literature, or books or music...'[1]

Sylvette missed Paris, but she found a number of European Jewish families who had settled at Castlecrag. She was particularly close to Friedel Souhami, a German woman who had arrived with her Jewish husband Manfred and daughter Renate in 1939 after fleeing Germany. The Souhamis bought one of the original 1920s Burley Griffin houses, and by the time the St Johns arrived, in 1948, they were local identities. The thick-set Friedel was a decade or more older than Sylvette but the women bonded quickly, and Sylvette, already seen as highly strung by her neighbours, often poured out her heart to Friedel.

But according to the standards of the time, Sylvette had nothing to complain about. She had a brand-new house with an open-plan living area and kitchen and lovely floors of local tallowwood, a husband making his way in the law, two pretty children and the freedom of not having to work to make ends meet. And the St Johns had a car—a maroon Vanguard—and enough money to decorate their modest home.

Built on the high side of the street, Number 9 The Rampart looked down to a gully and the harbour. The steep block had steps leading up to the front and side terraces made from local sandstone. A garage and playroom at the front was connected to the house with an internal stairway.

There were no fences between the houses in Castlecrag and few barriers between adults and children, who called their parents' friends by their first names and were encouraged to engage with other adults directly. Madeleine and Colette found friends close to home. Next door were Tina and Tonia Date. From the window in Tina's bedroom the four little girls could look down and spy on both sets of parents sipping cocktails on the St Johns' terrace.

The Dates were well known in the suburb. Albert Date was an economist who worked for the Rural Bank and later the Tariff Board. His wife Anita Aarons was a sculptor who used the garage at Number 7 as her studio. She was close to Sylvette but, unlike Friedel Souhami, was often impatient with her neighbour and less inclined to listen to her worries.

In the first couple of years at Castlecrag, the St John family held together. In 1949 Madeleine and Colette were all smiles when they were flower girls at their Aunt Josette's wedding to her teenage sweetheart Neville Jenkins. Their bouquets were made of gardenias and the perfume of the flowers drifted from one end of the marquee to the other.[2] It was a memorable and happy day, but there were strains in the St John marriage.

In 1950, Sylvette accused Ted of having an affair with a much older woman. When Sylvette offered to divorce him, Ted was alarmed.[3] Pom Stillwell thought Sylvette was wrong in her suspicions. She did not think Ted was the sort to have an affair, that the woman whom Sylvette had accused was Ted's confidante, not his lover.[4] Margaret Whitlam thought otherwise. She had no doubt Ted was having affairs with Castlecrag women. She recalled that Ted had made no secret of his interest in other women, indeed he 'almost boasted of it', and that this caused Sylvette considerable pain.[5]

There was a relaxed attitude generally to infidelity in the suburb. 'People knew about each other's affairs and there were affairs all over the place in the Crag,' Lorna Harvey said. She remembered Ted as a 'bit of a flirt. He was trying to flirt with me a bit. It was all the done thing to flirt.'[6] In later life, Madeleine never so much as hinted at having any notion that her father had been unfaithful—although she accused him of almost everything else. Colette recalled four or five women whom Ted knew and admired and with whom he had friendships in that period but she doubted her father had had an affair.[7]

Sylvette was witty, vivacious and charming. But she was also dissatisfied. She wanted more—more success for Ted, more parties, more of a leading role in fashion and society. Ted had done well at the bar but he believed Sylvette was disappointed he had not been a 'brilliant overnight success'. He was at a crucial stage of his career. His ambitions at the bar required serious work, and he struggled to understand his complicated wife. Sylvette kept the house clean and looked after the family well physically but not, in Ted's view, psychologically.[8] The tensions increased as his workload grew. Madeleine saw some of the arguments:

> I remember my mother saying [to Ted] if I only had one egg I would give it to my children but in your family if there was one egg, you would give it to the father, and my father denied it. But she was right, that was the way that family worked and it was the way my father expected his family to work.[9]

At other times, Madeleine saw Sylvette turn on the charm to try to lift Ted's mood. 'My mother must have been totally desperate,' she said.

> He would come home from work and she would have been slaving
> all day to keep the house and [put] wonderful food on the table and
> flowers in a vase and she gets this person who doesn't want to know
> [her] and sits like a stone and eats his dinner and you are chattering
> away and chattering away and trying to overcome this wall of silence
> and you are making more and more of a fool of yourself and finally
> the children go to bed and finally it's your bedtime and you have to
> get into bed with this block of concrete who doesn't want to talk to
> you…She must have felt, he doesn't love me anymore, he doesn't find
> me attractive anymore, he wants to throw me on the scrapheap.[10]

Sylvette had not been a particularly heavy drinker during the war, but as
the couple's marriage deteriorated, she began to drink. Madeleine recalled
her mother's behaviour and blamed her father:

> I think there were times when [Ted] would ring her up from his
> chambers or she would ring him and he would say something so
> horrific to her that she would have a few drinks or half a bottle to
> fortify herself or even more to blot out the whole of life. I think she
> was trying to be unconscious sometimes. I think unconsciousness was
> what she was after. She is trapped, she can't leave or she would be
> giving up her rights to the children. She is trapped in this situation,
> she can't fight and she can't flee. An animal in that situation would
> chew its leg off and I think that was what she was doing when she
> drank those dreadful potions—she was chewing her leg off.[11]

Ted was alarmed at the impact of Sylvette's drinking on the children.
When Madeleine chastised her intoxicated mother one night, saying, 'I
hate it when you talk in that silly way,' Ted was horrified.[12] One day he
came home to find Madeleine pinned against the wall, Sylvette slapping
her face and screaming at her.[13] On another occasion, Madeleine, just nine
years old, found her mother unconscious on the kitchen floor. When things
were particularly bad, Sylvette would shoo her daughters out of the house
and tell them to go next door to the Dates so they would not see her in

an intoxicated state.[14] But this was much worse. 'I ran straight out of the house and I can't remember where I went and what I did,' Madeleine recalled. 'It was my first inkling that something was very badly wrong.'[15]

Somehow, Madeleine and Colette continued with the business of childhood. Madeleine and Tina Date played Chopin duets on the piano and constructed elaborate fantasy games. The Date girls and the St John sisters were joined by Ingrid Relf. They called themselves the Famous Five and modelled their games on Enid Blyton stories. Mothers whistled up their children, running wild all day, as the dark set in.

Colette found Castlecrag an 'amazing place to live...We had Holocaust survivors living up there, we had schnitzel, we had dogs and fish and cats and the Dates had ducks, and we had the Castlecrag gullies.'[16] Creativity ruled. Colette was a born actor and a talented mimic. Madeleine was less of a performer but was very musical and had a natural eye, and she had plenty of encouragement to sketch and paint. Once Madeleine and Colette along with Tina and Tonia Date and Lorna's two children, Antony and Diana (Didy), put on a puppet show poking fun at the pretensions of a neighbour, artist Bernard Hesling. The adults loved it.[17]

Ted felt Sylvette was developing 'depressive and suicidal tendencies'.[18] His sister Florence felt he was desperately trying to 'contain the situation... he was at the bar and trying to be a success. Sylvette could not look after the children, she was not in a state to look after them.'[19]

The school holidays presented a particular problem. The family had often gone to the Blue Mountains for the May term break, but in 1950 Ted packed his wife and daughters off to his Aunt Lil's sheep station at Quirindi. Looking back, Madeleine thought Ted did it to save money: Sylvette could not spend up big at David Jones if she were in the country.

Sylvette, with her negative memories of the bush from the war years, was miserable, and the children were desperately bored by life at the station. The depression that had begun in Ryde in 1946 and hovered over Sylvette at Castlecrag worsened with her fury and frustration. One day, the misery was relieved when Madeleine and Colette found a rabbit. 'We were in raptures, we had this adorable bunny and we were perfectly ecstatic till it escaped the hutch and we were inconsolable.' The next day, Aunt Lil's adult son, Beau, announced he had found the rabbit—then he broke its neck. He thought it a terrific joke to pull on his city slicker cousins. Madeleine and Colette wept for days. Madeleine recalled the incident as an example of the St John family's lack of empathy, even though she conceded that Ted had been outraged when he learned what happened.[20]

By mid-1951, under pressure from Ted, Sylvette admitted she had a drinking problem and agreed to see a Macquarie Street physician. The visits continued for a year, but there was no improvement in her condition. Madeleine saw her mother in terrible states and realised she had 'been drinking or she'd been doing something to herself, [that] she wasn't well and [that] she smelt weird.' Colette was also aware something was wrong. One day, an inebriated Sylvette kicked the family cat, and Ted hurried the little girls up to Friedel Souhami's house for the night.[21]

The St John marriage was in crisis. The trouble was far worse than domestic rows or excessive drinking. Sylvette was suicidal. More than once, she tried to gas herself in the kitchen.[22] On one occasion, she tried to drown herself, and afterwards telephoned her husband to collect her, dripping wet, from the beach. Ted was not convinced these were serious suicide attempts, but he was at his wits' end with the deterioration in Sylvette's mental condition.[23]

In September 1952, Sylvette received her first course of electroconvulsive therapy as treatment for her depression.[24] ECT had been introduced in 1938, but it was not until the 1950s that the procedure, of inducing seizures by applying an electrical current to the brain, was widely used in Australian psychiatric hospitals. There was a severe stigma attached to 'shock treatment' and Sylvette begged Ted not to tell anyone she had received the therapy.[25]

ECT did not cure Sylvette's suicidal feelings. Two months later, in November 1952, she took an overdose of sedatives and was admitted to the Mater, the big general hospital on the North Shore. The link between her condition and her alcohol abuse was clear to doctors and she was transferred to Hydebrae in Strathfield, the first hospital in Australia to focus on the medical treatment of alcoholism. It was run by Dr Sylvester Minogue, a compassionate and influential psychiatrist who had launched Alcoholics Anonymous in Australia in 1945. During her three weeks at Hydebrae, Sylvette signed up to AA.

The St Johns traditionally spent Christmas holidays at Avoca Beach on the central coast of New South Wales, and it was there that Ted broke the news to Madeleine, aged eleven, that her absent mother was an alcoholic.

> My father decided one morning to wake me up at five o'clock and tell me quite brutally to get up and get dressed. I got dressed. I put on the clothes I had taken off the night before; there was a thin cotton dress I had been wearing with yellow and brown flowers on it, puffed sleeves. So I put this dress on and he told me to come out to the car. The leatherette-type seats were clammy and I wished I had a cardigan. So we drive straight to this cliff top and I was sure he would drive straight over the edge. He went right to the fucking edge of this cliff top. I was completely terrified, and he stopped the engine and staring straight ahead, he told me that he thought it was time that I knew that my mother was a drunkard, that was what was wrong with her and why she had to keep going into hospital, because she was an alcoholic.[26]

Madeleine felt Ted blamed her for the catastrophe:

> He was giving me the feeling in a tone of huge resentment and bitterness, he was telling me it was my fault, that I was totally responsible. I didn't understand what he was getting at. I didn't know what any of it meant. What I did know was that there was very bad trouble between my parents and that it was spilling out onto me.[27]

Madeleine's life went over a cliff that day. Ted was presumably desperate to give Madeleine a logical explanation for her mother's constant illness and absence, but Madeleine was unable, either as a child or later as an adult, to make sense of the information.

Sylvette was discharged from Hydebrae in early 1953. She dismissed Alcoholics Anonymous and argued that she could master the problem of alcohol unaided, declaring to Ted that she was not an alcoholic.[28]

CHAPTER FOUR

A Mother Lost

One lovely spring day in 1953, as Madeleine and Colette played with their cocker spaniel Candy, a petite woman arrived at Number 9. Margaret Michaelis was a professional photographer, an Austrian Jew who had come to Australia in 1939. She had photographed the Spanish Civil War and had been politically active, but was now specialising in portrait and dance photography.[1] She had artistic cachet, especially in self-regarding Castlecrag, where a European sensibility was taken for granted by a confident mob who were creating their own idea of what it meant to be Australian. A family portrait session with Michaelis, a reserved and stylish woman with a strong accent, was proof of good taste. And of ambition.

Michaelis set up her camera in the living room. Sunshine flooded the room as she arranged the furniture for a composition showing the family at leisure. The image suggested a weekend, perhaps Saturday afternoon or Sunday morning, although the man of the house holds a file of papers, adding a serious note to the scene. Madeleine and Colette pat Candy, while Ted looks at his wife and smiles. But Sylvette looks at no one. She stares beyond the camera, almost forcing her face into a smile. She is dressed smartly, but she looks physically uncomfortable and, like her husband, a little sad. Madeleine and Colette smile openly to the camera and seem untroubled. But the camera lied: the year had been a desperate one for the St John family.

Several months earlier Ted had driven his daughters across the bridge to their new life as boarders at St Catherine's School in Waverley. This was the same school attended by Ted's sisters before the war, the same school where Ted had been so captivated by Sylvette's charm when they had debated on rival teams in 1939. Now, just fourteen years later, Ted had decided that St Catherine's would shield his little girls from the domestic chaos generated by Sylvette's alcohol abuse and depression.

Madeleine was distraught about leaving Castlecrag. It was Ted's fault, she believed, but she recalled that Sylvette offered no solace:

> She never talked about it to us, she never sat down with us and said, this is a terrible thing for you to have to endure and terrible for me too but we'd got to be brave together. She was just blank about it, getting the uniforms ready and sewing on all the name tapes.[2]

The blankness may have been caused by sleeping tablets. Sylvette had temporarily stopped drinking but she was far from stable. Feiga came over to Castlecrag to help prepare her granddaughters' school kit—navy knickers, white knickers, laundry bags and shoe-cleaning bags, summer uniforms and winter uniforms.[3] She was sympathetic to her daughter, although she was losing patience.[4]

On the morning of their first day, Ted lined Madeleine and Colette up on the side terrace to take a look at them. Madeleine recalled she had been in a 'state of zombie-like mixture of dread and denial' about St Catherine's. She thought the uniform was hideous. Neither she nor Colette could really believe 'this horrific thing' was 'seriously going to happen':

> We are standing side by side being inspected by my father who is
> standing six feet away with his hands folded together in front, looking
> at us, and he says, 'Good Lord did you ever see such a miserable face,
> two such miserable faces,' and he roared with laughter and he laughed
> and he laughed and he laughed. Apart from causing such acute grief
> to my mother he was going to have the added bonus of causing the
> deepest kind of misery to us. He genuinely enjoyed the spectacle of
> other people's pain, or at least of our pain.[5]

Was Ted's behaviour due to nerves, a desire to break the ice, an effort to
jolly along his children on a dismal day, or the well-known tendency of
the St Johns to mockery? Looking back, the adult Madeleine was not
interested in such explanations. In her mind, Ted had been deliberately
cruel that morning.

For Colette, boarding school was a 'thunderbolt out of the blue'. It
was as if Ted had removed them from their own lives:

> One week we were getting on a bus and going to local public schools
> and everyone was singing on the bus and then a few weeks later we
> were transported to hell. [At Castlecrag] we were loved and adored
> by our nuclear family, by our extended family, we were connected
> to our extended family, we were connected to our grandparents,
> we were connected to our Aunt Josette and her babies, we were
> connected to everybody in Castlecrag by flesh, by culture, by trees,
> by our life.[6]

The transfer of her daughters to boarding school shamed Sylvette. It
was a public signal to Castlecrag that she could not properly care for
her children. 'She was labelled unfit, unworthy', Madeleine recalled. 'I
am sure he did it in order to punish her...[It is] one of those ultimate
crimes to separate a mother from her children.' Madeleine could not, or
would not, see that Ted had been pushed to the limit by Sylvette and
that he was trying to protect his daughters. Her grief was intense. 'I can't
describe even now, I am not going to attempt to describe, how it felt to

be separated from my mother and the pain I was in and the tears that we shed,' she said in 2004.[7] At St Catherine's on that first day, Madeleine wrote her mother a letter saying how much she missed her. Her sense of abandonment was acute.

Madeleine and Colette were placed in separate dormitories. The school was cold and institutional with heavy stone buildings and a routine defined by bells, abysmal food, prayers and evening study, known as prep. It was a punitive, Dickensian place, with an 'atmosphere of correction', Madeleine remembered. She likened it to Lowood, the notorious charity school in *Jane Eyre*, and she ridiculed the headmistress, Una Fitzhardinge, who suffered from Bell's palsy: 'Female from a good family, very grave, very Anglican. Your father is an archdeacon or your uncle is an archdeacon. Very good family, very good class of suits, and they have that handwriting that is like Greek. She was out of that box.' Madeleine's fellow students were also found wanting. They were 'great, lumping, uncultured, country hick girls and girls from the surrounding neighbourhood, which was not a posh neighbourhood in those days.'[8] Madeleine and Colette were united in their dislike of the school.

Boarders were allowed to go home every Saturday, and at the end of the first week, Madeleine and Colette cried all the way back to Castlecrag. Ted asked them to make a special effort to stop, but as soon as they saw Sylvette waiting at the top of the steps at Number 9, they burst into tears and spent the day weeping. Sylvette wrapped them in her arms, but she did not mention the letter Madeleine had sent her that week.[9]

Separation from her daughters did not help Sylvette's mental state. She had managed to stay sober for two months, but then began drinking heavily again. Then, on 13 March, she swallowed sixty Sedormid tablets, a prescription sedative, and was found semi-conscious at home. Ted had been unconvinced by her earlier attempts at suicide, but this time, he felt that she was serious. He called in her physician, Dr Hugh Fraser, and they decided that Sylvette, still groggy, should be committed to the Reception House at Darlinghurst.[10] This institution no longer exists, but at that time it was the main entry point into metropolitan psychiatric hospitals in Sydney. Patients were remanded under the Lunacy Act when they were considered a risk to themselves or to others. Dr Fraser wrote a letter, describing Sylvette as a:

> vain, self-centred, lime-lighting woman with a marked sense of inferiority masquerading under a superficially vivacious, witty social manner…Mrs St John has always been a demanding, dissatisfied woman, feeling she has never had a good deal. She is half French—half Jewish—born in France—parents' marriage unhappy, though never separated—now living in Sydney…[11]

He also said that Sylvette suffered 'delusions' that Ted was courting his secretary, noting that Ted was a barrister, with the implication that his version of events was the more credible. Finally, Dr Fraser advised:

> The husband would like to have his wife confined under the Inebriates Act if this offers the best chance of meeting her problem, though he cherishes the outside hope that the shock of R. H. [Reception House] admission might induce a belated sincere attempt at AA.[12]

Read fifty years later, the letter seems severe and judgmental, one written by an enemy, not by a doctor engaged to help cure depression and alcoholism. But it indicates the severity of Sylvette's illness and the lack of treatment for mental illness at that time, when it was often seen as a crime, not a medical condition.

Dr Fraser called the Chatswood police. When they arrived at The Rampart, they asked Sylvette if she had intended to take her life. 'Yes,' she said. 'I have nothing to live for, I want to die.' She turned to Ted and asked, 'Are they taking me to the Reception House?' When he said yes, she said, 'Oh well, it doesn't matter, I will do it again.'[13]

It was enough for the police. Sylvette was deemed insane, taken to the Chatswood Police Station, and charged with attempted suicide. Then she was driven across the bridge to the Reception House. It was just after midnight on 15 March and she was still drowsy and unsteady on her feet.

The following day Sylvette was brought before a magistrate who was informed that the 'wife of a barrister' was 'acutely miserable and depressed, lacks interest in self and surroundings, states she has only one plan for the future that is to die, says she will try to suicide if given the chance'. Sylvette's file was marked 'alcoholic' and she was remanded in the Reception House for seven days.

She was emotional. On 18 March, staff noted that she was uninterested, but at least over the next few days she slept. On 21 March she was given a drug to help her sleep and this was repeated the following night 'with effect'.[14] On 23 March, Sylvette was released to the Westhaven Private Hospital in Waverley, a specialist facility for patients with drinking or psychiatric conditions. When she was discharged some weeks later, she refused to go back to Number 9 and moved in with friends.

It is not clear how much, if anything, Madeleine was told, but she knew her mother had moved out of the family home. She wrote to Ted urging him to give Sylvette some money.[15]

Over the next few months, Sylvette controlled her drinking and, around October 1953, she and Ted decided to give the marriage another try. One Saturday, home from St Catherine's, the girls were told the news. Ted swept eight-year-old Colette into his arms, took her outside to the terrace and said, 'How about if I tell you Mummy's coming back!'[16] Madeleine and Colette were thrilled, but Ted kept them in boarding school while he and Sylvette tried to work things out.

At the end of her first year at St Catherine's, Madeleine won a scholarship for the following year. Things had improved at home and Ted decided the girls should stay at St Catherine's, but as day students—Sylvette was able to care for them again.

But life at Number 9 soon descended once again into arguments and recriminations. Sylvette had bouts of 'hysteroid' behaviour—depression triggered by the feeling that she had been rejected. She found Ted increasingly critical and later told a doctor that her husband embarrassed her in public and told people she was a drunkard and a suicidal maniac.[17] It seems unlikely that Ted would have used such words publicly—the comment suggests Sylvette was becoming increasingly irrational. She was dependent on prescription drugs as well as alcohol and she consumed high levels of both. She woke frequently in the night, crying, and complained of illnesses in every part of her body.[18]

It was no secret now in close-knit Castlecrag that Sylvette was in a fragile state. Her friends were concerned about her mental condition. The Whitlams noted the St Johns were no longer available for socialising.[19] On one occasion, Colette surprised her mother, who was clearly inebriated, trying to hide a bottle in the laundry cupboard. 'Can you keep a secret?' Sylvette asked her wide-eyed daughter.[20] On another occasion, Colette saw Sylvette embarrass Ted. The St Johns were visiting a male friend, also called Ted. When they arrived, Sylvette, who had probably been drinking, jumped on the couch, threw her arms around the man's neck to give him a hug and exclaimed, 'Oh Ted, what have you done to me!' The other Ted pursed his lips in disapproval.[21] By the end of first term in 1954, Madeleine and Colette were back at boarding school.

Madeleine was happier this time. New boarders arrived to start secondary school. Among them was Deslys Moody, Des as she was always known, and she and Madeleine became close friends. Des later recalled that Madeleine was 'bouncy and happy', joining in the hijinks and midnight feasts in Dorm Five on the back verandah of the school and excelling at her academic studies and the piano.[22]

Ted told his wife that he wanted to divorce her. Sylvette interpreted this as his desire to protect his reputation at a time when divorces were granted mainly on proof that one or other party was guilty of adultery,[23] and in May, after a 'severe drinking bout', she took more than a hundred sleeping tablets and was rushed to Royal North Shore Hospital unconscious.

The assault on Sylvette's body was severe, but after six days in a coma she regained consciousness. She was taken to the Winchester Private

Hospital in Darlinghurst where she was yet again given ECT.

Ted told Sylvette that the marriage was over, and she begged for another chance. But she was not well enough to leave hospital and, on 16 June, she was admitted to the Broughton Hall Psychiatric Clinic, part of the large mental health complex at Rozelle in Sydney. She was assessed and her personal history—based on Ted's account—was recorded. The document noted she was 'demanding, selfish, domineering and v. temperamental', given to 'much attention-getting behaviour, very ambitious... witty, vivacious, jealous, v. inconsistent'.

Two days later when she saw a psychiatrist Sylvette repeated her conviction that Ted had had an affair with an older woman in 1950, and she was diagnosed with a 'depressive state' caused by Ted's desire for a divorce.

A week later, it was Ted's turn to meet the psychiatrist. He did not make a good impression, appearing 'rigid and unrelenting' with 'nothing pleasant to say about his wife'.

After three weeks at Broughton Hall, Sylvette was granted weekend leave to see Colette, who was in hospital with scarlet fever. It proved a difficult weekend, and when Sylvette returned to the asylum, she reported that Ted had 'ordered her out of the house' at Castlecrag and moved members of his family in. This was an exaggeration, but it was the case that Ted's sister Pat and her husband, Maitland Buckeridge, had moved in to help look after Madeleine and Colette when they were home from school.

Ted was worried that Broughton Hall staff would release Sylvette to allow her to nurse Colette, and he wrote to psychiatrist Dr Marie Illingworth and the superintendent of the institution urging them to keep Sylvette in their care:

> Having regard to the fact that my wife seems to react badly when responsibility is thrust upon her & to her recent history, I would not be happy about my wife nursing Colette from the point of view

of mother or child. Yet if she is discharged and is *not* permitted to nurse Colette I think she will take it badly. I do not pretend to be a psychiatrist; but I know my wife pretty well & I would respectfully suggest that it would be premature to discharge her now. She is capable of a deceptive brightness of demeanour which belies what goes on beneath the surface.[24]

Ted's entreaties were successful and Sylvette was held at the asylum till 22 July. Her discharge was recorded in her file but there was no account of her treatment or of her state of mind on release. ECT was the most common treatment at Broughton Hall in the 1950s. Overseas, psychiatric patients were given alternative help such as psychotherapy or insulin treatment, but at Broughton Hall, due to the large number of women, sometimes more than seventy, there was not the time or staff for psychotherapy. A shortage of supervisory staff meant that the women lined up naked in a corridor waiting their turn for a bath because there was no time for them to undress and dress in the bathroom. Dr Illingworth said later that patients were often discharged with insufficient or no treatment.[25] It is likely that Sylvette was in that second category.

Sylvette did not return to Castlecrag—she moved into a shared house in Chatswood. One Saturday, Ted took Madeleine to see her mother there. He let her out of the car and she walked up to the door and rang the doorbell. There was Sylvette. 'I am just making the bed, come in and help me,' she said. Sylvette introduced her daughter to the other people in the house and she and Madeleine spent the day together:

> I had my mother to myself that day and I remember walking up the street to the cinema and we had our arms linked…we just go into this instant mother–daughter [relationship] as if nothing is wrong. We are not pretending, it is just a happening thing.[26]

They walked past a chemist shop and Sylvette pointed to a manicure set in the window, telling Madeleine she would buy it for her if she stopped biting her nails. Madeleine would have had a lot to tell her mother: the night before, she had performed a piano solo at the St Catherine's annual concert.[27] Madeleine remembered this day fondly: a day when she and Sylvette were alone and completely united, a perfect day.

Sylvette and Ted argued over the divorce and about who would live in the house. After a short stay at Chatswood, Sylvette moved back into Number 9, and Ted went to stay with Pat and Maitland. Sylvette was alone and worried about how she would survive without a job and without a husband. Henriette and Marcel Pile found her a job in a shop in the Chatswood area, selling home goods. She was to start in the last week in August.[28]

On Saturday 7 August, Madeleine and Colette were waiting for their mother to collect them from school for a day out, when Madeleine was told that she had been grounded for a misdemeanour. Sylvette eventually arrived at the school, and Madeleine was allowed to go into the driveway to talk to her for a moment. Sylvette was wearing the Dior copy, the 'New Look' black suit that her daughter adored. Madeleine recalled:

> I told her how sorry I was that I was not able to go out with her and she had these very big brown eyes and she was just looking at me and there were great big tears welling up in her eyes, and there were kids all over and I was terrified that she was going to cry—not because I minded her crying but because I didn't want the other kids to see her. [So I was] patting her arms and telling her everything was all right.[29]

Sylvette told the girls that Ted was going to divorce her and that she was frightened about the future. The three of them clung together, sobbing, in the St Catherine's driveway. Colette remembered:

> It was horrific. We had the last interview with our mother on the driveway, in the freaking driveway of the school, late in the day, they could not or would not accommodate the visit in any other way… My mother was saying that the marriage was over, and over forever, that this was it…Madeleine was saying, 'What are you going to do?'

and my mother was saying, 'I will be all right, I will be fine, I will just get a job in a factory or something.'[30]

That night, Ted responded to his wife's calls for company and went around to the house to see her. He was concerned about her fragility, but he was reassured—Sylvette did not mention suicide, which she had so often on other occasions.[31] But all was not well.

Sylvette told friends she was going away to the coast for a few days before starting her job, but on Tuesday 10 August, she was still at Castlecrag.[32] She telephoned Friedel Souhami and invited her over for a drink. Friedel walked down the side path from her home in The Parapet to the St John house to be greeted by a distressed Sylvette: 'I am lonely and I wanted you to come over and keep me company.' But by the time they parted, Sylvette was calmer and Friedel did not think she was suicidal. They agreed to have lunch the following Friday.[33] On Thursday night, 12 August, Sylvette again phoned Friedel to ask her to come over but Friedel was busy and declined.[34] Anyway, she thought, they would see each other the next day.

Anita Date always kept an eye out for her neighbour, and on Friday morning she was concerned. The St John house was locked up and silent, and Sylvette had not surfaced. Before long, Anita was so worried that she raised the alarm.[35] Ted left work and drove over. He no longer had a key to the house and had to force his way in. Anita went inside with him.

Sylvette was lying on the double bed. She had been dead for a considerable time. On the bedside table was a glass with a small amount of water in it and a spoon, but no suicide note. Ted called a doctor and Sylvette's body was taken to the city morgue.[36]

Across the city at St Catherine's, the boarders were getting ready for evening study when the headmistress announced that Madeleine and Colette were to go to her study. Madeleine knew instinctively what was about to unfold. 'I knew there was no other reason that we could be summoned to the headmistress's study...she would not be going to tell us to go to her study just to tell us my mother was sick.' Miss Fitzhardinge told the girls there was 'something very hard' that they had to contend with.[37] It was a terrible moment. Over and over she said: 'Your father loves you very much, you just have to carry on as usual.' Ted was on his way, she told them, then left the study to get them some hot milk. Madeleine began to cry. 'I think she's dead,' Colette told her older sister.[38]

When Ted arrived, accompanied by his brother-in-law Bill Baker, Colette rushed into her father's arms but Madeleine held back: '[He] turns up, he is a block of concrete, he doesn't want to touch me, he doesn't want to know me, he doesn't even put his arms around me. He just stares at me in this totally block of concrete way.'[39]

Bill embraced his nieces and the men disappeared into the study with Miss Fitzhardinge, leaving Madeleine and Colette on a bench in the corridor outside. When they emerged, Ted and Bill said goodnight and left.

No one told Madeleine and Colette that their mother was dead. They had to put the pieces together for themselves. And there was no talk of the girls going home to Castlecrag, but Miss Fitzhardinge asked if they wanted to sleep in adjoining beds rather than in their separate dorms. Madeleine declined. 'We did not want to have anything to do with each other,' she recalled. Looking back, she was scathing about Colette, who had asked Miss Fitzhardinge whether Sylvette was now in heaven. 'I mean, pass the sick bag, Alice! It was a pure performance, it was completely bogus,' Madeleine said.[40] Her bitterness was extreme but not surprising: the death of a mother would have been devastating for any child.

Bill Baker had rushed to Ted's side when he heard the news. As a clergyman, he had to enforce the church rules that barred suicides from full religious rites. He wanted to know if Sylvette had deliberately killed herself or whether it had been an accidental overdose, and he went to the morgue to investigate. The medical advice he was given was equivocal and Bill, with some relief, decided Sylvette's death was not suicide.[41]

Some time later, Dr Stratford Sheldon performed the autopsy and gave as the cause of death 'poisoning by pentobarbitone'.[42] Sylvette's body was released to the family and funeral arrangement were made.

The *Sydney Morning Herald* carried the death notice: 'St John, Sylvette—August 13 1954 at her residence 9 The Rampart, Castlecrag, beloved wife of Edward Henry St John.' There was no mention of Madeleine or Colette.

At St Catherine's, Madeleine's friends knew her mother had died but there was little time for tears: 'I was just expected to get up and proceed as usual, and some of the girls came and gave me their sympathy and condolences. But apart from that I was expected to proceed as normal, which is what I did.'[43]

On Monday, at 1.45 p.m., the funeral service was held at St Thomas's Church of England in North Sydney. Henriette Pile remembered it as a cold ceremony filled with an atmosphere of blame towards Sylvette.[44] Neither Madeleine nor Colette attended and they were given no details of the funeral or their mother's cremation at the Northern Suburbs Crematorium. In retrospect their exclusion seems harsh, but Ted doubtless thought his daughters, aged nine and twelve, should be protected as far as possible from the tragedy.

Madeleine's cousin Antony Minchin, just eleven years old, sent her a letter of sympathy, but Madeleine and Colette had no contact with Feiga and Jean Cargher, who would have been of such comfort. It was the last week of term and the girls stayed on for the school routines of morning prayer, class, meals and prep. Over in Castlecrag, the adults whispered of suicide and the children knew something terrible had happened, but a veil of secrecy was drawn over the event. Ted wrote to Florence, who was living in London: 'The poor girl is at peace at last.'[45] Madeleine and Colette knew never to speak of it again.[46]

During the school holidays, the girls finally saw their Cargher grandparents. They also visited Bill Baker and his family. Years later, Madeleine claimed that, during that visit, her cousin Felicity Baker told her that Sylvette had suicided.[47] For Madeleine, the question of whether or nor her mother had intended to kill herself became a defining issue. There was a lot at stake. A suicide would mean that Sylvette had abandoned her; an accidental death allowed Madeleine to believe she had not been rejected by her beloved mother.

It was some months before the inquest was held, but on 27 October Coroner Frank McNamara held a brief hearing. Constable Aubrey Goodyer went first, citing the details of 13 August when he had gone to Number 9. Ted was then sworn in. He said he had been 'temporarily away from home' after Sylvette's discharge from Broughton Hall at the end of July. It was a potentially embarrassing situation for Ted, who was in and out of the courts on a daily basis. Now he was being interrogated about the circumstances of his wife's death. But the coroner asked only one question: 'Any medical man ever give you notice of the cause of her condition?' Ted said he had never had a satisfactory explanation, and the coroner did not delve deeper.

The report from the government analyst noted the presence of the drugs pentobarbitone and carbromal, often used together as a sedative to induce sleep. It did not record any alcohol present in the blood. The coroner ruled Sylvette had died 'from poisoning by pentobarbitone wilfully self-administered', but made no finding on whether her death was deliberate.[48]

On 24 November, the *Sydney Morning Herald* carried an extensive report detailing allegations of bad conditions in Broughton Hall and other mental hospitals in New South Wales. Among five statutory declarations from psychiatric staff was one from Dr Marie Illingworth, who had treated Sylvette just weeks before she died. She had since resigned: there was such a shortage of staff and so many new patients that she was not able to give satisfactory psychiatric treatment, she stated.[49]

Madeleine found the months after her mother's death very hard, and her headmistress noted her behaviour was 'not all that might be desired'. But by October, Madeleine had pulled herself together and started working steadily again, and her scholarship was renewed for the next year, 1955. But Madeleine must be warned, Miss Fitzhardinge said, that the grant would not be renewed again if her behaviour and work were not satisfactory.

The first Christmas after Sylvette's death was always going to be difficult for Madeleine, but it began well enough with the St John clan gathering at Number 9. Madeleine played the piano brilliantly and Ted was back to his witty self. Madeleine and Colette were grieving, but the rest of the extended family, including Marion and Bill Baker, Margaret and John Minchin and Pat and Maitland Buckeridge, were more relaxed without Sylvette.[50] But that Christmas Day ended in tears. Madeleine and Colette, ordered to bed by Ted, sobbed inconsolably.

The girls scarcely saw their mother's side of the family in this period. When Ted occasionally took them to the Carghers' flat, the visits were awkward. Feiga and Jean had once adored Ted, but now, mourning Sylvette, they must have been conflicted. When she looked back years later, Madeleine believed her grandparents had come to see Ted as having 'trashed their daughter'.[51] And Colette recalled that Ted 'severed our relationship' with the Cargher family.[52] When Josette wrote to Ted, inviting her nieces to come for a visit to the hotel that she and her husband managed in New Guinea, Ted told the girls he could not afford to send them. Madeleine was angry. Aunt Josette would have been a comfort.

Madeleine never saw the coroner's report on her mother's death, or any of the reports on Sylvette's psychiatric history. She knew her mother had been given ECT, but she never asked why such treatment had been deemed necessary. She spent many years constructing a story of her parents and their marriage that blamed Ted for the problems and ignored any evidence that pointed to her mother's mental illness.

CHAPTER FIVE

Flower Girls for a Stepmother

A round the middle of 1955, less than a year after Sylvette's death, Madeleine received a letter from her father. Ted was in London attending an international legal conference. He had some exciting news for his thirteen-year-old daughter—he had met a 'wonderful woman' and planned to marry her. Madeleine and Colette were to have a stepmother: Valerie Erskine Winslow, just twenty-seven years old.

Years later Madeleine spoke of the news from Ted as 'abominable'. She felt she was not being given time to accommodate her loss. She wrote to Ted and pleaded to be allowed to remain at boarding school. She told her father that she was very happy and wanted to remain there even when he and Valerie returned from London.[1]

It was a lie. Madeleine was doing well academically and had recently represented St Catherine's, playing the piano at a schools' musical festival in the Sydney Town Hall, but she was not happy. Des Moody had seen her friend become very sad after Sylvette's death, 'not just sad in a normal mourning way, but perhaps depressed'.[2] Madeleine still joined in the dormitory fun, but she was now more solitary and she suffered from mood swings. Sometimes at morning prayers, she wept silently over her prayer book. But boarding school was better than going home to a stepmother. St Catherine's was her 'only insurance' against that pain.[3]

Ted readily agreed to Madeleine's request: he was focused now on Val and the prospect of happiness after a marriage that had gone so wrong.

Valerie Winslow was a pretty young woman with a neat figure and dark hair like the young Sylvette. She worked with newly arrived migrants, teaching English in the camps set up in New South Wales after the Second World War to house the many thousands of 'new Australians' from Europe. She had been an outstanding student at North Sydney Girls High School before studying languages, including French, at Sydney University.

Valerie was a decade younger than Ted but, by the time they met, she too had spread her wings. In the mid-1950s, she had convinced her family to return to the UK and to settle there. She was teaching in London when she landed a dream job: a wealthy German industrialist hired her to accompany him and his wife to Australia by ship. Val was to teach the businessman enough English to talk to potential partners in Australia, and her payment included a return trip. Mission completed, she was on the way back to the UK on the *Iberia* when she met Ted on his way to London.

The couple sat on the deck and Ted told Val of his nightmare years with Sylvette. He claimed he had been tricked into the marriage, and Val could see he was in 'a very bad way'. Sometimes, this man who seemed so contained wept as he recounted his wife's multiple suicide attempts. Sylvette's psychiatrist had spoken to him as if he were a monster, he said. But he wanted Val to meet his daughters. 'They are so special,' he told her.[4]

Ted and Valerie left the ship in Marseilles and travelled through France, Switzerland and Italy. In Florence they chose an engagement ring; in Paris Val bought a glamorous dress; and everywhere they went Ted sought gifts for his daughters.

When the couple finally arrived in the UK, Ted rushed to a phone and told a rather startled Florence that he was engaged to be married. Over the next few weeks Ted and Val enjoyed socialising in London. The Commonwealth and Empire Law Conference opened in July amid great fanfare in Westminster Hall. This was the first of what would be regular five-yearly conferences, and the Brits turned on the ceremony with a garden party at Buckingham Palace. Ted delivered a paper on law reform and, characteristically, he went out on a limb: law reform attracted limited support in Australia at that time, but Ted was an enthusiast and argued the case strongly.[5]

The time in London was exhilarating. Ted had been overseas during the war, but this was different. This was England, the country his parents had always regarded as home. Even so, he convinced Val and her parents to return permanently to Australia.

Ted had seen the conference as a circuit breaker, a way to 'distance myself from the tragedy I had been through'.[6] It had been successful beyond his wildest dreams, but he had left behind in Australia two daughters still devastated by their mother's death. Aunts and uncles in Castlecrag scarcely compensated. At St Catherine's, Des Moody noted the lack of warmth and care in Madeleine's life. Des's mother, M'Liss, regularly despatched supplies of biscuits and Granny Smith apples to her only child, but Madeleine never seemed to bring back food from her Saturdays at Castlecrag. She never had much in her 'tuck tin'.

Ted's sister Pat was busy all week teaching at a nearby school but, on Saturdays, she and Maitland were on hand to care for the girls when they were home from boarding school. In 2004, Madeleine recalled their presence with bitterness:

> After my mother died, my father had the brilliant idea of getting [Pat and Maitland] to come and live with us in our house so he had an instant housekeeper, cum nanny cum cook and bottle washer and then he could fuck off and do what he liked. He often had lots of little holidays and then finally he cruised off to England...and had

a wonderful time and left us in the house with…this ghoulish pair, it was like something out of Dickens.[7]

Colette was dismayed too. She shrank from Maitland with his badly arthritic hands and his psoriasis. 'Dead skin came off him all the time, he smoked a stinking pipe…he was grotesque to a kid,' she recalled. Castlecrag had meant a French mother 'who smelt good, whose linen press was a sight for sore eyes and whose domesticity had been immaculate'. Now Pat and Maitland were sleeping in Sylvette's bed and Number 9 was dominated by this bluff man who wore a tweed peaked cap and tried to ingratiate himself with his nieces by winking at all the wrong moments.[8]

Sylvette's death had destroyed Madeleine's world, but the years of stress leading to that death had also damaged her relationship with her father. Colette also felt Ted's emotional withdrawal. 'He had been a doting father till we went to boarding school,' she remembered. 'It was like the tap had been turned off. It was the end of holding and touching, it was the end of the relationship we had with our grandmother. It was the end of everything good.'[9]

Madeleine believed Ted was deliberately humiliating and threatening her:

> He starts coming and waking me up in the night…I am now in a state of depression. He would have this routine of fifty minutes of coming to the door and barking my name at me, barks and wakes me up in a really peremptory fashion in order to get up and clean his shoes…He goes into a rage and suddenly he pulls back the bedclothes and looks down. My sister is witnessing this entire scene. He stares down at me and I get this really disgusted feeling that he is looking at something he despises…he is telling me that I am disgusting—sexually…I am not even thirteen yet.[10]

On some occasions when her father woke her up late at night, Madeleine recalled, he ordered her to stand in his bedroom while he enumerated her misdemeanours 'as if from a charge sheet' read out in court.

> He no longer had my mother to humiliate so he transferred the whole operation onto me...I could not open my mouth without him turning it around and ridiculing [me]. I was just this laughing stock, I was repulsive and I was this evil person...I got a feeling that my father's routine might have originated in a sexual dysfunction. I think maybe he was a man who could not perform...I would stand there, practically fainting, and he would be telling me something I had said or done, and he would go on about how disgusting and loathsome I was and I must not wake up my sister when I went back to bed and not let anyone know.[11]

In 2004, Madeleine speculated whether this had been the only way Ted could 'get off'. 'Maybe the humiliation of my mother was a sex thing and he could not fuck her till he humiliated her...' She thought that Ted transferred the humiliation to her: 'It turned into a regular feature till he got married again.'[12]

Madeleine felt that Colette joined Ted in humiliating her. 'Part of that operation was to make a great fuss of Colette and [hold] her up as this perfectly good daughter that he loved as opposed to [me].' Not that Colette escaped:

> [Ted] would completely lose it because of something [Colette] had done...She would inadvertently wind him up and so I remember one time this happened and he gave her a terrible bollocking and she dissolved into a puddle. It ended up with him staring at her and [saying] 'You are not worth a damn'.[13]

These incidents were as raw and painful to her as an adult as they had been fifty years earlier. They had wrought damage on Madeleine that no amount of time could repair.

Val's entry into Madeleine's life when the teenager was so vulnerable would prove debilitating for both, even though their first meeting, at

Sydney Airport, when Val flew in from London in 1955, was positive. Madeleine 'did not take her prejudice to that first meeting', Colette recalled.[14] But events moved swiftly, and within a couple of months, Ted and Val were preparing for their wedding. It was common for widowers with children to remarry quickly, in part to secure a regular domestic life for their families. But Sylvette had been dead for hardly more than a year, and Madeleine and Colette had had little time to adjust.

Ted and Val married in October at St James' Church in the city, with a reception at the Australia Hotel. No one, it seems, saw anything odd in the decision to have Madeleine and Colette as flower girls. Madeleine was astounded that no adult intervened to stop it:

> I can feel my stomach turning at the whole experience…To me the grossest thing in the world was for my father to remarry so quickly. Completely impossible. And if he was going to do it at all—to have this big lavish wedding and for no one to see that it should have been a quiet wedding. That I should be expected to be an attendant, and that no one concerned could see that and I had to play this out.[15]

Ted doubtless wanted his daughters to share in his joy, but Madeleine grew only more resentful. After the reception, she and Colette, in their pretty dresses, were driven back to boarding school—and their separate dormitories.

The newlyweds moved into Number 9. It must have been hard for the young bride, living in the house where Sylvette had died. And it must have been hard too for Madeleine and Colette to have another woman in their mother's bedroom, another woman using the same pots and pans in the kitchen.

Val made an effort to accommodate the girls' needs. Madeleine and Colette came home on Saturdays, and sometimes Val went to see them at St Catherine's on Sunday afternoons when visitors came carrying cakes in tins, to sit on rugs spread out in the school grounds for afternoon tea. She

tried hard but there was always a coldness between Val and Madeleine.[16]
Colette recalled their relationship in the early days of the marriage:

> Val didn't have too much trouble getting to me, I was open and ready
> for that, and Madeleine in no way was. I think she was open and
> ready for it up until she actually met and encountered Val face to
> face...Val played a huge, unwitting part in blocking [our] experience
> of accepting and mourning and grieving our mother.[17]

Ted and Val had a couple of months of married life alone at Castlecrag, but
in December, when Madeleine and Colette came home for the holidays,
Val began to discover what she had taken on. She had no experience as
a mother,[18] and to Madeleine and Colette, she failed in every way. She
could not compete with the girls' memories of their stylish French mother.
Sylvette was a 'sensuous Parisian', Colette recalled, while Val's 'sensuosity'
was limited to her beauty routine of 'cleanse, tone and nourish'. Worse,
she served up burnt chops with boiled potatoes and peas. It was as if
she was 'from another planet'.[19] Val scored badly on everything from
her housekeeping skills to the shape of her ankles. The adult Madeleine
labelled Val a 'swot...not a party girl', and snidely noted that she did a
lot of ballet but did not have a dancer's body.[20]

Val was no match for Madeleine's wit and unerring ability to wound.
'Those girls were so mean [to Val]; they were vitriolic, so horrible that I
felt she could not have been so bad,' Didy Harvey said.[21]

None of it was helped by the residents of Castlecrag taking sides
with the girls. Sylvette had been exotic, and she suited the Crag, even
if she was highly strung and difficult. But Val was reserved, even stiff.
Ted had always been more conservative than the left-leaning artists and
professionals who dominated the Crag, but now he was tagged a Tory
by some, and he no longer seemed to fit in at all. 'None of the kids liked
[Val],' Didy's brother Antony recalled. 'She was probably a very nice
person but she came across as pretty cool, as did Ted.'[22]

Val, left to cope with her stepdaughters, was on guard. Yet she was secure in one thing: her husband's love. Ted believed his young wife could do little wrong. Florence told the adult Madeleine that Ted could not be seen to fail again at marriage after Sylvette's death and so acceded to Val's requests. 'She [Val] sussed this out and used it to manipulate,' Madeleine said in 2004.[23] She and Colette recalled their father taking Val's side against them when they argued with their stepmother. Val rarely reprimanded them, but saved their misdemeanours to recount to Ted when he got home. He would then deliver the punishment. 'She never tried to stick up for me! I was this dogsbody and if I said something and she took exception she could not talk to me about it, but would wait and go to my father,' Madeleine recalled.[24]

Ted's belief in Val was reciprocated. Sylvette had mocked Ted at times and challenged his views, but Val took a different approach. She understood Ted's need for approval and an audience, and if she managed to get her own way on issues, it was rarely through a direct challenge. But managing two stepdaughters, with a new husband busy building his career in the city and with few friends nearby, was very difficult.

Colette handled the new family dynamics more easily than Madeleine did. Colette still had friends in Castlecrag, and when she was home from St Catherine's, she made herself scarce. 'Always the flighty one,' according to Margaret Whitlam, Colette was a charmer.[25] She was far more gregarious than Madeleine, whose friendships had petered out because of her absence at boarding school and because she was busy with long hours of piano practice and housework. 'I was meant to be the kitchen maid and the laundry maid…I had this scullery maid job on a full-time basis.' But she sought refuge in books. 'I was just too wounded and stunted to pick up relationships in Castlecrag, so I was left to my own devices really and I just read books.'[26]

Val had been keen to start a family quickly but soon realised that it was 'a huge mistake' to become pregnant at a time when she was trying to build bridges with her stepdaughters. Things hadn't been too bad when the girls came home for a day or a weekend, but by the long summer holidays in December 1955, Val was suffering the morning sickness that would dog her pregnancy and things became more difficult.[27] Instead of the traditional holiday at Avoca Beach, the family repaired to Jamberoo, south of Sydney. The holiday was not a success—Madeleine had no sympathy for Val:

> She was a complete and total pain in the neck. She could not bear to be with us and I think it was not because she was feeling sick but because she had suddenly been confronted with what she had done—taking on these kids. She didn't know how to form a relationship with us so she would go off into her bedroom and hide away from us for the entire day.[28]

It wasn't all darkness in these teenage years. Des Moody's mother, M'Liss took Madeleine under her wing during the holidays at Cessnock, including her in picnics and other activities in the town. Sometimes, on a drive into the country, Des and Madeleine helped M'Liss collect cow manure for the garden and sat in the dicky-seat at the back of the Hillman, their hair streaming in the wind, on their way back to town. Sometimes they drove from Cessnock to nearby Lochinvar to see Madeleine's grandfather Frederick de Porte St John, who was running the town's Anglican church. After one holiday, Madeleine brought home a present for pregnant Val. Deep inside layers of tissue paper was a handmade, embroidered satin dressing-gown for the unborn baby. M'Liss had made it for Val, whom she had never met.[29]

During term, M'Liss, turned out in hat and gloves, met the girls in Sydney and treated them to a movie matinee and afternoon tea at the seventh floor restaurant at David Jones. They walked out of the lift of the department store to be met by two women dressed in black who directed them to their table overlooking Hyde Park.

Boarders were permitted to catch the tram to the city, to attend dental or hair appointments or to go to David Jones or Farmers—wherever their parents had an account—to replenish their uniforms. On some afternoons,

Madeleine and Des walked over to Denman Chambers in Philip Street to visit Ted. Des felt warmly towards Ted but noted that 'he did not pay much attention to the girls'.[30]

When school started again in 1956, Val offered her stepdaughters a choice—stay home and go to Queenwood School for Girls or continue at St Catherine's. Colette came home; Madeleine continued to board, but she began to resent Colette's improved relationship with Ted and Val. They 'had this thing in the house as she started as a day girl and that made a huge difference because she was the sole daughter of the house'.[31] Colette was an astute child. She saw what happened when Madeleine stood up to Ted and incurred his wrath, and she decided there was no more room for 'screaming and yelling and hair tearing' at Number 9.[32]

Oliver St John was born on 31 July 1956, after a difficult pregnancy. Ted was thrilled to have a boy and gave him the St John family name of Oliver. In spite of herself and her mistrust of Val, Madeleine joined in the excitement.

Baby Oliver made his presence felt, screaming constantly. 'I wish I had a nickel for every time I babysat that child and he screamed,' Madeleine said later.[33] But both sisters loved the little boy. Colette shared her bedroom with him and changed his nappy in the mornings.[34] However, Oliver drove Ted and Val to the edge. He was hard to settle at night and often woke at 3 or 4 a.m. and stayed awake.[35] By the time he was two, his hyperactivity and disturbed patterns of behaviour indicated far deeper problems.

Madeleine was fond of Oliver, but years later she could see her half-brother only in terms of the father she so denigrated. In 2004, she said that Ted had seen Oliver 'as a contribution to the family line and God took note of this and made sure that Oliver was not going to contribute anything whatsoever to the aggrandisement of my father's reputation or the family. Nice work, God.'[36]

Madeleine was doing well at school and wanted to matriculate well enough to get a Commonwealth scholarship and go to university. She decided to leave St Catherine's and move to Queenwood to improve her chances. She later described Violet Medway, the headmistress, as:

> One of the classic, monumental girls' schools headmistresses. They were a brood, a breed apart, the headmistresses of the girls' schools of Sydney. They were the ones who devoted their lives to female education. None of them was married. The idea that you could be married and be a headmistress [was never entertained]. They were magnificent and Ms Medway was the greatest of them all.[37]

Madeleine saw herself as a painter and pianist, but Ms Medway peered down at Madeleine at one point during her entrance interview in 1957 and announced: 'You know, dear, I think you might write.'[38]

The school was small and had superb views from the classrooms. In the summer, the girls filed down to the baths at the southern end of the beach at Balmoral or sauntered past the rotunda and across the little bridge to the tiny Rocky Point Island at the northern end.

Many of the girls had been at Queenwood since kindergarten. They socialised with each other at weekends, and their parents were friends. Madeleine was the new girl, from a different suburb. She was never disliked, but she was a little different with her red hair and pale skin and her bookish ways. In her first year at the school, she was an enthusiastic helper in the library, and she co-authored the notes for the end-of-year school magazine, listing some interesting additions to the library as *Gone with the Wind* and *The Guns of Navarone*.[39]

She was always writing, and her work was published in the magazine. In 1957, she wrote a piece about Mrs Thring's Azalea Garden—a landmark in the northern Sydney suburb of Wahroonga. 'Azaleas! And even more azaleas! A profusion, a richness, an astronomical figure of azaleas!'[40] A year later, competition for publication in the magazine was strong and Madeleine was one of only two students from her class whose work was chosen. Her piece 'Shells' was highly imaginative and showed a love of wordplay. 'So here I am, lying almost dazed on a beach with hair flying ragged-flaggedly, sand and heat mixing up with one another and enclosing me in the sea symphony which has spread over me from my finger-tips up...'[41]

If Madeleine was 'desperately plain' in the eyes of some of her class-mates,[42] her view of them was equally blunt:

> The main gang was gorgeous and if you weren't gorgeous you didn't belong to that gang and I was not gorgeous so I didn't belong. It was a small class with the gorgeous gang and the others, and so the others took me in. There was a thin one and a fat one and another thin one and me. One of the thin ones was Armenian, the other thin one was the daughter of refugees born in Australia, and the fat one was the daughter of Plymouth Brethren.[43]

Sue Manion, like Madeleine, started at Queenwood in her final years and the two were thrown together, partly because they were the outsiders and they studied advanced English. 'She was just different,' Sue remembered. 'She didn't try to be trendy like the rest of us did. She could have been beautiful but she was not interested in the girly stuff.'[44]

But the school was a positive space for Madeleine. As an adult, she said that Queenwood had been a 'respite to me from my utterly Gothic family life'.[45] Even so, she must have been lonely at times, not really fitting in at the school and drifting away from many of her childhood friends in Castlecrag. Her closer connections were with older women—her aunts and Pom—rather than her peers.

Madeleine's talent as a pianist saw her take the stage as the accompanist when the school choir performed at a schools' festival at the Sydney Town Hall. Ted paid for her music lessons at the Sydney Conservatorium. But the Con meant serious practice, three hours a day, and two afternoon lessons a week, and Madeleine was also busy with homework and spent long hours on the bus and trams getting to school. She felt the pressure, and she was becoming increasingly jealous of Colette. Years later she described her life at that time as a nightmare, noting that Colette had a 'charmed existence' while she was 'this fat girl that nobody loves, except Pom!'[46]

Ted was worried about Madeleine and he asked Florence, who was back in Australia for the first time since 1950, for advice. Florence was a social worker and she told Ted that Madeleine was still grieving for Sylvette and needed help. But she felt it was not what her brother wanted to hear.[47] Ted had put the devastating events surrounding Sylvette and her depression behind him, and may well have found the idea of professional therapy for his daughter to be threatening.

Madeleine was miserable. There had also been a distressing scene in the St John household one Sunday morning when Ted asked Madeleine to go to church with him and she declined:

> He went completely ballistic and he started beating me over the head. He had these great big fleshy hands and he was hitting me on the head, one after another. But hard. And he completely lost his rag and he was right off his trolley and he was shouting abuse at me and hitting me on the head. He was in a total rage. He wasn't a pretty sight. It was the first and only time that he actually did this thing. If he had been alone with me, he would have killed me…he would not have been able to stop…or at least I would have ended up with permanent brain damage. And Val managed to pull him off… After bashing me up…after beating me up to within an inch of my life, to an inch of what my stepmother could tolerate seeing him do, my father expressed the view that I should pull myself together, and get dressed and come to church, which I did and which I thereafter continued to do every Sunday.[48]

The incident was a major issue for Madeleine. Around 1990, she told Felicity Baker that: 'Ted beat me up once. Every year I force myself to write out that memory, and I keep what I've written to compare my efforts, to measure how my control over the experience is improving.'[49]

Ted had been upset when he had seen Sylvette slap Madeleine two or three years earlier, but now he too was under considerable pressure with a new wife and baby and two daughters who were testing his emotional reserves. As a child, Ted had become accustomed to violent physical punishment at the vicarage where his father had routinely strapped the boys with a razor strop. In 1983, he told an interviewer that while he had sometimes smacked his sons, he had never hit his daughters.[50]

Most support for Madeleine in these years came from Pom and her husband Os Jarvis. They were a warm couple who provided a family atmosphere. The St Johns shared regular holidays with the Jarvises and other families at Avoca Beach. There were prawning trips and shared meals, and the children took off without the adults to the outdoor picture theatre in the evenings. Madeleine was the eldest of the group and she was its natural leader, even if her pale skin and love of books often kept her indoors. She was funny and imaginative during those summers. She ran charades and devised elaborate games and theatrical performances for the group.

Pom's daughter Jonette remembered these times as carefree, but Madeleine looked back through more jaundiced eyes. As an adult, she claimed the last time she went to Avoca before she left school in 1958 was 'boring, dismal and dreadful'. Indeed, life generally with Ted and Val was a drag. 'There are painful memories, but mostly it was odious and boring, one was never taken anywhere, one was never given any kind of treat. Perhaps one was taken to the ballet once a year very occasionally...'[51] Things had been different with Sylvette, who had taken both little girls to ballet lessons in the city on Saturday mornings. 'My mother was always [up] for an entertainment, for whatever was going on,' Madeleine said. 'With my mother [the idea] was to have as much fun as possible and with [Val and Ted] it was to have as little fun as possible.' Madeleine felt her only contact with 'normal family life was the time I spent with the Jarvis family'.[52]

Madeleine's anger increased when Val vetoed her French studies. Val had studied French at university, but if Madeleine thought she would be an ally in her bid to take advanced French for her Leaving exam in 1958, she was disappointed. Madeleine and Colette's French heritage had been ignored since Sylvette's death, but Ms Medway encouraged her student to study the language at a higher level. Val thought Madeleine already had too much on her plate. Madeleine sat the Alliance Française exam that year and attempted the higher level Leaving exam but, without the extra lessons she needed, she did poorly and she resented Val's intervention.

There were more black marks against Ted, too. Madeleine would go to Ted's chambers after her piano lesson and do her homework while she waited for him to come back from the courts or other meetings. Then they would drive home together. One afternoon, she was hunting for a pencil or eraser in a drawer in Ted's desk when she found the letter she had written to Sylvette in 1953 on her first day at St Catherine's, pouring out her sadness about leaving home. Now, years later, here was the letter. Madeleine was horrified. What was it doing in this drawer? Why did Ted have a letter that she had written to her mother? Madeleine ripped it into small pieces and threw it into a wastepaper basket.

Looking back, Madeleine said that it had only occurred to her years later to ask herself whether Sylvette had even seen the letter. If Ted had kept the letter from Sylvette, Madeleine said, 'we have to assume he did not want her to know that she was missed, unless—to put a charitable interpretation on it—he wanted to spare her'.[53]

CHAPTER SIX

Sydney Uni and the Octopus Girls

Madeleine St John may not have been in the gorgeous gang at Queenwood but she landed on her feet at Sydney University. Too plump, too plain, too different at school, the seventeen-year-old Madeleine began to find her way in a student body that boasted some of the smartest talents of the time. She still carried the hurts of Sylvette's death and what she saw as Ted's rejection. But this was a time in her life when her talent and creativity helped her to shine.

Much of her stability in this period came from the group of girls who found each other early in first term in 1959 when they signed up to the Sydney University Dramatic Society (SUDS). There were eight of them and soon they had a name, the Octopus, and a regular meeting spot in the cafe in Manning House.

The Octopus moved in a pack on campus, finding strength in numbers in an environment where beauty could still trump brains and where men almost always had the best parts. Coming of age almost a decade before the start of the feminist revolution—Germaine Greer had not yet arrived at the campus—they teetered on the brink of an independence taken for granted by later generations.

The glue that held the teenagers together was their love of the theatre and writing and their determination to be different. They scarcely realised it at the time, but for many language was an obsession.[1] Madeleine threw herself into the avant-garde SUDS with its repertoire of Pinter and Genet and Ionesco. And the girls attached themselves to the office of the student newspaper, *Honi Soit*, where Clive James and his mentor Philip Graham, known across the campus as Chester, were accorded rockstar status.

University life was exciting for Madeleine. She was still living at home, which was now at Balmoral on the North Shore. Val had long wanted to move out of the house that Ted had built with Sylvette in Castlecrag. Finally Ted was making enough money at the bar to move from Castlecrag, and the St Johns sold Number 9 and were renting a flat at Balmoral while they looked for another house. The flat had lovely views but it was cramped—not that Madeleine was around much.

She thrived on the academic work in her Arts course, especially English literature, and she also threw herself into campus life, relishing the freedom and the exposure to young men after life in a single-sex school. She stayed out late for meetings, rehearsals and parties, having a 'grand old time' and a life of her own.[2] But the tension was growing between Madeleine and Val, who was pregnant again. One day after making breakfast for the family, cutting Colette's lunch and settling Oliver with his toys, Val sat down in the living room with a tray to have a quiet breakfast. Madeleine was at the piano. 'She banged away as loudly as she could and when I asked if she could play something more restful while I had my breakfast, she took no notice. I took my tray back to the kitchen and I was so upset, I could not stop shaking. Later that day I had a miscarriage,' Val told Florence, decades later.[3] Ted ordered Madeleine to stop playing the piano, and Madeleine was aggrieved. She believed Ted blamed her for the miscarriage.[4] They were both determined, stubborn characters and they clashed more often as Madeleine became more independent.

On campus, 1959 was proving to be a very good year. Those who

hovered around *Honi Soit* and SUDS in that period read like a list of
Australia's culture shapers: Clive James, Les Murray and his rival in
poetry Geoffrey Lehmann, Richard Walsh, Mungo MacCallum and,
later, Robert Hughes, Bruce Beresford and John Gaden.

Honi Soit reflected the literary rather than the political enthusiasms
of its editors and staff. It was a vibrant and intellectual atmosphere for the
Octopus members, but in those pre-feminist days women were heavily
outnumbered by the men who ran student clubs and activities. Men
edited *Honi Soit*; men decided what plays would be produced; men were
selected to head the Student Representative Council. Women were good
for conversation, as well as sex, but everyone knew that the men would
take the best jobs. Clive James recalled that women were required to be
'decorative...In those days, the glamour girls ruled, and we men were
unreconstructed in every way.'[5] Madeleine was definitely not in the
glamour camp in her first year.

Some of the Octopus women were writers, but they were discour-
aged by the men, and the university revues and the articles in *Honi Soit*
were dominated by the male voice. The girls spoke the lines on stage
(sometimes) and sub-edited the boys' masterpieces. Looking back, Mungo
MacCallum recalled that his generation of students 'talked as equals, but
the assumption was that the leading roles would be taken by men'.[6] The
October edition of *Honi Soit* carried pictures of the (male) 'stars' and the
(female) 'subs'—with Richard Walsh holding 'the distinction of being the
only male on the sub-editing staff'.[7]

Madeleine was among the sub-editors, but the future Booker Prize
shortlistee was never published by her student paper. Colleen Olliffe,
one of the Octopus girls, remembered that in 1959 'we all wanted to
write, but most of us were persuaded out of it'.[8] Another member, Jane
Iliff, said, 'Most of us came from all-girl schools and had no experience
of boys, of how they show off and bully.' Once, having managed to get a
poem published, Jane found that Clive James was not impressed.[9] When
Colleen was also published—with a parody of one of Clive's poems—he

bailed her up in the lunch queue: 'Not bad kid, but don't do it again.'[10] Sue McGowan, who later married Mungo, was roped into long meetings of the Writers, Artists and Composers Group, which consisted largely of Geoffrey Lehmann and Les Murray reading their poetry while the girls listened.

The Octopus struck back, making a pact to write regularly for each other and to swap their pieces for peer review. It was a short-lived experiment that included a joint poem, one line each. But the girls took their studies seriously. They didn't skip lectures. Sue remembered regular meetings in each other's homes to talk about their academic work.[11]

But for both sexes, university was life-changing. Mungo found university liberating. 'It didn't matter which schools you had been to, whether you had been a prefect or not,' he recalled.[12] Richard Walsh and his friend Peter Grose, later a journalist, advertising executive, publisher and writer, also signed up for *Honi Soit*, gathering their courage and bursting into the office to offer their services. 'It seemed like a citadel,' Richard recalled. He and Peter were allowed to stay, working alongside the Octopus girls who had signed up as subs. 'It was fabulous, we went to *Honi Soit* every day. It was a great thing to do—and of course it was good to be with the girls.'[13]

Madeleine found university more inclusive than Queenwood. 'This is what it is all about,' she told Jonette Jarvis when the younger girl attended a SUDS performance. 'Don't worry if you don't fit in at school, you will fit in here.'[14]

There was no bar on campus so the *Honi* set drank at the Forest Lodge pub on the other side of Parramatta Road, where Clive James held court at his own table. Sue McGowan was stunned one day when he announced: 'What is meant by the word, intellectuals? It's us!'[15]

At the Forest Lodge, the young men and women plotted the next theatrical production and worked out where the party would be on Saturday night. They discovered Vadim's, just off the main strip of Kings Cross, virtually the only late-night eating spot in Sydney. They drank wine from teapots to avoid the police and gawked at the city's intellectual class, among them Harry Kippax, the legendary theatre critic from the *Sydney Morning Herald*, who would repair there as the curtain came down to write his review in leisurely fashion, calling it in to the copytakers for the morning edition.

Madeleine and her friends spent hours in Manning House, drinking bad coffee and styling themselves as pre-Raphaelites. They were mad about Baudelaire and Oscar Wilde and they didn't mind being labelled beatniks. Madeleine was becoming confident in her new style and identity. One day, in the city, she ran into former Queenwood classmate Angela Wills. Angela was dressed for the office while Madeleine was sporting a dark dirndl skirt, black stockings and an oversized black jumper. She was off to a coffee shop in Rowe Street, a popular 1950s Sydney laneway that offered a taste of the alternative life.[16]

Sometimes the men circled the women at Manning House in the mating rituals of the time, often more in hope than deed. 'A great many of us were from single-sex schools and the reason why we could not sleep with the girls was not the lack of the pill but inexperience,' Mungo said. 'There was no great women's lib push, but it would be unfair to say they were regarded as nothing more than objects of seduction.'[17]

In 1959, the Octopus girls were still only seventeen—this was before New South Wales added an extra year of high school. While some were keen to lose their virginity, they lived at a time when it was difficult to avoid pregnancy. You had to know which doctor would prescribe the pill or you risked a shotgun wedding, adoption or a dangerous illegal abortion. Keeping a child as a single mother was almost unheard of.

Winton Higgins, later a lawyer and academic, was one of Madeleine's best friends. Their relationship was platonic but Madeleine's intellect and personality thrilled Higgins. He had known few girls growing up. To Winton, Madeleine, with her French background, love of literature and individual style, represented 'Life with a capital L'.[18]

The freshers watched French movies and competed to recommend the latest novel. In this febrile atmosphere, Madeleine was intellectually able, but she was overlooked by the leading men on campus. Clive James recalled those days: 'I had absolutely no idea she was such a writing talent…she was a writer, a real one. But at that stage she hadn't written anything, so perhaps we can forgive ourselves for not spotting that there was a genius in our midst.'[19] Bruce Beresford was a close friend in later years, but in 1959 he didn't pay her much attention. Like almost everyone else, he was in love with Danne Emerson.

Danne was the adored beauty from a Catholic girls' school let loose, first on the Newman Society on campus and then later on the *Honi Soit* set. Tall and beautiful with a natural sexual magnetism, Danne could easily have been the model for Gillian Selkirk, the mistress in Madeleine's 1996 novel, *A Pure Clear Light*. Among those who longed for her that year was a young Bob Ellis. Much later, he would write that she was 'beautiful, blonde, international, proud and doomed'.[20]

Madeleine, known now as Maddy, may have been somewhat less sought after, but Richard Walsh noted her high sexual energy.[21] She had a crush on Chester and later on Charles Manning, a close friend of Colleen. And she made no secret of her determination to 'have sex'.[22]

But it was on stage that Madeleine shone, surprising everyone by being cast in a lead role in the University Revue in May. The show was called *Dead Centre*, with skits by Clive James among others, and Madeleine's appearance as Lolita in 'The True Story of Lolita Montez', a piece written by Chester and John (later Katherine) Cummings, became part of Octopus lore.[23]

Madeleine was not the only Octopus member who made it into the revue that year. It was unheard of for freshers to get parts, yet in 1959 Marilyn Taylor was also in the show, appearing in four different guises. Marilyn had arrived on campus with the express purpose of joining SUDS and becoming an actor. Colleen Olliffe had nursed a similar ambition and would later score serious acting parts on campus. Some of the Octopus members toiled behind the scenes for *Dead Centre*. Libby Smith did costumes; Sue McGowan was on makeup. Madeleine was not a natural actor, although she had inherited the St John gift of mimicry. But she saw herself as something of a *femme fatale*, even if she was buried in a duffel jacket and oversized jumpers. The role of Lolita Montez appealed to those fantasies, and she adored the vintage dress she wore on stage. She also appeared as Nancy Mitford in another skit and as a shopper in a third. Madeleine was doing well.

In September of that first year, most of the Octopus were involved in Victoriana, the music-hall-style entertainment organised by Pam Threthowan. Pam had brought the idea with her from the UK and produced it as a SUDS fundraiser in 1959. It eventually spread off campus to the North Shore and the city. Maddy, Colleen, Marilyn and Sue as well as Helen Goldstein, Libby Smith and Judy MacGregor-Smith, who were also Octopus members, were all part of the scene.[24]

Libby spent her fresher year boarding at a Salvation Army hostel in South Dowling Street, Surry Hills, and Madeleine took her under her wing. 'She was very generous and kind,' Libby recalled. 'She had a strong impact on my life. Everyone else was city and I was country. I had never been exposed to the plummy accents, the domestic standards.'[25] Madeleine saw herself as Libby's teacher and guide, intent on schooling her in the right style, the right food, and the right table settings. The kindness was real, but Madeleine was also tricky. As the Octopus girls spread out on the tables in the Manning House cafe, Madeleine occasionally sighed: 'I like Colleen and Libby best because they are always the nicest to me.'[26]

At the end of first year, Libby and Jane Iliff gravitated to the more political group, the Sydney Push. Madeleine was more cautious. Years later she wrote to her cousin, Antony Minchin:

> Oh, and, The Push. Oh God, the big P. I used to get glimpses of them around Syd Univ; they scared the wits out of me, with their combination of Total Self-Assurance verging on love, & air of being thoroughly unwashed, not to say Filthy & basic thoroughgoing cynicism

I can see that the whole package would've been irresistible to a girl with a bit of Spirit but I, e.g. wasn't.[27]

Libby soon had a boyfriend, Albie Thoms, who would go on to become a radical filmmaker. And Jane horrified her parents by moving in with her boyfriend. Madeleine's gang was branching out and she was being left behind. Marilyn knew that Maddy, despite her social self-confidence and outspoken manner, was sometimes unhappy about not being pretty and not having a boyfriend. Clive James recalled that she 'wasn't your average soubrette...She wore a lot of psychic armour, obviously feeling she was being got at'.[28] By then her circle knew about her 'wicked stepmother' and the mother whom she idealised. Madeleine's story of abandonment and loss set her apart. It became her calling card and invariably engendered sympathy. No one who met her throughout her adult years was left in doubt about the childhood trauma she had suffered.

Madeleine was still under her father's financial control, but she was trying to carve out a life separate from Ted and Val and Colette. During the swot vac before the university exams, Madeleine chose not to study at home. Instead she joined other Octopus girls in a house at Avalon on Sydney's northern beaches, enjoying a holiday atmosphere as they revised their first year of university work. When the exams were over, the Octopus joined Mungo MacCallum and others in an Angry Penguins–style prank in the *Australian Women's Weekly*, posing as members of the 'Students' Progress Association' who were 'proud to be squares'. Madeleine smiled coyly for the camera, along with her friends.[29]

In February the following year they were back on campus. The *Sydney Morning Herald* published a series of photos about events being held at the university for Orientation Week. There they all are, with the assurance of students heading into second year—Madeleine and Marilyn and Jane and Sue and Helen dutifully helping Clive James prepare a special issue of *Honi Soit* for a new group of freshers.[30]

Late in her life, Madeleine was bitter about her university experience. She said she had arrived on campus thinking it was an institution devoted to the truth but had been badly let down.[31] She overlooked the happy times on stage or gathered around the tables in Manning House. Friends' recollections show a more complex and varied experience.

Madeleine's novels do not touch on campus life, and in 2004 when she recorded several hours of tape about these early years she scarcely mentioned her time at Sydney University. She forgot the joy of that first, brilliant year when she threw off her duffel coat and took to the boards as Lolita Montez.

CHAPTER SEVEN

Adrift in Castlecrag

B y early 1960, Ted and Val were living in their dream home over-looking magnificent Chowder Bay on Sydney Harbour. They took out a hefty mortgage to pay the £16,000 for Vino del Mar, a Spanish mission-style mansion built in 1936 for a Swedish sea captain.[1] Designed by the Sydney architect Alan Stafford after he returned to Australia from California, 30a Morella Road, Clifton Gardens, had a touch of Beverly Hills glamour, with its high ceilings, heavy timber work, wrought-iron chandeliers, stone-flagged terrace and manicured gardens running down to the harbour. There was even a maid's quarters at the back. The craftsmanship was superb, but it was a derivative building, light years away from the innovation that drove design at Castlecrag.

Moving to Clifton Gardens drew a line under Ted's first marriage and family. Val had suffered three miscarriages since Oliver's birth, but was now pregnant with the couple's second child, Edward, who would be born in September. And there would be a third son, Patrick, in 1963. Ted's second family would grow up in Vino del Mar, but he gave

Madeleine, aged just eighteen, her marching orders at the end of 1959, not long after her first-year university exams.[2] He felt he had no choice given the tensions between Madeleine and Val. He offered Madeleine a regular allowance to live away from home, but Madeleine was distraught; once again she believed her father was rejecting her. She and Tina Date had composed a ditty:

> We're moving our house of strife
> To Mosman to start a new life
> I'll drown Madeleine as soon as I can
> And kill off Colette with a knife.[3]

Now it was coming true. Madeleine dashed out of the Balmoral flat and ran through the dark to Pom Jarvis. She lacked the confidence to search for digs in Sydney. She was witty, not worldly—in her own words nothing less than a 'blithering idiot'.[4] Madeleine was unhappy at home and she wanted new experiences, but the outside world filled her with trepidation. Later, when Pom tackled Val and Ted about the decision, Val replied, 'That girl made me lose three babies.'[5]

Madeleine turned to Edmund and Lorna Harvey in Castlecrag. Lorna wanted to help but had two teenage children and could not see her way clear to taking Madeleine in.[6] Friedel Souhami came to the rescue. Her husband had recently died and her only child Renate had left home. Friedel welcomed the company and she was happy to do Ted a favour by looking out for his daughter. She still felt a little guilty that on the night before Sylvette died she had not responded to her invitation to call by.

Madeleine moved back to a suburb filled with memories and a secure group of adults whom she had known since her childhood. It was a family of sorts, and she found support again from older women—Pom, Lorna, Friedel, and her aunts Margaret Minchin and Pat Buckeridge, who lived just streets away. The Souhami house at 14 The Parapet delighted Madeleine. It was built from sandstone that had been quarried in the area. Inside, a huge fireplace dominated the living area and the Bauhaus furniture that the Souhamis had brought with them from Europe before the war looked perfect.

Friedel was excellent company for a young woman: she spoke openly of contraception and sex, and her independence impressed Madeleine and the friends she sometimes brought home from university. When Libby Smith visited she was struck by Friedel's strength: the older German woman was a powerful role model for the wide-eyed teenager.[7] Friedel was a good cook—her Russian Salad was renowned throughout the Crag. 'For thirty people', the handwritten recipe went, 'take sixteen pieces of potato, eight pieces of beetroot, six herring, four apples…' Four nights a week, Friedel was home late from her job at the Berlitz language school and Madeleine went over to the Harveys' to watch television with Didy and Antony.

Madeleine spoke openly to friends about her sense of rejection. Winton Higgins was sure that Ted was paying her to stay away.[8] But Madeleine still visited Ted and Val at Clifton Gardens and enjoyed being part of an extended and privileged family that was listed in *Debrett's*. She seemed immensely proud of being the daughter of a barrister, while still dismissing her stepmother.

Left at home in Clifton Gardens, fifteen-year-old Colette began to clash badly with her father. Ted had directed most of his anger at Madeleine, but now he turned to Colette, who found his wrath 'crashing down' on her. Colette was upset at the transformation in her father. Ted had been different before Sylvette's death—he was warm and playful. 'The local children used to jump on his stomach; he used to give us aeroplane rides,' she recalled. Now he was severe: 'What's your grievance, girl?' 'Where's your gratitude, girl?' 'Look me in the eye, girl!' Colette dreamed of dying her hair red and escaping to a country town and a job at Woolworths.[9]

Ted and Val held regular play readings in the house where the raised entrance hall and sunken living room created a stage and auditorium. Ted was passionate about literature and the arts and had loved being around artists at Merioola and Castlecrag. Clifton Gardens was far from bohemian, and the play readings were an effort to pursue those interests in a more suburban setting. Ted was thrilled by classical music, turning it up to full volume at weekends.[10]

Sometimes Madeleine used Vino del Mar for an evening of the occult with the Octopus girls. Val and Ted welcomed the group but left them alone to experiment with contacting the supernatural using a Ouija board.[11]

On campus, the Octopus girls had a lot of fun. In May 1960, Madeleine performed in Armand Salacrou's *The Plate Breaker*. Richard Wherrett, who would go on to be the founding director of the Sydney Theatre Company, played the stagehand. In July and August, Madeleine had a role when the other campus theatre group, the Players, staged the e. e. cummings surrealist play *him*, directed by Ken Horler, another student who would go on to be an important director. Colleen Olliffe featured alongside John Bell; Sue McGowan was on makeup; Richard Walsh was business manager.[12] Madeleine demonstrated strong physical presence on stage: in one role she had to stand and do nothing. A reviewer noted that she did so with verve and aplomb![13]

Madeleine was acquiring some notoriety, swanning into lectures draped in layers of clothing and wearing oversized sunglasses. One day she took on Gerry Wilkes, the colourful professor of English who had a strong following among the undergraduates. They enjoyed his lectures, which were punctuated by quotes from poems such as Louis MacNeice's 'Bagpipe Music':

> It's no go the Yogi-Man, it's no go Blavatsky,
> All we want is a bank balance and a bit of skirt in a taxi.[14]

But this day, it was Madeleine who received the plaudits. She arrived late and was ordered out by an angry Wilkes. She refused to leave. He insisted, then slowly left the podium and walked up the stairs as if to remove her physically from her seat. There were howls of disapproval and Wilkes was left looking foolish as Madeleine held her ground.

By now some of the Octopus girls were going their separate ways. Sue McGowan and Mungo MacCallum were lovers, and Danne Emerson and Bruce Beresford were among the most glamorous of the couples on campus. Madeleine was ready for a boyfriend. And he came in the shape of Christopher Tillam, a second-year student who lived at St Paul's College. Chris had noticed Madeleine around campus even though the 'Paulines' traditionally held themselves slightly apart.

It was at a party in the Vaucluse flat of John Fenton-Smith that the arty mob from SUDS and *Honi Soit* encountered the St Paul's men. It was the end of 1960, just after exams. Madeleine, at close quarters, was intense: Chris recalled much later that she had been a 'fierce kisser' that night. Madeleine knew Chris had a girlfriend but, as the party ended, she announced, 'I'll be your holiday girl.' Within days, she had arranged to meet Chris again, inviting him to her Cargher grandparents' flat, which was close to where he was staying with his mother for the university break.

Chris's mother, Joan, had separated from her husband, Roger, the previous year and was living independently in a gracious block called Brantwood Hall in New South Head Road. Roger, like Ted, was a lawyer, although a senior partner in a law firm rather than a barrister. Joan was an artist who studied at the Julian Ashton Sydney Art School in the 1920s and later at the George Street studio run by Grace Crowley and Rah Fizelle.

Chris grew up in a bungalow in Morella Road, Clifton Gardens, just two houses from Vino del Mar, but by the time Val and Ted moved into the street, he had decamped for college. He was an only child and had spent most of his life at boarding school, but he loved coming home for holidays, which were filled with swimming and sailing. Joan was thirty-nine when Chris was born in 1941, and in the following years was often ill with asthma and tuberculosis. Her family was financially comfortable and well connected but Joan held a deep secret about the circumstances of the death in 1930 of her father, Harry Vernon Dixon, a successful company executive who ran the Colonial Sugar Refinery company.

Chris's classmates at Barker College included Richard Walsh and Winton Higgins. Richard and Chris were academic rivals although they were very different children—Richard was constantly in trouble throughout high school, and Chris was more studious—but they both wrote for the school's end-of-year revue. Barker College emphasised high academic achievement, and Chris did the school proud, obtaining one of the highest scores in the 1958 Leaving examinations. When the results were released, his photograph appeared on the front page of the *Sydney Morning Herald*, alongside Mungo MacCallum, another precocious scholar. Chris told the reporter from the *Herald* that he planned to study law and become a barrister.[15] The reporter did not have to go far for the interview: Chris was a copy boy at the *Herald*, a summer job secured by his father.

Leaving school and going to university was the start of a new phase for Chris, but his world imploded when his parents separated. He felt his family had evaporated overnight—just as Madeleine had after Sylvette's death. During the term, he lived at St Paul's, but he spent his holidays with Joan, who lived in a series of hotels and boarding houses after the family house was sold. For several years Chris felt that he did not really have a home.[16]

When Madeleine took Chris to meet her grandparents, he felt their 'incredible sadness'. He took away a strong impression of Feiga and Jean with their heavily accented English, their Jewish culture and their framed photographs of their daughters—Josette, away in New Guinea, and Sylvette, dead now for six years. Chris wrote later that he and Madeleine had found 'refuge in the shadows of the ruins of two families'.[17]

That summer of 1960–61, Chris dropped his girlfriend and took up with Madeleine. 'I don't know if we were in love,' he recalled. 'We were very interested in each other. I was fascinated by this person who was A, so literate, and B, so voracious in everything that she did. I know she read Proust—that was grist to the mill. Airmail editions of the *Observer* were *de rigueur*.'[18] Chris was clever and well read, but Madeleine led her boyfriend into new intellectual areas. They read Claude Lévi-Strauss's *Tristes Tropiques* in translation, when it was serialised in *Encounter* magazine. They went to art-house movies at the Savoy Cinema in Bligh Street and the Embassy in Castlereagh Street. Chris, especially, was interested in film, and they lapped up French and Italian movies.

Madeleine kept a copy of *Debrett's Peerage & Baronetage* on her bedside table, announcing at any opportunity: 'I'm in *Debrett's*!' Chris, too, had a sense of his heritage—his father was a member of the Pioneers Club, which had been established for the descendants of early settlers. But he was surprised at Madeleine's interest in her genealogy: she and Ted did not get along, yet she was obsessed with her father's ancestry.[19]

In the early months of their courtship Madeleine occasionally spent time with Chris at the Souhami house in Castlecrag, where his presence was tolerated by Friedel, and around the corner with the more welcoming Harveys. Madeleine took Chris on a walking tour past the St Johns' old house in The Rampart. She told him her parents had been so poor at one stage that they could not afford blinds. After his visits, Chris would walk to the crossroads at Castlecrag, well after midnight, and take a taxi back to St Paul's. Once, he stayed the night at Friedel's. But Madeleine and he did not sleep together. They were taking things slowly.

Madeleine moved across the harbour to a boarding house at 18 Billyard Avenue, Elizabeth Bay. Her room had a view with water glimpses. It was here that Madeleine and Chris finally became lovers. But in the early days of their relationship, Madeleine was not monogamous. She had other boyfriends at times but she never talked about them to Chris. He knew of one or two of them but claimed later that he was not particularly jealous. 'It wasn't a hanging offence as far as I was concerned,' he said.[20] But Chris, by his own account, was probably depressive in this period, although the condition was not diagnosed.

He was happy with Madeleine even if her moods could be 'volcanic'.[21] She could easily lose her temper and when she did, she became sarcastic.

Chris recalled that throughout their relationship 'she could freeze up; she could occasionally be violent…it was like a cloud would come down and a glitter in the eyes and you would feel this incredible bursting anger.'[22] Similar comments made by many others who knew Madeleine described a pattern of inexplicable anger towards those she loved. It was as if she tested her most intimate relationships by constantly inviting rejection. Chris blamed himself for her eruptions and adopted the role of peacemaker, looking for ways to help Madeleine through the crises. One day at Billyard Avenue he gave her a Robert Graves poem, 'Lovers in Winter', to try to calm her.

Madeleine helped support herself with babysitting jobs and she tutored her cousin Annabel Minchin in high-school maths. She was an excellent teacher and her quirky way of looking at things made the lessons a pleasure for Annabel.[23] But Madeleine was constantly short of money. On one occasion, Chris gave her some funds. When Ted found out, he offered to repay the money, but Chris was insulted and refused: he and Madeleine were a couple.

Some Sundays Madeleine went with Chris to see his mother. In October 1961 Joan gave Madeleine a picture, which she hung proudly in her room at Billyard Avenue. A month later, on her twentieth birthday, Madeleine received more gifts from Joan. 'Dear Mrs Tillam,' she wrote on 14 November, 'The elephants have settled in and look divine and I can't tell you how much pleasure the Japanese book gives me.'[24] Later, Chris could not recall the gifts but said the elephants might well have featured in a museum calendar from the British Museum or the Victoria & Albert Museum.

Madeleine was close to finishing her degree and Ted urged her not to enrol in an honours year. The St John women were encouraged by their men folk, and by the times, to set their sights low and 'just be very nice girls with minor accomplishments and a future as wives and mothers'.[25] Madeleine rebelled. She was determined to do English honours, but Ted refused to support her for the extra year. Not for the last time, Madeleine turned to Pom Jarvis, who agreed to give some financial assistance. Lic Walsh—who had shared her Mosman flat with Sylvette when Madeleine was a toddler—and her husband, Brian Alcorn, also agreed to help.[26] With this money and her jobs, Madeleine would get by. Chris helped her find a cheaper place to live, in a rundown mansion called Springwood in Cameron Street, Edgecliff. It was old, romantic Sydney—terraces, little wooden cottages, gum trees, wild gardens. Madeleine loved it:

> [It was] this absolutely divine old house in a part of Edgecliff that most people didn't know about then. It was on the Glebe land belonging to St James' Church…I had a room on the top floor with a bit of a verandah, French windows, the kitchen on the verandah. I had to share the bathroom. It was totally primitive and really squalid.[27]

To Madeleine, everything was an adventure. Even the cockroaches. Beside Springwood was a big garden of overgrown grass and jacarandas. When they were in bloom, the residents took their washing in from the line covered in blue flowers. Madeleine loved the 'fly-by-night' grocery shops that were open late and offered only the basics. One day she asked to buy chocolate biscuits only to be told they were not stocked in the summer because the shop did not have a fridge.

Madeleine put her stamp on her own space, and Chris helped her paint the room red and hang prints on the walls. Springwood became a favourite meeting place for the Octopus girls and their friends. The English honours students sat about endlessly debating their texts and life in general. In the makeshift kitchen, which was in danger of collapsing through the verandah, Madeleine and Chris cooked elaborate meals from Elizabeth David's newly released *French Provincial Cooking*.[28]

In June, Madeleine and Chris went to a cocktail party to celebrate Des Moody's twenty-first birthday. The friends from St Catherine's had gone in different directions: Des was now a nurse and had already met her future husband, Peter Hunter.[29] But the young women enjoyed seeing each other again and Madeleine wrote Des a warm letter of thanks. Madeleine usually hit the right note regarding matters of style. Denise Haren (later Professor Denise Bradley, the vice-chancellor of University of South Australia), who had been close to the Octopus gang, was married around this time. She recalled that Madeleine's gift was a crafted wooden salad bowl. Denise had never seen one before but Madeleine, of course, knew they were the coming thing.[30]

That final year at university was difficult for Chris. He struggled to cope with his father's remarriage to Elvira Nettlefold, the adopted daughter of the owner of the Tivoli Circuit, Ernest Nettlefold. Elvira had inherited a fortune when Ernest died, along with a waterfront mansion in Carrara Road, Vaucluse. Chris reluctantly agreed to Roger hosting a twenty-first birthday party for him at the house. All his friends got drunk 'because none of us was having a good time'.[31] And Roger was outraged to see Madeleine making out with one of Chris's college mates.

Chris had been involved in a long dispute with the history department over his honours thesis topic. He lost the battle to focus on American history, and, as time ran out, turned to methedrine to keep himself going as he cobbled together a thesis on an Australian subject. He handed in the document and then disappeared for two weeks, staying alone in a friend's house in Newtown, sunk in a 'huge depression'. He recalled: 'I eventually found my way back to life.'[32] But his absence alarmed Madeleine and when he turned up again, she persuaded him to see a psychiatrist. After one session, Chris decided he did not want to talk about his problems: he wanted to concentrate on his future. He applied for a job with the Department of External Affairs but missed out. Roger came to the rescue and organised his son a job as a cadet journalist at the *Herald*. Chris began covering the courts, the morgue and the airports round, and moved into a flat at Rushcutters Bay.

In early 1963, when Madeleine graduated, she gave tickets to the ceremony to the Jarvises and the Alcorns as a thank-you for their financial support in her honours year. It was a very public signal that Ted had failed as a father. He was furious. Although he had not supported his daughter's decision to do honours at university, he paid for the professional typing of her dissertation. But Madeleine was unrepentant. Her father had not backed her study and she was not going to allow him the glory of her graduation.[33]

Like so many other women of her generation, Madeleine's options for a career were limited. Other Octopus members took diplomas of education and went into teaching. Marilyn Taylor scored a permanent job as an actor/presenter on the ABC radio program for children *The Argonauts*. From her very earliest years Madeleine was tagged as the smart one, the scholar destined for success. Now real life was upon her. She had the brains and the style, but in the end she had to settle for a clerk's job in the Commonwealth Department of Education at North Sydney. She worked on *Hemisphere*, a departmental magazine that promoted the Colombo Plan—an aid scheme that sponsored Asian students to study in Australia. The job was far below her capacities. Ted St John could doubtless have pulled some strings for her, but it seems he did not.

Madeleine's work was unsatisfying, but her social life was interesting. Chris often collected her from the North Sydney offices in his blue Renault and they went to concerts at the Sydney Town Hall. They visited Pom and Os Jarvis, with Madeleine regaling them with her latest adventures. Jonette thought the couple well suited, that Madeleine's extroverted personality was nicely balanced by Chris's reserve. Pom worried that Chris was too close to his mother, although Madeleine got on famously with Joan.[34] Madeleine and Joan shared a fascination with words and a distinctive visual aesthetic, and it is likely Joan felt a special bond with this well-mannered girl who, like her, had been scarred by the death of a parent. Writing much later, Chris described the women as having 'much in common, sensibilities honed to the point of excluding most of the local quotidian, a delight in small beauties, in the juxtaposition of words and of objects'.[35]

Sometimes Madeleine and Chris visited Feiga and Jean, but looking back Madeleine realised she did not appreciate their sadness at the loss of Sylvette:

> I did not have a clue. By the time I was 19 or 20, I was this cold-hearted, unloving, ungiving little bitch...I was trying to find a nest for myself and burrow down into it. I had no sensitivity to other people...I had no sensitivity to my grandparents. I could see they were in pain but I didn't know what to do about it. It was only later on that I realised that the only hope that they had for any type of happiness was in their children and grandchildren.[36]

When the young couple drove over to Clifton Gardens to have dinner with Ted and Val, Madeleine fussed over her half-brothers, Oliver and Ed, and baby Patrick, but the atmosphere was brittle. There was still great tension between father and daughter. But Madeleine had found stability with Chris. He accepted her behaviour. Spikiness was part of her nature and her sharp tongue was accompanied by a distinctive intellect that he found very attractive. He took on the role of the rock to withstand her eruptions and weather the storms.

CHAPTER EIGHT

Till Death Us Do Part

In the years after university, with her job at *Hemisphere* providing a regular income, Madeleine lived in a series of flats and houses around Elizabeth Bay and Paddington in the eastern suburbs of Sydney. Usually Chris was with her, although the couple always maintained separate rooms. Their first shared locale was at 55 Elizabeth Bay Road, in a boarding house run by Chica Lowe, the same Chica Lowe who twenty years earlier had managed the Merioola artists' colony where Madeleine had lived as a child. The Elizabeth Bay house was not as bohemian as Merioola, but Chica took in a motley crew, from men who had left their wives to teenagers who had left home. Madeleine's room was upstairs at the front. Chris set himself up in a smaller room at the back of the premises.

Around this time, they became engaged. Chris recalled: 'I can't remember why we decided to get engaged but we did.'[1] They went to Steiner's jewellery shop in Castlereagh Street and bought a ring, a floweret of bright emeralds on a gold band. The ring was second-hand but it was not cheap—Madeleine did not do cheap.

Madeleine was happy, but her pleasure was short-lived. Colette also headed for Chica's. Her friends Lyndal Moor and Yvette White were there and Chica, who remembered Colette as a baby at Merioola, had offered her a room. For Colette, it was freedom from Ted and Val.

When Colette arrived at Chica's, Madeleine felt her space invaded. She had begun to carve out a life for herself and now Colette was on her turf and was hostile:

> As soon as I appeared on the scene, she would start ridiculing me or say what a terrible dress I was wearing. She would generally set me up as this person to ridicule. I became completely socially incapable; I could not participate as an equal person in any gathering as long as she was one of the people in it. I realised that I could not have a life with her, [that we] had to have separate lives. But only in Sydney you can't. You know the same people. So if we ever happened to run into each other, [if] we happened to be at the same party or whatever, she gave me a bad time.[2]

Madeleine assumed she had offended Colette, but did not know how. Colette was battling to find a direction. Unlike Madeleine, she did not have a clear path to university. She wanted to be a photographer, and, after she left school, had been apprenticed to a photographer. Ted and Val had bought her equipment to set up a dark room under the house, but in 1963 Colette moved into Chica's and went to work at the PMG as a telephonist.

She had a strong circle, among them, her gay American friend, Geoffrey Humphries, whose parents rented a mansion in Billyard Avenue. He spent most of his time hanging out at Chica's along with another American, Jill Roehrig, who became friends with Chris and Madeleine. Jill was fond of Chris. She recalled him as 'a rock…a very sweet, patient man' who spent his time trying to calm Madeleine down. Jill saw several 'enormous fights' between the couple: their relationship was difficult and Madeleine had a lot of issues.[3]

Living in the same house, Colette, too, saw her sister and future brother-in-law up close. She was surprised that Madeleine did not seem to care how she behaved in front of her boyfriend. 'She did things to me in front of him, she behaved in the Madeleine way, she was not trying to hide it from him. I never saw her being vile to him, she was vile to me…She would create and destroy at such a rate I knew she had to be doing that to him.'[4]

Chris was unperturbed. It did not seem to him that his life with Madeleine was so difficult. His tolerance of her behaviour, an acceptance akin to resignation, was now a key element of their relationship. Madeleine was struggling with self-esteem, but her intellect and her intensity exerted a powerful hold on her boyfriend.

Around this time, Chica Lowe moved her boarding house to 55 Grosvenor Street, Bondi Junction, and Chris and Madeleine went with her. Colette went her own way, sharing with friends in a $20-a-fortnight house in Oxford Street, Paddington. She was well known on the Sydney party scene. Madeleine had steered clear of the Sydney Push while at university, favouring the theatre and literature over politics, but Colette dipped in and out of the Baby Push, a slightly younger crowd who hung off the edges of the original group. She was sexually attractive—men could sense her wild streak. And she was a risk-taker, in a way that Madeleine could never be, embracing the 1960s zeitgeist with enthusiasm. One day, as a dare, Colette took the bus from Paddington to the city, braless in a see-through shirt, to the consternation of passengers.[5]

Despite their clashes, Madeleine and Colette were soon sharing a house again: Madeleine and Chris fled Chica's when the atmosphere soured after Chica began an affair with one of the tenants. In Oxford Street, Madeleine squeezed onto the enclosed back balcony and Chris camped on a sofa in the adjoining sitting room. Chris recalled that one morning as he lay in bed, Madeleine, barely awake, came in and punched him in the eye. She was mortified when she realised what she had done.[6]

*

After a year or so at the *Herald*, Chris knew reporting was not for him. He was asked to interview again for a foreign affairs job, but his lack of confidence ruled him out of the diplomatic life. He was accepted as a trainee talks officer in radio and television at the ABC, and when an information sheet was sent around for Fulbright scholarship applications, he wrote to half a dozen American universities to see if he could get a place as the first step in applying for a the grant. By chance an old St Paul's friend, Mike Rubbo, who had used his Fulbright to go to Stanford the year before, saw Chris's application to the Mass Communications course there and urged the department to take him on. There was a specific grant available to Australians—the Melville J. Jacoby Scholarship—and soon it was sorted. Chris would go to Stanford in the middle of 1965 for a boutique documentary-making course. It was a big break for the young Australian.

Chris parked the Renault down at Mrs Macquarie's Chair on the harbour and broke the news to Madeleine. They should both go, Chris said, but first they should get married.

Madeleine responded: 'You don't have to.' She was giving Chris a way out. To Chris, there was some attraction in breaking off the engagement, yet it was also unthinkable given their shared history.

Whatever his own hesitations, Chris insisted they would go to the US together, and they drove to Clifton Gardens to tell Val and Ted that they were getting married. Ted made a wry remark about wanting to 'recover the sofas' that year but there was never any question that he would pay for the wedding.[7] A date was set for shortly before Chris's departure by plane for San Francisco. Madeleine decided she would follow by ship. A long sea voyage met her desire for living in style, and Chris was happy enough to confront the first few weeks at Stanford without the extra pressure of Madeleine's volatility.[8]

Some of Madeleine's friends were surprised when the wedding invitations arrived in the post: they had not realised the relationship was serious. Colette wondered if her sister's decision to marry had been a way to win

Ted's approval. Despite their fractious relationship, Madeleine often tried to gain his attention and love.[9] Felicity Baker recalled that Madeleine had always had a 'deep ambition' to marry, to attain a 'respectable married status, to create a home and family for a respected man'.[10]

At 5.30 p.m. on Friday 4 June 1965, Madeleine and Chris were married. There had been a small crisis when Ted decided he did not want to walk his daughter down the aisle to 'give her away' and had to be persuaded by Val.[11] Madeleine was almost hysterical by the time she battled her way through the Friday afternoon traffic to enter the church. Her uncle, Bill Baker, performed the ceremony at the Church of St James—where Val and Ted had married a decade earlier. Madeleine's choice of venue startled her friends, who had expected something less 'establishment' from the woman who had played Lolita Montez.[12]

Madeleine had refashioned herself since university. She had lost weight and looked stunning in an expensive Chris Jacovides dress. But she banned photographs. She controlled every aspect of the wedding, and she enjoyed being perverse. She wanted to be different. Colette recalled that Madeleine thought being in the social columns was terribly *infra dig*, 'the lowest of the low'.[13] Not having photographs was about showing she did not care a toss about such things. Madeleine was also sensitive about her appearance, so may not have wanted pictures. Looking back, Chris wondered whether she refused to be photographed because she did not want to be recorded as married.[14]

Colette was a bridesmaid and she, too, wore a white Jacovides number. A superb dressmaker like her grandmother, Colette had planned to make the dresses for Madeleine and herself and had even bought the fabric. But at the last minute, Madeleine changed her mind. Colette was upset, even more so when she found the Jacovides bridesmaid dress did not suit her.

Chris recalled that he felt 'incredibly alone' that day. He had given up his rented room as he prepared to fly to the US, so he dressed for his wedding in a stranger's house. Then he met the groomsman at the

Pioneers Club in nearby Bent Street. The wedding ceremony was a blur, and years later Chris could not recall the name of the groomsman. It was a strange period for the twenty-four-year-old. He was getting married, but within a few days would be separated from his bride as he headed for Stanford alone.

Seventeen-year-old Annabel Minchin was overwhelmed by the romance of the day and cried her way through the proceedings. Winton Higgins was an usher, even though he had had little contact with Madeleine in the previous couple of years. Marilyn Taylor was intimidated by the whole show, despite the fact she was already 'on the wireless' at the ABC. Many of the Octopus gang had not been invited, so rapidly had their lives moved apart since university. But Colleen Olliffe and Richard Walsh were among the guests. Richard was not close to either Madeleine or Chris, but assumed he was there due to his connection to Ted, whom he had come to know through the *Oz* trials the previous year. Ted had defended the printer of the magazine, Francis James, in the court case in which Walsh, Richard Neville and artist Martin Sharp had been charged with publishing an obscene issue.[15] At the church, Richard shocked Colleen when he whispered, 'Imagine her being the first of you to go!'[16]

As they walked back down the aisle as man and wife, Madeleine dug her nails into Chris's arm and whispered, 'Too fast!'[17] She had a picture in her mind of how the event should unfold and she had no hesitation in trying to control Chris. But it was a stressful day for Madeleine. Chris recalled, 'We were both taking a leap, escaping Oz, escaping family.' Looking back, he felt it must have been confronting for Madeleine to have chosen the kind of church of which Ted approved, yet to know that Sylvette was not there to see her wed.[18]

The reception in the sunken living room at Vino del Mar turned out to be a 'spiffing affair' according to Colleen.[19] But there was an awkward moment when Ted rose to say a few words. He loved making speeches, but when Madeleine announced ironically, 'Well, you won't get a speech out of him!', Ted backed off.[20] At the end of the evening, Madeleine changed from her wedding dress into her going-away outfit of a grey woollen pants suit. She was glowing.

As they prepared to leave, the new Mr and Mrs Tillam stood in the elevated entrance area of Vino del Mar gazing down at the guests. 'It was as if she was saying, look at me, this is my moment,' Marilyn Taylor recalled.[21] Her pants suit had been made by a men's tailor but had not been entirely successful, according to Colette. Madeleine thought the suit made her look like a lesbian; Colette thought it was the kind of suit worn by little Italian boys at a wedding.[22] Nonetheless, Madeleine wore it.

The young couple drove in the Renault to the Bundanoon pub, about 150 kilometres from Sydney in the Southern Highlands. A couple of days later they were back in the city, at the stylish Belvedere Hotel near Kings Cross. Colette recalled that Madeleine had been enchanted with the Belvedere when they had seen the hotel as children. The next morning the newlyweds took photographs on the balcony, Chris in his tweed jacket, cigarette in hand, Madeleine in her grey suit.[23] Then Roger Tillam drove them to Sydney airport for their goodbyes, and Chris flew out to San Francisco. It was 10 June 1965.

Three days later, Madeleine wrote to her mother-in-law to thank her for her wedding gift of a necklace 'which I shall wear with the greatest pleasure'.[24] Joan had given Chris a Sidney Nolan painting, and Madeleine, staying temporarily in Paddington, told Joan that she could not wait to have a household for the painting. It was 'heart rending' to leave the wedding present behind for a year but the Nolan was too valuable to cart to Stanford and she asked Joan whether she could leave the painting in her care.

Joan had grown very fond of Madeleine. A few days later, she sent a box of flowers to her daughter-in-law's cabin as her ship departed for San Francisco. From Auckland, Madeleine posted a letter of thanks and enjoyed the blooms all the way to Honolulu.[25]

CHAPTER NINE

American Dreams

In his first days in the US, while he waited for Madeleine to arrive, Chris bought a second-hand Chevrolet and rented an apartment at 1159 Bay Laurel Drive in Menlo Park, the suburb closest to the Stanford campus at Palo Alto. It was the top floor of a two-storey house set back from the street on a circular drive. There were huge trees everywhere in the slightly unkempt garden, as well as bird-baths and a sundial, squirrels, jasmine, Virginia creeper and bees, and magnificent magnolia trees lined the streets.[1] The Tillams' land-lord lived below, but upstairs was private and roomy with casement windows, a large living room and a study as well as a double bedroom. It was, Chris told his mother, 'sylvan, airy and quiet'.[2]

Chris threw himself into his course, which was led by Henry Breitrose, one of the most influential film and mass communications academics of his generation. When Chris arrived in the summer of 1965, Breitrose's Documentary Film Program was at its height. His students, including Chris, were smart, highly educated, artistic and literary. Many were being exposed to the technical side of film-making for the first time, and the department buzzed with experiment and energy.

'It looks like being exciting & tough,' Chris wrote to Joan ten days before the course began.[3] Mike Rubbo was showing him the ropes, but Chris was apprehensive. Mike was leaving big shoes to fill: he had been a social and academic success in the course and was about to leave for a job at the Canada Film Board, the Mecca for documentary makers in those years.

Around the middle of July, Chris went to the San Francisco wharves to collect his wife after her sea voyage. He was late and found a grumpy Madeleine, shoulders slumped, sitting on her suitcase. The trip had been a disaster, her cabin mate appalling, the whole experience nothing like her dream of a stylish ocean journey.

Chris had always been her rock, but now he was torn between his role of Madeleine's pacifier and the demands of his course. Madeleine, to her credit, stumped up early the next morning to accompany him to the Central Valley to record some audio of a horserace for one of his projects.

She found work house cleaning in Palo Alto for $14 a day while she looked for a proper job. She told Joan in a letter at the end of July that America was 'too exciting for words—there is so much of absolutely everything, both good things and bad, and everything is so much bigger! There are marvellous shops near us without even going into San Francisco. But of course, San Francisco is—superlative.'[4] She loved the 'posh department stores' in San Francisco, with their scented air and floors of beautiful clothes:

> It's all terribly clean—like the rest of these parts—and the climate is perfect—cool, crisp and sunny...there are the most wonderful old houses...flowers and vines grow in every available space—you see a lot of window boxes, with geraniums tumbling down onto the foot-path.[5]

The letter was upbeat and positive. Nothing less would have been expected back home at the start of such an exciting American experience. But

Madeleine was already becoming adept at presenting an image that was not always based on reality.

Chris was 'frantically busy' with his course and Madeleine apologised for his not writing to Joan.[6] When Chris did write to his mother, he grumbled about the workload in his course, saying, 'there isn't really enough time to do any one project properly'.[7] In fact, it was worse than that. Chris knew he was not coping with some aspects of the course, and this was confirmed when Henry Breitrose told him that he was not performing at an appropriate level.

Madeleine, too, was under strain. She was still trying to find a proper job and she was using sleeping pills. Things improved when she found work at the university bookshop. She was to work five days a week, with Fridays and Sundays off, and at last she would have an income rather than relying on savings.

But just a few days after Madeleine started her new job and less than three months into their marriage, the couple argued. This was nothing new, but this time Chris retreated to the study, taking with him a bottle of Madeleine's sleeping tablets. He spread the pills out on the desk and then swallowed half of them. Madeleine discovered him, blue in the face, and he was rushed by ambulance to the Palo Alto State Hospital. Four attendants held him down as doctors pumped his stomach. When he regained consciousness, Madeleine was there. His first words to her were 'I'm sorry I did not make a proper job of it.'[8]

It must have been devastating for Madeleine. In Sydney, she had been aware Chris's moods could swing, but now she was far away from family and friends. In the past she could rely on Chris, but now the future must have looked uncertain. There had been silence around the details of Sylvette's death, but she knew enough of her mother's history with sleeping tablets to be alarmed by this latest development.

Yet, on the surface, life quickly returned to normal. After a couple of days, Chris came home from the hospital. Madeleine was at work at the bookshop so, still in his dressing-gown, he took a cab back to their apartment. He began attending weekly psychotherapy sessions, with a month or so to pull himself together before term commenced at the end of September. There was little or no discussion of what lay beneath Chris's behaviour. The young couple were becoming practised at papering over the cracks in their relationship.

Madeleine was cheered by a letter from Colette in London. Her sister was 'adoring' the metropolis, and Madeleine wrote to Joan that she was 'so pleased to get in touch with her again'.[9] But life at Stanford was still a challenge. Madeleine told Joan that she enjoyed her work at the bookstore but arrived home 'terribly tired & not feeling terribly prosy or creative'. The Tillams were short of money and were watching a lot of television rather than going out. But the cultural offerings of the area beckoned and Madeleine hoped that 'by mid-October we'll be more straightened out & able to do more'.[10]

A couple of weeks later Chris typed a long letter to Joan, and filled it with details of things seen—including a football game between Stanford and the Navy—and books read. He did not mention his recent crisis and the letter was chatty but distant. Term would start the following day, the holidays had been 'pretty quiet', the car was costing Chris more in oil than in gas, and the weather was 'getting a bit cooler'. Madeleine had a twenty per cent discount on books from the bookshop where she worked and she and Chris were buying up. Chris was reading 'a Canadian English professor, Marshall McLuhan, who has some revolutionary ideas about how the electronic media are shaping our sensibilities'.[11]

It was a time of cultural and political upheaval in the US. In August, Congress had passed the Voting Rights Act, which finally outlawed the discrimination against blacks that remained in several US states. It was history in the making. That year also saw a dramatic escalation of American involvement in the Vietnam conflict amid controversy at home. Stanford was relatively quiet, a 'hotbed of rest', as Henry Breitrose recalled.[12] But across the bay, Chris told his mother, Berkeley was 'the spiritual home of practically all civil-disobedience groups in America. It's here, on the west coast, that feeling against US Vietnamese policy runs strongest and there are the biggest and most regular demonstrations.'[13]

The cultural change transforming America was taking shape in California and it was impossible to ignore. The Summer of Love—when 100,000 hippies flooded into the Haight-Ashbury area of San Francisco— was two years away, but sex, drugs and creativity were breaking out all over. 'There is a bit of a local cult here, centring on the author Ken Keesey [sic],' Chris told Joan. 'Keesey has written one novel so far, *One Flew Over the Cuckoo's Nest*.'[14] At Stanford:

> one meets characters who appeared in the books of Jack Kerouac, there is a flourishing drug coterie—and a lot of serious investigation goes on as well into the whole psychedelic question. Rumours at the moment of a campaign to be launched this fall at Berkeley, over the bay from SF, for the legalisation of marijuana…[15]

In the second semester, Chris was much happier. The emphasis of the course, with new lecturer George Stoney, a well-known documentary maker from New York, suited Chris, and his work improved.

Now Madeleine was the watchful, wary one. The power had shifted slightly in Chris's favour, now that he had 'punished' Madeleine by taking an overdose.[16] She could no longer take his fortitude and devotion for granted. If, as she later claimed, she had married Chris in search of security, she must have had cause to wonder in those first months at Stanford as her new husband became more independent.

Madeleine made an impression on campus. She was far more memorable than her quiet and civilised husband, according to Chris's classmate Tom Bell. She was an extrovert who loved to talk literature and 'spoke in complete sentences, if not paragraphs. There was a kind of acute articulateness to her speech.' Tom recalled that her style of dressing set her apart: she was 'carefully put together'.[17] She smoked constantly, usually unfiltered cigarettes such as Gauloises. Jill Roehrig, who was now back in San Francisco, noted how Madeleine flicked the tiny shreds of tobacco from her lips with the edge of a fingernail.[18] Madeleine had always yearned to be a *femme fatale.*

She also proved to be a consummate performer in her letters. At the end of October, she wrote to Joan extolling Chris's virtues as a filmmaker and artist:

> He really is remarkably clever, I don't think it can be too long before we are not the only people aware of it…He wrote a wonderful poem on Sunday, to cheer me up when I was feeling 'blue'. He is working very hard & doing a lot of reading & I think, finding life altogether stimulating.[19]

Madeleine made some 'lovely muffins' for her appreciative husband and announced she wanted a white kitten for her birthday. The praise for Chris was just a touch excessive, even for a young bride.

Madeleine and Joan swapped book recommendations and ideas. 'I don't care very well for H. Miller,' Madeleine told her mother-in-law:

> I think his ideas are a little simple, but I haven't read *Maroussi*—Chris says it's wonderful. I too didn't care for *Lady Chat's Lover*—in fact I found it a very poor novel. What I really love is Henry James—please try, say, *The Portrait of a Lady,* and tell me how you find it. Have you read any of Marianne Moore's poetry? You'd love her.[20]

After a Thanksgiving spent with Jill Roehrig, Madeleine was in bed with a cold, rereading Blake and encouraging Joan to have a go at the modern Greek poets Cavafy and Seferis.[21]

Chris's life had taken off. He told his mother he was 'way past my ears with work' and thrilled by George Stoney's leadership. 'The points he keeps hammering home are psychological rather than technical…you can't make a film by standing on the sidelines—you have to be in the thick of it…'[22] Chris was making two films: his own three-and-a-half-minute 'boy doesn't meet girl' film featuring Jill Roehrig and an MG; and another with a colleague, Saad Raheem, about the campus of the University of California being built at Santa Cruz, sixty-five kilometres away on the coast. Students and staff were living in trailers among the redwoods while the residential colleges were built. Chris wrote an expanded treatment for his film and successfully applied for $500 from the University of California to reshoot it as a ten-minute documentary.

Madeleine had a nine-to-five routine at the bookshop, but Chris spent hours in the basement editing room at the university. 'Time passes quickly and sometimes I'll go down at 7 p.m., and emerge a little before dawn,' he wrote home. 'It's common practice for someone editing his film to take a sleeping bag & toothbrush & camp there.'[23] Madeleine never hinted at it in her letters, but she must have been lonely in this period as her husband's horizons expanded.

Colette turned twenty-one in December 1965, and Madeleine and Chris sent greetings to her in London. Madeleine made a multi-leaved card with US dollars hidden between each sheet and Chris sent a poem to his sister-in-law:

> Nor think to falsify your hair with wigs or rinses, tints or dyes
> Forbear such foolishness for men, low creatures, find
> less interest in a head than a behind.[24]

Christmas 'wasn't quite Christmas' that year for Madeleine and Chris, who felt 'rather bereaved, having Christmas in a cold & strange climate'. Madeleine had never professed a great love of Australia but, after six months in the US, she was homesick and hoped to be back in Sydney for Christmas 1966, although she admitted this looked less likely. Playing the dutiful wife, at least on paper, she wrote: 'Chris's career comes absolutely first & if it is necessary for him to stay on a bit longer here, then stay we must.'[25] Chris had finished his short film, and Madeleine announced it was 'a lovely thing with perfect jazz music score and titles, all of which should gain him an A grading'.[26]

The Tillams were disappointed that they received only one Christmas card from Australia. Madeleine had little correspondence from Clifton Gardens and noted that Val's letters were 'somewhat staid', while Ted didn't often find time to write. Joan was a far more dedicated correspondent. She and Madeleine exchanged letters independently of Chris, an indication of a closeness that exceeded the usual relationship between in-laws.

In many ways, Madeleine grew closer to Joan as she sensed her husband drawing away. In the new year, Chris grew a beard and Madeleine reported he was turning into 'rather an extrovert' who worked very hard and was 'rather witty & loves film-making'.[27] The power was moving further away from Madeleine.

The couple soaked up the culture on offer. They heard Rosalyn Tureck play Bach and listened rapt through four encores; they went to a John Coltrane and Thelonious Monk concert [28] and another with Dizzy Gillespie and the Modern Jazz Quartet; they saw the film of *My Fair Lady*, which Madeleine found 'frightfully disappointing' apart from the Cecil Beaton costumes, the Ascot scene and the performance of actor Gladys Cooper as Henry Higgins's mother. Cooper was 'quite perfect, & she has the loveliest sitting room, which we see right at the end—all blue and white, leading into a little conservatory. One longs to have a blue and white room just like it,' she told Joan. Not to mention a 'moss-green dining room one day...with white woodwork'.[29]

In January 1966, they attended a screening of Sergei Eisenstein's movie on the October Revolution, *Ten Days That Shook the World*. In the audience was the octogenarian Alexander Kerensky, the last survivor of the government overthrown by the uprising. It was the first time that Kerensky, who lived near Stanford, had seen the film.[30]

Madeleine was beginning to look to England. Colette wrote from London to say she had been invited to a wedding. Madeleine relayed the news of the 'chi-chi' event to Joan and said she hoped Colette would:

meet some nice young men there, anyway—she complains that she hasn't met anyone (male) really gorgeous yet, so I hope she will soon, since everything I learn about London makes me think of it as the ideal setting for a love affair—all those Bond Street shops, spring flowers, quaint nooks, courtyards & streets, millions of intimate restaurants, etc. and plenty of cold weather.[31]

Madeleine surprised friends and family back home with her embrace of America. She wrote to Antony Minchin:

I think you mean to flatter me when you say you didn't imagine me & the USA hitting it off. Annabel wrote and said the same. So I've asked her to tell me why, so that I can explain. [America] is really not what one imagines it to be—it's really a marvellous, exciting country. Very bad things & very good things too. I could never live here for ever (mainly because I'm too much of a socialist to do so, also because Australia is my place) but for a while it's just divine.[32]

'Don't believe everything you read in books, Anna darling, or you will never see the world!' she wrote to Annabel. 'After all, is all of Australia like Patrick White's Sarsaparilla?'[33]

Madeleine was a keen observer of human nature and the physical landscape and now she absorbed the style and mores of her temporary home. She asked if Antony had read Robin Boyd's *The Australian Ugliness*, published in 1960, which had cast a highly critical eye over the Australian aesthetic:

[Boyd] makes a very just comparison of Aussie chrome & brashness and American ditto. So you wouldn't see, in these parts, anything very much more startling than you can see in parts of Sydney. For the rest, there are millions of Americans who are anything but brash—there's a tradition of politeness & good manners here which one hadn't expected—a sort of fine old American thing. There are a lot of 'fine old American' traditions and practices that make us Australians seem very young and raw & undeveloped. I'll explain at length one day.[34]

She noted cultural differences between American and Australian men. American men 'didn't hate women' in the way she sensed many men did back home. Years later, Madeleine recalled that the men at Stanford opened doors, treated her with respect and 'liked women, quite frankly and quite unselfconsciously'. It was taken for granted, she said, that 'men and women were made to have pleasure in each other's company'. It was 'quite an extraordinary thing to experience for the first time'.[35] One day in the refectory, she saw a golden Californian boy buy a glass of milk, pour it into a saucer and gently feed it to his little kitten. No Australian man would be seen doing such a thing, she thought, for fear of being torn to shreds as a sissy.

Madeleine fell hard for a colleague at the bookshop. 'There was something about him that was kind of foreign', and she was drawn to this man who looked so different from her own husband. Madeleine's interest was reciprocated. 'You could practically hear the violins,' she recalled. 'It was just amazing. It was one of the great *coups de foudre* of my life and I couldn't do a damn thing about it.' When she told the man she was married, the affair ended before it had begun.[36]

Around her the social rules were in flux. The increasing availability of the pill made it a time of experimentation with sex and lifestyles. Yet Madeleine was more cautious than many of her generation. In later life, she said that in sixties California she had been 'far too young to take advantage of it, far too crazy to use this experience to grow up and get away from the mess I had got myself into'.[37] The mess she referred to was her marriage to Chris. But if that was her state of mind at the time, she gave little away.

The Tillams entertained visitors from Australia. Tina Date dropped in for five days, fresh from her success with a hit album, *A Single Girl*. Playing guitar Joan Baez–style, she was now one of Australia's leading exponents of folk music. Madeleine welcomed Tina, but she was privately disparaging of her in a letter to Antony, thanking him for the 'hysterical cutting' he had sent about Tina. Antony kept Madeleine up to date with developments back home: he sent a new Australian dollar shortly after the switch to decimal currency on 14 February 1966. It was 'greatly interesting to see, though I don't think I like it; in some ways it's good. But marvellous to have; thank you again so very much,' she wrote back.[38]

Her restlessness was obvious to her Stanford friends. Tom Bell thought she 'looked like a person who couldn't wait to move on, as if she was parked in Palo Alto on the way to someplace else'.[39] Madeleine told him that given the education system in Australia considered London to be the 'centre of the cultural universe, the least [the government] could do would be to give us an airline ticket there'.[40]

Madeleine maintained her composure in letters to Joan. She wrote of her latest purchases—an expensive navy blue and 'frightfully French' overcoat and a 'marvy new pr. of sunglasses—big circular white frames'. She had spring-cleaned the apartment, washed curtains, sewn on buttons, mothproofed clothes, and made a 'divine' cheesecake for Chris's birthday. Colette had sent her a 'gorgeous Jaeger jumper—pale blue, quite plain' from London.[41]

She was now spending more time alone. Chris went on the road making a documentary film of the famous 300-mile protest march of striking farm workers from Delano to Sacramento. His world was opening up, and Madeleine resented her role as 'the main bread-winner. It was just horrific, it was all work, work, work.'[42] At the end of April, Chris spent almost a week at a television conference at Monterey Bay. Among the participants was Marshall McLuhan.[43] When he returned home, Madeleine found her husband tired and 'undervitamised looking' after days of staying up till 2 a.m.[44] Chris was planning to spend three months in Europe to make a documentary on the Stanford courses offered there, but Madeleine was not happy about it, even admitting this in a letter to Joan, saying 'how vile' it would be without her husband around.[45]

In the end, the project did not go ahead, but Madeleine was sounding tired—and almost sad—in letters to Joan:

Very sunny, the sprinkler playing outside & Brahms on the gramophone, leaf shadows flickering on the page as I write—a pretty scene. I wish life had this quality more often. But there is so much rushing about, one barely has time to enjoy these simple pleasures of mood & moment.[46]

The Tillams exchanged gifts for their wedding anniversary on 4 June—an amber cigarette holder for her and a book on the Aztecs for him—but they were tiring of their relatively suburban existence.[47] 'We are both mad to get out of the Stanford area and move to the city,' Chris told his mother. They had friends in San Francisco, where rents were cheaper and there was more to do. 'Palo Alto doesn't exactly swing at the best of times, and in summer it's…incredibly motionless. And the last three days there's been a heatwave, 95 all day.'[48] It's likely they were hoping the move would alter the state of their marriage, but they had to wait. Chris got a job in Henry Breitrose's department for the summer and so they stayed on in their apartment at Menlo Park.

Madeleine's letters to Joan were shorter now, often mere thank-you notes for gifts received. The news they contained was trivial. She had seen a wonderful set of steak knives—French, stainless-steel blades with ivory handles hafted on with tiny brass rivets. Madeleine loved beautiful objects and she was determined to twist Chris's arm to buy them. They were not, after all, 'terribly expensive'. She was weary but she maintained her pose with Joan in that same letter: 'Have just had a shattering bulletin from Chris—"We're out of tea!"—which I cannot live without. Will have to get some tomorrow, or dreadful derangement will set in!'[49]

Madeleine was bored. 'Nothing much happening,' she wrote to Joan. 'Went to an open-air concert, L'Orchestre de la Suisse Romande doing Honegger, Debussy & Pétrouchka—lovely setting in the Frost Amphitheatre at Stanford, beautiful summer's evening…but orchestra somewhat disappointing. Their American debut. Ansermet very, very old—a figure of the past.'[50]

In the fall of 1966 the Tillams finally packed up and moved to San Francisco. Strong winds whipped the leaves as high as their rented second-floor apartment in California Street, next door to the fire station. From Sydney, the ever-thoughtful Joan sent dozens of yellow roses and white carnations to welcome them to their new home with its white walls and woodwork, billowing light curtains, honey-coloured timber floors and woven mats. Madeleine and Chris bought white chairs and art nouveau lamps from a charity shop and daisies from the Union Square flower stores.

They were not far from Jill Roehrig's flat, which she shared with her friend Kathy Kettler, who had grown up on the fringes of the Hollywood movie set in Los Angeles. Madeleine and Kathy got along well. The young Australian was funny and sharp and Kathy found her a pleasure to be around.

Once again, Madeleine found some casual work in a bookshop and began keeping house. And she painted an image of domestic harmony in her letters. 'I must attend to the *poule au pot. Au revoir* and write soon,' she signed off to Joan in September. It could almost have been a line from a novel.

San Francisco was pleasant, and Madeleine had family around. Ted's sister Florence and her husband Frank Heller and their three children had arrived for Frank's teaching appointment at Berkeley and were living across the bay. Madeleine was delighted, although she told Joan: 'I felt I ought to apologise to Chris for not being able to escape my voluminous family—fancy a branch of it turning up on our doorstep like this!'[51]

They had yearned for the move to San Francisco, but almost as soon as they arrived, the Tillams were hatching plans to leave. Chris could not find a permanent film job in the city and Madeleine applied for unemployment benefits. Out of the blue came a phone call from George Stoney, who had taught Chris at Stanford. He had recommended Chris for a film-making job with Dr Edward A. Mason of the Laboratory of Community Psychiatry at the Harvard Medical School. Mason, a psychiatrist, had pioneered the use of film to teach students more effectively, and Harvard had funded him to expand his work. Chris and Madeleine were excited by the thought of 'working for Harvard and having $7,200 a year'.[52]

They waited to see whether anything would come of it, where Chris's work would take them. It was an unsettling time and old tensions resurfaced. Indeed the relationship was worse than ever. Jill Roehrig had seen huge arguments between the couple when they all lived in Sydney. But now she thought Madeleine was 'disturbed'. Chris was 'just trying to stop her jumping off the ledge', she recalled.[53] Jill thought things were so bad between them that Chris was trying to leave her.[54]

Early in October, on a fleeting visit to America, Ted St John called in to see his daughter. He had decided to stand for federal parliament at the November election and he was about to enter a grueling preselection contest. He had only a day in San Francisco and spent the afternoon at the apartment in California Street. Madeleine organised a small party for his recent fiftieth birthday and the Hellers came over. It went well, yet, as always, Madeleine judged her father harshly. She wrote to Annabel Minchin that 'T talked about himself most of the time, but don't breathe a word, *ma cousine*'.[55]

Madeleine was at pains to hide the problems in her marriage. She and Chris were 'as happy as 2 birds in a tree', she told Annabel. She had stopped work and her cake making '& general kitchen repertoire' had improved enormously.[56] The Hellers saw it differently. Madeleine nagged Chris endlessly and he seemed no match temperamentally for his intense wife. Frank, a social scientist, was blunt. 'I don't think that will work,' he told Florence.[57] Perhaps Madeleine knew it too. Despite the fictional domestic idyll she presented in her letters, she knew she was in trouble. 'I was out of my mind,' she recalled years later. 'I was totally screwed up.'[58]

She was anxious about the idea of moving to Boston. She had found Jill and Kathy to be good friends. Kathy had lived with a suicidal mother and she had quickly become a strong support for Madeleine. For the first time, Madeleine felt that she was among people who understood her pain. Now she was about to lose that support. But the Harvard job made sense for Chris, who needed to show practical skills in film-making as part of his Stanford degree. When the job offer came through, Madeleine claimed she was delighted. She wrote to Annabel Minchin:

> I greatly look forward to living in Boston…one of the oldest American cities, full of Pilgrim Fathers & the wonderful Georgian architecture, a 1st class symphony orchestra, Harvard University (Chris will be on the staff), a fabulous museum, marvellous New England countryside nearby & New York 4 hours away![59]

On the surface, she was embracing the move to the east coast, but she was in a highly emotional state.

By mid-October it was settled. Chris would take the Greyhound bus across the US to Boston on 19 October, and Madeleine would follow. But the impending move crystallised Madeleine's anxieties. When Chris left, she moved in with Jill and Kathy. Years later, Madeleine said, 'After I had been away from my husband for a week I realised that I should stay there.' She flirted with independence, but she could not make the break.

Around mid-November, Madeleine left San Francisco to join her husband in Boston. It was, she said later, 'a really bad move'.[60]

CHAPTER TEN

Letters Home

Madeleine's reunion with Chris after their month apart went badly from the start. Whether through anger or fear or depression, she could scarcely speak to her husband. She was hunched over and frozen, her silence an accusation. Later, she recalled arriving in Boston and thinking: 'What the fuck am I doing here?'[1]

Soon, Chris discovered that Madeleine thought he had been having an affair. She pointed the finger at twenty-three-year-old Allegra May, who had been employed, like Chris, as a filmmaker to work with Edward Mason at his Fenwood Road unit in Cambridge.

Allegra was the daughter of the famed psychologist Rollo May and had grown up in a privileged, intellectual family in New York. By the time she arrived at Harvard she had trained as a filmmaker and spent time working in Montreal. She invited Chris to stay in her share-house while he waited for Madeleine to arrive from San Francisco. Working together, Chris and Allegra bonded quickly. Allegra loved talking philosophy and literature with her new Australian buddy. Chris thought she was a little 'mixed up', but he admired her views on film.[2]

They had become close when they went with Edward Mason on a two-day business trip to New York. Then, one weekend, Allegra invited Chris to Manhattan to stay at her parents' house on the Upper West Side. Chris wrote to Madeleine in San Francisco to let her know his plans. When he and Allegra arrived at the May apartment, he was surprised to discover her parents were out of town. He felt he was on 'thin ice', but he slept alone, in the high, book-lined study.[3]

Madeleine's wordless accusation when she arrived in Cambridge distressed Chris. He tried to calm her fears, denying an affair and explaining the circumstances. Madeleine was unconvinced, but she held herself together well enough to spend the Thanksgiving weekend with Chris and Allegra at the New York apartment. In early December, she seemed to accept that there had been no affair and Chris reported to Joan that 'Madeleine and I have found [Allegra to be] a good friend'.[4] They had also become friends with Allegra's sister Caroline and her husband Frank Mazer.

Around this time, Edward Mason offered Madeleine a part-time clerical job at the Mason unit. She leapt at the chance. The Tillams moved into an apartment at 10 Agassiz Street, just a three-minute trolley ride from Harvard Square. Across the street they had ready-made friends—Tomas Kalmar, who had been at school with Madeleine in Sydney and was now doing graduate work at Harvard, and his Australian girlfriend, Jennifer Kemp. Tomas was an exuberant man and a talented pianist and guitar player, and the friends made music and sang together. Sometimes Madeleine played the piano. The group read novels aloud, and there was always plenty of talk—of politics and society and education and of the new world that seemed about to emerge at the end of the 1960s.

A few weeks after she arrived, Madeleine dashed off a note to Joan to thank her for a gift. On the surface, there was no hint of her feeling that the move to Harvard had been a mistake:

> We're terribly behind in our mail; there simply hasn't been a minute

for anything lately. All very exciting however. I adore Cambridge. And Boston. Horribly cold but really I rather like it. We're buying me high boots next Saturday as preparation for the real cold which will come with the snow, probably soon.[5]

Chris told Joan that life was 'pretty good'. The couple listened to Bach and Mozart on Harvard Radio and the thick Irish accents of the streets of Boston. There was a Rembrandt exhibition in town and Madeleine had a 'spate of cake making'.[6]

But they were not as happy as they made out. The weather was appalling. Feiga visited, and Madeleine panicked: she felt she was in no state to entertain her grandmother. Her fears about Allegra May had returned. She told Annabel that Allegra was 'very mad and dreadful'.[7] Working at the Mason unit, she saw the rapport between Chris and Allegra. The tension built until one day Madeleine tore strips off Allegra in a very public display, then locked herself in the bathroom.[8] The situation was irretrievable. Madeleine knew she could never return. She had done herself out of a good job.

Chris tolerated the outburst—her behaviour was nothing new. 'It was obvious her eruptions right from the beginning were coming from a fire that preceded our relationship,' he recalled.[9]

Madeleine and Chris went to the edge then retreated from the abyss, knowing they could not live at that level for more than a few minutes at a time and understanding that they had to get on with their lives. 'There would not be reconciliations,' Chris recalled. 'They weren't needed.'[10]

The Tillams stopped socialising with Allegra, although she and Chris continued to work together. But Madeleine remained suspicious. Once or twice she was physically violent towards Chris. He recalled that her 'curved fingers and nails' once left a mark. It was enough for one of their friends to remark that Madeleine was not behaving well.[11]

Chris did not always trust himself when Madeleine flared up, sometimes screaming abuse at him. He retreated to the boiler room below the apartment, waiting in the dark till her outburst subsided and he was calm enough to go back. He did not confront her about her behaviour: 'I just felt, well, here's another volcano to deal with...I retreat, I don't stop her, I just ride it out somehow. I go out for a breather.'

After an eruption, they would click back into familiar patterns, each of them trying to create a domestic calm of work and shopping and cooking meals and attending cultural events. Looking back, Chris said that he 'must have been terribly unaware of Madeleine's angst...I don't think I was terribly sensitive when you think about it. I almost literally rolled with the punches.'[12]

Madeleine was in severe distress. She had known in San Francisco that she needed professional help. But now she was far worse. Looking back, she said that she had a complete nervous breakdown when she lived in Cambridge and had been 'more or less incapable of a normal life'. She felt she should have been treated in hospital.[13]

As Madeleine spiralled out of control, her father began one of the most exciting times of his life. Ted had long harboured a desire to go into politics, but what he later described as 'family problems' prevented him from doing so earlier. A decade after Sylvette's death, with a supportive second wife in Val, he won the safe Liberal seat of Warringah at the 1966 federal election. Ted was ambivalent about party politics; he always said he had first made a decision to go into politics and only then decided to join the Liberals rather than Labor. He felt that he could not support Labor because he believed unions were too heavily influenced by Communists, although he was not 'whole heartedly in sympathy with the Liberal Party or everything it stood for'. As a private citizen, he had campaigned against apartheid, and he conceded he was 'an odd bod, with my small l liberal views, so they [the Liberals] were distrustful of me'.[14] He was stubborn when it came to politics, and intensely emotional on the floor of the House of Representatives. His parliamentary career was a high point in his life.

Life was not so satisfactory for his eldest daughter. Madeleine's first few months in Cambridge were terrible although once again she dissembled in letters home. She told Annabel that Harvard was:

> all very American-colonial; puritanical, high minded and quaint. The newer buildings are just as much of the best of their times—the Carpenter Centre for the Visual Arts is the most beautiful and exciting building I have ever been in; it was designed by Le Corbusier. There are other buildings by World Famous Masters but I have forgotten their names...[15]

Madeleine was reading her way through Proust and was busy writing. Chris admired her work. It was original, he told Joan, and had been influenced by her reading of the French writer. But the calm did not last. Madeleine wrote to Colette in London, telling her she was low. Colette did not reply and Madeleine wrote again asking what she had done to 'cause this freeze'. In mid-May, Colette sent a postcard and promised a letter. On 30 June, when no letter arrived, Madeleine complained to her cousin Felicity:

> Meanwhile I hear she [Colette] is writing to various people, has a nice flat and everything is going well. So I concluded that sympathy from the family was quite out of the question if my own sister could be so indifferent.[16]

Madeleine, as always, was quick to arrive at negative conclusions. Colette had been through a tough period. Her adult years were plagued by bouts of suicidal depression. A few months before Madeleine's letter, she had gone to Henley, on the river outside London, had lunch and drinks at a local pub and then sat for hours near the water. She wanted to kill herself but was not quite sure how to do it. Eventually a local bobby took her back to the station and called a psychiatric institution. She was admitted and had to be 'rescued' from it a few days later by her friend Philip Hedley.[17]

Madeleine, too, was desperate to get help. Unable to afford private care, she went to the outpatients departments at two big public hospitals. At one, they wanted to admit her immediately, but she could not face it. At the other, her name was added to a waiting list for therapy. But she would not be seen for three months and the therapy would cost $10 a session. Madeleine wondered where she and Chris would find the money.[18]

Chris wrote to Ted, asking for help. Ted was supporting a young family, including ten-year-old Oliver who had been diagnosed as intellectually handicapped, as well as coping with the demands of a political life. The St Johns were finding that Ted's parliamentary salary was not a fortune, and Ted wrote to Chris declining to send money and saying that Madeleine's condition was inevitable, given her mother's history.

Ted wanted the letter kept secret but Chris revealed its contents to Madeleine. She knew her mother had been mentally ill. Now Ted was saying she was on the same path. It was a devastating judgment. Madeleine told Felicity, in a letter in June 1967, that Ted had written that he 'couldn't spare anything for psychotherapy—nor did he feel it in any way to be his duty. He did express some sympathy for Chris.'[19] Chris was knocked by Ted's response, but for Madeleine, it was just another rejection by her father. She realised she would simply have to wait her turn at Beth Israel public hospital.

Madeleine had worked for a time at the Co-op Book Shop in Harvard Square, but she found her mental state improved after she stopped working. 'The mess is still there [but] I can control it,' she told Felicity:

> When I start therapy, I hope to get that mess cleaned up. I want to be a good person, even a wonderful person, if that is possible & I hope I can do it. In some way, I hope eventually to come to terms with my mother's death and to make up for that terrible loss; to stop mourning for her & to keep her memory alive in me, not as the wound of having lost her, but as the spring of having spent 10 perfect years as her daughter, and 2 years, which tho' marred, were redeemed entirely by her good periods. [20]

More than a decade after Sylvette's death, Madeleine's wounds were still raw. Her grief was almost overwhelming, and she had identified her mother's story as central to her own mental health. However, she blamed her father, telling Felicity that she now understood that:

> since I was about twelve years old [when Sylvette died] my father's feeling for me has been hatred shading into indifference. Once I put this horrible fact down, everything falls into place—all his vicious cruelty, all his rages, everything down to the fact that he didn't want to give me away when I was married & had to be persuaded into it by Val.[21]

Madeleine had always accused Ted of siding with Val and rejecting her, but now her anger was white-hot. She had expected love from Ted, she told Felicity, but now realised she had 'got something else, repeatedly & repeatedly & it has taken me all this time to learn'. Ted, she said, had 'died about the time that my mother did'. Madeleine wanted to become 'as indifferent to him as he is to me'. Indifference would stop the horrifying disappointments she had suffered over the years. 'When I learn to stop cringing before him I hope I shall learn to stop cringing before the rest of the world. All the years I have wasted, that what talents I have have been dissipated, I hope to make them up.'[22] She was equally unforgiving of her stepmother:

> I have just had a letter from Val that so upset me that I am going to go on trembling all day unless I write about it to the only person who is likely to preserve some discretion on hearing what I have to say...I do not think I will write to Val...It is really impossible for me to deal with people who I don't trust and who don't understand me—that sounds very egotistical but it isn't really, it is a matter of my keeping calm, it really is something that I have to work at, and it is something I have learnt here in this country; for all its faults, I've found wonderful friends who really accept me & I try to give people the trust and affection that I like to get & so cannot cope with other relationships at the moment.[23]

It is impossible to know what it was in Val's letter that so upset Madeleine, but by now almost everything Val said or did was interpreted as an attack. Madeleine sent her letter to Felicity, complete with criticisms of Val, care of Clifton Gardens. Val sent it on, unopened, to Felicity.

On the surface, life went on in the Tillams' apartment in Agassiz Street. As usual, their letters to Joan were cheerful. Chris was busy repairing their kitchen chairs and a rocker they had bought for $5.[24] He and Madeleine regularly shopped for food at the North End Italian section of Boston on Saturday afternoons, and they planned a trip to Long Island Sound in September for the America's Cup races—Chris had loved sailing ever since he was a boy. They had been to the Royal Ballet. And they socialised regularly with Tomas Kalmar and Jennifer Kemp. Madeleine was upbeat, but Tomas could see it was an act.[25]

Then came a calamity that swept aside concerns about Madeleine's mental state. In Sydney, Roger Tillam, now separated from Elvira and living at his club, suffered a severe stroke. Chris worried about how he could afford to go home, and decided against it. But his financial worries ran deeper than that. Since his departure from Australia, he had lived in part on an overdraft guaranteed by his father. Now he would be solely responsible for repaying those funds.[26] It was the start of a stressful time for Chris as he tried to help his mother and his father over the long distance.

It was a hot and humid summer in Boston and the roses were in full bloom. The Tillams walked in the evenings, and Madeleine became adept at stealing flowers for her vases. Chris had three weeks' leave while the Mason unit worked out some funding issues, but he was concerned about how he would complete the thesis film for his Stanford degree.

Roger Tillam died on 22 July 1967. Chris took a day off work but felt disconnected from the event. He recalled that Madeleine could not bring herself to comfort him because she feared it would unleash grief over her mother's death. 'It wasn't that she wasn't concerned,' he said.[27] Chris was preoccupied over the next few weeks with the impact on his mother's alimony and her living arrangements. But by September, with

Joan sorted, Chris spent a 'fantastic week' at the Flaherty Film Seminar for documentary makers, held at the Harriman estate outside New York. Allegra May also attended. It was a week of wall-to-wall movie-watching and film discussions. There was a swimming pool and copious amounts of alcohol for the eighty filmmakers attending.

Madeleine, back home in Cambridge, finally started psychotherapy. She was probably on medication but, after Chris's overdose at Stanford, she kept her pills well away from her husband. She was upbeat in a letter to Felicity, who was about to start a lectureship at the University of Pennsylvania. Madeleine invited her cousin to Cambridge. She was open about her therapy, joking that she was not 'greatly boring on the subject of myself for I HAVE STARTED, LIKE, PSYCHOTHERAPY at last. So after my weekly hour I am more than ready to change the subject.' Felicity should arrive in Cambridge after about 11 a.m. on a Friday, 'this being the hour I exit from Beth Israel Psychiatric Clinic'. Madeleine wrote that her shrink was 'wonderful' and even after three weeks, she felt she was making progress and not going around in the same circle.[28]

Three weeks later Felicity arrived. Madeleine was low in spirits. The cousins and Chris walked around Harvard Yard, Madeleine clinging like a limpet to her husband. At home the Tillams entwined on the sofa, reading the newspapers. Madeleine could scarcely operate without Chris and did not venture out alone. She was miserable. Felicity thought that Chris was angelic towards her and that the couple seemed very loving. But the therapy was having little effect and Madeleine's mood plummeted. She was often tearful and leaned constantly against Chris, almost 'piggy backing' on her husband.[29]

Madeleine found Felicity's visit intense. 'Oh what a weekend,' she wrote to Joan. '[Felicity] talks a lot & has a lot of problems & some rather inflexible opinions. I must say tho' that she is far prettier at 27 than she was at 22.'[30] Once again, she managed to sound quite cheerful on the page, yet a week earlier she had seemed in a state of near-collapse. The real Madeleine was hiding between the lines.

Chris was busy, travelling down and back to New York for work, but he managed to pop into La Cuisiniere, an upmarket cookery shop on Madison Avenue, to buy a decorative ladle for Madeleine.[31] He knew how much his wife loved beautiful objects and, even at this stressful time, he found moments to seek them out for her. It was now settled that after Christmas he would head back to Stanford to finalise his degree by making a film about managing difficult children in the classroom. There was only one problem: Madeleine did not want to go back to California.

The Tillams were at a critical point in their marriage, yet they did not confront this directly. Instead they came up with a plan that, on the surface, was about travel, not separation. In a letter in October, Chris told Joan that they were:

> seriously thinking of packing M off to London for the three months: we are so near, and may never for a long time be nearer; it would (hopefully) be fairly easy to get a job…But what a wrench—we have circled round the notion and said 'yes, that's what we'll do' but the feeling in my bones at least is that the die still has to be cast.[32]

Years later, Chris recalled the London trip as Madeleine's idea, one based on her desire to see the city and to see Colette.[33]

Madeleine had scarcely written to her mother-in-law from Boston—an indication of the strain she was under. Now she too wrote to Joan. She made no mention of the London trip but the letter was chatty. Madeleine and Chris had taken a trip to Rockport on the Massachusetts coast, which was 'pretty & strange & lost & lorn looking,' she told Joan. 'There is something chilling about it.' Chris had recently bought her a thick white china pot from their favourite junk shop in Cambridge, and she included a sketch of it for Joan. She had visited the Boston Museum and decided the Renoirs 'are so badly hung that…it's still not possible to look at them comfortably'. There was baseball fever with the Boston Red Sox fighting it out with the St Louis Cardinals, and Madeleine reported that

she was interested 'in spite of myself'. She was reading *Persuasion* aloud
to Chris who was, instead, 'mad about Stendhal at the moment, having
just read *Scarlet & Black*'. She passed on some gossip about Sidney Nolan's
penchant for dashing off paintings. And Chris, she wrote, was:

> really the funniest person in town. While the rest of us strain he quietly
> comes out with one perfect & enormous joke. I'm sure this kind of
> dead-on sense of humour is another thing which is very necessary
> for making good films, wouldn't you say so?[34]

Madeleine was an accomplished performer by now, managing to conjure
a picture of domestic harmony and stimulating intellectual life that was
only half the story.

She was deeply frustrated by her lack of creative outlets, and she and
Chris began to plan a film based on her grandfather, Jean Meer Cargher.
Madeleine had found a book of photographs by French photographer
Eugène Atget, which included pictures of little shops in Paris. She wondered if the Atget might have taken a photograph of the Cargher shop. Part
of his collection was held in Maine by American photographer Berenice
Abbott, who had worked in Paris in the 1920s and been close to Atget.
So Chris and Madeleine drove north to investigate. They stayed overnight
at a motel on the coast, but Chris went on alone to contact Abbott. He
did not see the collection, but back in Cambridge, inspired by the Atget
pictures, Madeleine wrote a short monologue about Paris—a city she
had never seen—and Chris filmed her reciting it, noting that there was
a beautiful rhythm in this homage to her grandfather.[35]

Back in Australia in 1967, Ted St John was about to become a household
name. He was determined to make a difference as an MP, even from
the backbench. His maiden speech on 16 May is one of the most famous
in Australian political history. Ted called his own leader, Liberal prime
minister Harold Holt, to account for failing to hold a second inquiry into
the controversial HMAS *Voyager* incident.

During exercises on 10 February 1964, the Navy destroyer, *Voyager*, had collided with the aircraft carrier HMAS *Melbourne*, killing eighty-two crew of the *Voyager* including the captain, Duncan Stevens. Ted believed the royal commission, which criticised the *Melbourne* captain John Robertson, had been a whitewash of Stevens. Ted was among several politicians, journalists and members of the public who agitated for further investigation. Robertson resigned 'in disgust' after the royal commission reported that while the *Voyager* was responsible, it could not say who was to blame.[36] Ted was convinced that Stevens had a history of drinking, and he played a crucial role in forcing the second inquiry when he outlined the evidence in his maiden speech. It was extraordinary for a new MP to use a maiden speech to attack his own party. Career suicide. But Ted also directly embarrassed the prime minister when Holt interjected—also unheard of during a maiden speech—and Ted ticked him off. The second royal commission, which reported in February 1968, found that Stevens had been medically unfit for command, and Robertson was paid $60,000 in lieu of a pension.[37]

Ted had angered a lot of people in the party and he was becoming increasingly isolated in Canberra. He was uncompromising and fearless when his mind was made up, and he had supreme confidence in his own moral rectitude:

> I really wasn't so much concerned with self-advancement...my chief concern basically was to form my own views. I rather foolishly thought that I could and should exercise my own independent judgment and I don't regret having done so, but I mean, with the wisdom of hindsight, I could see it just wasn't on...[38]

In May 1967, when her father made his infamous speech, Madeleine was absorbed in her own problems. Just after Christmas, Chris told his mother that he and Madeleine would be separated for six months, till he finished his course at Stanford in June 'and then we'll come home. By what route and to what work...and even for how many years, who can tell.'[39] Madeleine was going to London. She would fly out a week later. Chris knew his mother needed an explanation:

> because we are obviously very much in love and happy: why not stick to the very good thing? Well, it's not easy to explain but we both, for different reasons, want to be on our own for a while. M because she sees herself as too dependent—discontented with herself, not with being married or me—she wants to try living without a 'total protector'. I think she is ready to do this and will prow through… Her psychotherapy has helped tremendously and even has made her able to sense the tremendous possibilities she has…[40]

Chris saw the separation as a fresh start and believed that he too could gain from being less dependent on Madeleine. 'I hope there's a really productive period starting & you shan't see me for smoke,' he told Joan.

> I want to devote total time and energy to work for a while, and M thinks I need to as well. The point is, we both think it will do us good to break up the present way we live our joint life: too much dependence. But, oh, how we love each other: you mustn't fear that things are wrong, or that we won't be together again in six months' time.[41]

Chris told Joan that they were sad to break up the household at Agassiz Street, but they had itchy feet and a 'real sense of wider horizons'. He understood what the separation looked like to outsiders and he asked Joan to be discreet: 'Would rather things about M & I were paraphrased by you as you think best—but the letter is really private.' And he asked his mother to sell the Nolan painting she had given him as a wedding present. He needed the money.

Meanwhile, Madeleine was focused on a special project. She made a book with a blue cardboard cover, grey paper and hand-sewn binding to send home to Joan. It contained the photographs of the couple's life in the US, at Menlo Park, San Francisco and Cambridge. She was making her mother-in-law the custodian of the years she shared with Chris. In

2012, he recalled that 'at the time there was a sense of, why are we tearing up all these records of our marriage and sending them home? Why are we not keeping them?'[42] Chris had reassured Joan that they would be together again in six months, but it seems he was already wondering whether Madeleine had another agenda.

The news of a separation must have worried Joan. She had never seen Madeleine behaving badly: 'We would not have wanted her to see that.'[43] And in 1967, when Chris wrote to his mother about Madeleine's departure for London, he continued to shield her from those details of their life.

Soon it was time to leave. Madeleine and Chris had recently moved their bed into the sitting room so they could 'wake up with the snow'.[44] At 8 a.m. one day, the men from the second-hand furniture shop arrived to take out the chest, the table and other pieces they had sold. Madeleine slept on—whether through exhaustion or denial that her American sojourn was over—and woke up to an empty room.[45] Agassiz Street was no more.

The next day, the Tillams flew to New York. Madeleine went to Bergdorf's and spent a hectic hour buying up with her travel money. Then she and Chris met friends for dinner at the Algonquin Hotel. It was 'quiet, sedate, red plush, New Yorker staffers; redolent of Robert Benchley and D. Parker', Chris wrote to Joan.[46] Then suddenly it was time to take the shuttle to Kennedy.

It was snowing and there were no taxis. Madeleine and Chris ran four blocks to the Pan Am Building, took the lift fifty floors to the helipad and bought helicopter tickets. They circled the Empire State Building, and pressed their noses to the window to see a receding Manhattan. Ten minutes later they landed at the international airport. Twenty minutes later, Chris waved his wife goodbye.

The next day, 6 January 1968, Madeleine sent a cable to Chris from London. She had arrived.

CHAPTER ELEVEN

An Expat in London

In the 1960s, London became the destination for a generation of young people determined to break from the past—and their country. Madeleine's friends were all 'desperately seeking something other than Australia'.[1] For the Octopus girls and the *Honi Soit* crowd, Australia 'was a lost cause, sunk in banality, Catholicism, censorship. Life began when you got to London.'[2] In those years, the Australian diaspora in London included people such as Clive James, Germaine Greer, Peter Porter, Barry Humphries, Bruce Beresford, Robert Hughes and Richard Neville.

They were the stars among the thousands who washed up in the capital. Many travelled for a year or two; others for much longer; some never came home. But the era produced a remarkably clever batch of expats whose experience of London was shaped by a time when travel was still relatively expensive and when telephoning home was a rarity. Once away, they stayed on for years, seeking a new community in their adopted country.

Madeleine was looking for a fresh start. That first day, she made her way, as agreed, to Colette's shared flat in Upper Berkeley Street, near Marble Arch. There were several Australians in the building; friends had joined friends as rooms became available. Tonia Date was there, so too was Didy Harvey with her new American husband, film student Daniels McLean. Richard Wherrett shared the basement flat with Jim Anderson (who would go on to edit *Oz* magazine in London with Richard Neville), the theatre director Philip Hedley and Colette.

Colette was excited about seeing Madeleine after two and a half years. She gave her older sister her bedroom and her warm quilt and slept on a couch in the boiler room.[3] Madeleine did not mention Chris joining her, or her suspicions of an affair, but Colette was in little doubt Madeleine had left Chris and that the marriage was over. She blamed Madeleine for the couple's marital problems: 'I could only imagine that she must have done a number on him as I had seen her do on others…I could not spend two weeks with her and I could not imagine how any guy could live with her.'[4] Even so, Colette urged a reconciliation. She liked Chris.

Madeleine found work at Collet's London Bookstore in Charing Cross Road and met some new friends through the Upper Berkeley Street crowd. Tonia Date had a new French boyfriend, Daniel Le Maire. He flirted happily with Madeleine and teased her about trying to be more English than the English, even to the extent of adopting the upper class British habit of adoring anything vaguely French. They danced together at parties, and Daniel was struck by Madeleine's physical fragility, and her sadness.[5]

The St John sisters had long had a fractious relationship. Within days of Madeleine's arrival, they argued. 'She just had this talent for alienating people and it didn't matter what you did. That's what she did with relationships, she was terrified of intimacy,' Colette recalled.[6] Madeleine, in turn, blamed Colette for their arguments.[7] Some friends in London thought Madeleine was jealous of her younger sister. But Madeleine insisted that:

even in my worst period after my mother died and my father obviously found me completely repulsive and made a huge fuss of Colette and showed her off as this adorable kid...I don't think, even then, that I thought 'it's not fair, she's got the looks and I am just this fat person that nobody loves'. I just accepted her, much more than I accepted myself.[8]

At other times she patronised Colette and questioned her authenticity:

Colette was this little blonde girl, she was terribly fey and vague, she was like a little fairy. That was her persona. Maybe she was really like that, but that was what you had to deal with. Ted just adored it, but it got up Sylvette's nose. [Colette] was a pain in the neck, she was always going off on some trope or other and making things difficult; she liked to wind people up.[9]

Madeleine claimed that Colette had not been able to 'develop a proper moral sense' because Sylvette had died when she was nine. If only Colette had had the advantage of 'my mother and I on her case together' it would have been different. Instead Colette had 'gotten away with acting the role that suits the audience all her life. [She] was the poppet and she was going to make damn sure that she stayed a poppet.' Colette was 'the dumb blonde—that was her role. She was clever, but the clever thing she did was to decide she was going to be the stupid one.' At close quarters in London in 1968, the St John sisters soon fell out.

Chris stayed on in New York after Madeleine left, dossing down with a friend and doing some casual film work. He planned to leave for Stanford in a few weeks. He and Madeleine were still in contact—she sent two letters, a postcard and some photos of herself in the snow in Trafalgar Square taken by Didy Harvey's husband, and wrote that she was having a good time, renewing dozens of friendships. When Chris saw the photos, he wondered if Madeleine had already found a boyfriend.

In the last week of January, Chris went back to Boston, picked up a hire car and film equipment and went on to Maine to pursue the Atget photograph. He was still committed enough to seek out the material for his wife. He spent four days in an unheated house at Moosehead Lake without finding a picture of Jean Meer Cargher's shop.[10]

Back in Boston, Chris went to stay with Martha Kay, whom he had met the previous year at a party. Madeleine had not been at the party but she knew Martha slightly and had babysat her toddler son, Matthew, in Cambridge. Martha's husband had moved out and, alone with a young son in a tiny house in the poorer end of Cambridge, Martha was finding life tough. She was attracted to Chris. She too wanted to be a filmmaker, and, indeed, under her maiden name of Ansara, she would go on to have an important film career. Within days she and Chris were lovers. Martha was besotted. Madeleine was out of the picture and Martha scarcely gave her a second thought.[11]

The relationship escalated quickly and by February, when Chris left the east coast to drive to Stanford, it was decided that Martha and Matthew would go out to California for the summer. Madeleine and Chris were still corresponding.

Madeleine had joined a number of loose, overlapping friendship groups among the floating population of Aussies on their UK and European adventure who shared houses, boyfriends, dope and a sense that they were on the brink of huge change. Everybody survived on the smell of an oily rag, went to the same parties and moved in and out of each other's flats, turning their floors over to other people's brothers and sisters as they travelled in and out of London. There were defined subcultures. Madeleine and her crowd sniffed at the 'Kangaroo Valley' set who flatted in Earls Court. Didy Harvey lived in Earls Court when she first arrived at Christmas 1966 but found it a relief to get over to Marble Arch.[12] The *Honi Soit* mob headed for South Kensington or Bloomsbury and tried to get jobs in the arts. The *Oz* editors had moved to London and were producing a UK edition of the paper from an office near Hyde Park.

Colleen Olliffe and other friends from Sydney were in London, and Madeleine became close to Christine Hill, one of three sisters who had known the St John girls in Watsons Bay in the 1940s. Madeleine was sending mixed messages to her friends about the state of her marriage. She told Christine that she was in London for six weeks and would then go back to the US.[13] She appeared hopeful of a reconciliation, but she did not yet know of Chris's relationship with Martha.

Around her, other expats, including Robert Hughes, Bruce Beresford and Clive James, were trying to get a start. Hughes had married Danne Emerson, and the couple were living in a huge flat in Hanover Court Gardens with their baby son, Danton. Madeleine stayed with them for several weeks, often babysitting while Danne cut a promiscuous and drug-fueled swathe through sixties London.

In London in her late twenties, Madeleine emerged from her awkwardness to become, Christine Hill thought, stunningly beautiful. 'It was her moment. She had this very thick, dark curly red hair and she looked exotic and interesting.'[14] Madeleine certainly saw herself as a romantic figure as she wandered London with a little hat pulled down over her cascading hair.[15] She smoked heavily; a Golden Virginia roll-your-own was constantly between her fingers. And she was developing a dope habit.

At some stage in those first few weeks, Chris telephoned Madeleine and told her he was seeing Martha. Madeleine was devastated. In the spring, Martha wrote to Madeleine asking to 'borrow' Chris for the summer. It was the sixties, when all the rules were broken, but, looking back, Martha was alarmed at her careless approach to Madeleine's feelings.[16]

Martha and Matthew arrived at Stanford in mid-April and, a few weeks later, Chris began breaking the news to Joan. First, he told his mother that he had:

> decided against bringing M and self home separately when I finish here at Stanford at the end of June. Coming home at this stage represents a commitment to settling down, and all that this entails, which I'm

just not prepared to make. I know that sounds selfish, but it's better, I hope, to be honest about it, than to do something because others expect it of one.[17]

He said he was going to go to England to 'sort things out' with Madeleine, but that he wanted to stay in the US in the long term. He was about to start work on a documentary about the resistance to the Vietnam War draft.

Meanwhile, Madeleine moved in and out of shared houses, usually taking a single, sparsely furnished room. She hung her carefully chosen clothes from pegs on the wall, collected odd cups and saucers and invited friends to high tea served from an upturned crate that did duty as a table. Madeleine was obsessed with her weight, often eating only rice for days. Once, so weak from this diet, she collapsed on the Tube.

There was camaraderie in the Aussie 'club'. One Christmas, a group of Madeleine's friends went to the food hall at Harrods and shoplifted the ingredients for a feast, stuffing chickens and sausages and hams under their commodious winter coats and cloaks. Madeleine was not among them, but she joined the illicit Christmas dinner. London was her place. She would come to love the seasons and the flowers, the fact that you could rent cheaply or squat in the heart of the metropolis, the access to culture, the buses, and the buzz.

Chrissie de Looze, an Australian art teacher who was part of Colleen Olliffe's circle, felt Madeleine was often wary: 'It took Mad some time to warm up to a person, but she was also very endearing.'[18] She had presence. She could be still and observe. But she was always broke, thanks to her erratic work pattern, and her friends made concessions for her lack of money. Chrissie did a lot of listening as Madeleine pined for Chris and anguished over her lack of a boyfriend. She had met Michael Chesterman, a young Sydney lawyer who was teaching at University College. He would eventually become one of Australia's prominent legal academics and law reformers. He was handsome and charming and Madeleine fell for him. It was not much more than a one-night stand, but Madeleine was inconsolable when Michael did not pursue the matter. For months she drove her friends crazy with talk of her unrequited love. It didn't help when Michael began seeing Colleen Olliffe. He knew Madeleine was disappointed that nothing had come of the dalliance, but he was shocked in 2012 when told how obsessed Madeleine became with him.[19]

At the end of 1968, a year after Madeleine's arrival in London, Chris acknowledged the marriage was over. On 18 December, he told his mother that he had written to Madeleine about going to London to see her before coming back to Australia with Martha and Matthew. Madeleine was still wearing her wedding ring and wondering what exactly Chris was up to. But she was also still infatuated with Michael Chesterman. Early in 1969, she wrote to her cousin Felicity:

> I went to a party that M. Chesterman was at. I think I gave a brilliant performance—very self-assured, contained, detached & so on. Stole sideways glance at him, enough to assure me that a direct & proper look would be fatal, & talked brightly to simply everybody else, & all like that. I see I am still in love with him—absurd phrase, whatever can it mean—but the whole thing, because of the way I am & so on, lives in a realm of its own which I suppose is no bad thing—see Marvell: 'My love is of a birth as rare/As 'tis for object strange & high/ It was begotten of despair/ Upon impossibility'.[20]

Madeleine told Felicity that she had not heard from Chris and did not know 'where on earth he can be', even though she knew Chris was still on the west coast.[21] He was sharing a flat with others in San Francisco, having completed *Narodniks*, a documentary on draft resistance. Their contact was now intermittent, but Madeleine was happy to ask Chris for favours. In one letter, she requested a book she could not find in London, some 'Skippy' crunchy peanut butter which was not available in the UK, and some pot. Chris laughed at Madeleine's assumptions he would run after her, but nonetheless set about filling the order.[22]

Madeleine wanted a divorce and arranged with Ted to launch

proceedings in Sydney. She blamed her father for her psychological distress, but she turned to him to help her with the divorce. Chris told Joan: 'I haven't yet heard on what grounds, or whether she is seeking alimony. We each, when we write, try to deal gently and honestly with each other, but it's very unsatisfactory as so many things on each side seem to get misinterpreted.'[23] Chris was determined to have a life with Martha, and he continued to reassure his mother that the breakup of his marriage was rational and to some extent amicable.

In London, Madeleine was far from rational as she tried to get treatment at the Tavistock Clinic for her depression. She admitted to Felicity Baker that she was in a 'very boggy state':

> Not very brilliant at all darling. Am about to go and create Big Scene at Tavistock Clinic & Freak Out in their Foyer if we don't see some action soon. I rang them the other day. 'Wot's Happening?' I said. 'This won't do you know'…and they apologised and seemed to be saying that there had been a mistake or a file mislaid or something & they would fix me an appointment soon & I say it had better be. So that is the story of my life recently. In fact you see, I am not making a success of anything at all at this point, except the utterly necessary—going to work.
>
> On my day off, the effort has utterly debilitated & exhausted me & I spend almost all of it sleeping. On Sunday, I watch clouds, if there are any, for most of the day & I think—about very little, I must add. I've written one more poem, about animals at Cambridge. It isn't finished yet. This is such a dull letter, and really I did not mean it to be. I wouldn't say that *I* am dull exactly—it's just that anything real I have to communicate now is terribly hard to sort out and write down, or even say. For a start, I am finding people very threatening & much time and spirit seems to get wasted & every issue is confused by various defensive manoeuvres. And so forth. I am really very alone; it is the only state where I can feel at all safe; and I think I have absolutely accepted a state of constant unhappiness, a perpetual garment. Anxiety and despair in any unbearable degree are precluded by the hope of

therapy—I should say the whole trip is a kind of Micawberism.

I've quite given up every kind of endeavour, until, until—like a cripple sitting motionless in a chair, waiting for the crutch to be delivered. He sees the others walking about on the green with a detached envy, knowing that any attempt to rise and join them is perfectly futile till the crutch is there. The difference between my trip—I having had therapy before & knowing where it's at—and the trip of any other neurotic, is that the latter doesn't realise that his efforts to rise & walk are bound to failure; he will keep trying & the anxiety of his continual falling & failing quite exhausts him & makes him worse all the time. Of course I could go on just sitting here but it remains my ambition not merely to walk there with all the other cats but even to run and perhaps even leap up and down every now & then. So I think that's enough about that. In this state of refrigeration, to change the metaphor, thought it time for a bit of variety, I've not done/seen much lately that would provide interesting news for you...

Madeleine apologised for unburdening herself but said she was really trying to 'say something I really mean' rather than 'merely inventing a self for the purpose of the letter which is something I am still capable of tho' it becomes harder & is really rather despicable'.[24] Almost two years earlier, she had written to Felicity from Boston, identifying Sylvette's death and Ted's subsequent treatment of her as the cause of her psychological problems. Now, she seemed to take responsibility for herself and tried hard for a more honest conversation.

Chris too was trying to be honest. Joan had asked, in effect, 'who left whom'. In March 1969, Chris wrote back:

Madeleine and I both thought the original separation was a good thing for both of us, she in London, me in California. Maybe we were too young, too unsure of ourselves to understand what we both meant by doing that—that we really wanted to part; perhaps—but the important question isn't allocating the blame, or even allocating the responsibility. About each other, as persons: we were never, during

> our time together, sufficiently at home and comfortable with our own
> selves to be able to view our relationship detachedly—which is the
> first necessity in working out problems together.[25]

Chris told his mother that he had been low in spirits for the previous
couple of months but that things were now much better. He was not sure,
however, about his future with Martha.

As Madeleine struggled in London, back home in Australia Ted was
making waves. The Liberal member for Warringah had been lauded for
his principled stand on the *Voyager* inquiry but, in March 1969, he risked
the ire of his colleagues again by denouncing his own prime minister,
John Grey Gorton, whom he considered a 'dangerously irresponsible'
playboy.[26] Sex was in the air in Canberra, just as it was in London, and
Gorton was a party boy, a drinker and a man at ease with himself and with
women. For months there were rumours about an evening in November
1968 when the prime minister turned up at the American Embassy with
nineteen-year-old journalist Geraldine Willesee after a press gallery dinner.
The Americans wanted to talk about the crisis in Vietnam but the prime
minister spent the next two hours in conversation with Willesee. The story
became a source of gossip around the press gallery and then seeped into
the public arena. It gripped the country for weeks, with voters divided
between those who saw Ted as a prude and those who saw the incident
as proof that Gorton must go.[27]

The prime minister was popular in the press gallery, and so was his
American wife Bettina. A few days after Ted's outburst, she circulated a
poem, adapted from one by William Watson, to the press gallery:

> He is not old, he is not young,
> The Member with the Serpent's tongue,
> The haggard cheek, the hungering eye,
> The poisoned words that wildly fly,
> The famished face, the fevered hand,

> Who slights the worthiest in the land,
> Sneers at the just, condemns the brave
> And blackens goodness in its grave.[28]

Ted copped further criticism for his actions. Alan Reid, the veteran reporter, later described him as:

> Napoleonic in stature, thin faced and lipped, precise of speech and manner, religious, abstemious in his habits, bespectacled, proud of what he considered to be his morality and high principles, and possessed of a Savonarola-like zeal to secure their adoption by others, a zeal which earned him a high reputation and a wide berth.[29]

At a meeting of his parliamentary party colleagues, Ted refused to back Gorton. He resigned from the Liberal Party and went to the crossbenches. He was undeterred and decided he would contest the next election, later in 1969, as an independent. He wrote *A Time to Speak*, an account of the sensational events that justified his actions and laid out his views on democracy and society. He wanted his version of history to be recorded and his reputation retained.[30] Ted fought a strong campaign but lost his seat.

Madeleine must have known of these events—Ted's sisters were in contact with her in this period—yet she gave no indication in letters of her views on the matter.

By May 1969, Chris was back in Cambridge, living with Martha and Matthew and planning their journey to Australia. Madeleine wrote to him saying that despite her depression, she was very happy, liked her job, her flat in Belsize Park, and—especially—London. He had not heard from her for about three months, and was relieved to receive the letter.[31] They continued to correspond even as they contemplated a divorce. Sometimes the exchanges were happy, 'sometimes less so'.[32]

Chris, Martha and Matthew booked a passage on a freighter to Sydney. Martha had divorced her husband and was now pregnant to Chris. Chris wrote to Madeleine to tell her about the baby. 'I am afraid it will make her sad, especially as she has been pleading with me to just visit her in London,' he told Joan.[33] Madeleine must have been devastated by the news. She wanted a divorce, but the speed with which her husband was creating a new family must have been difficult to accept.

Martha was advised not to tackle the sea voyage because of the risk of miscarriage. The boat left without them, but Martha still lost the baby. A few weeks later she flew with Chris and Matthew to Sydney and they went almost immediately to visit Joan. Chris quickly signed up for casual work back at the ABC and stevedore work on the wharves.

Soon he was served divorce papers. Madeleine cited adultery as the grounds and named Martha as the co-respondent. She also sued for a share of her husband's estate. Martha, in a move she would later deeply regret, did not spare Madeleine's feelings. Charged with committing adultery, Martha and Chris responded by naming in court documents dozens of locations across the US and Australia where they had had sex. Chris also attempted to argue in the proceedings that Madeleine was the one at fault because she had deserted him.

It would be another three years before the divorce was formally granted by the New South Wales Supreme Court—on the grounds of adultery—but by late 1969, the 'marriage of children', as Madeleine once called it, was over.[34] Thirty-five years later, Chris would write that Madeleine, like his mother, blossomed after parting from her husband. But, for Madeleine, that blossoming would take a very long time.

CHAPTER TWELVE

To the Edge and Back

M adeleine's psychological state deteriorated in 1969. Some of her friends realised she was in a bad way. They were worried, too, about Colette, who had spent the summer as a hippie in Ibiza, but then wandered around London trying to live, in effect, without money. The sisters had little contact with each other, but one winter's night Colette called on Madeleine at her rooms in Belsize Park. Colette was shoeless, homeless and penniless, but Madeleine would not allow her to stay.[1]

Madeleine had just turned twenty-eight. Her efforts to find appropriate therapy for her depression had yielded little, and she was desperate. She took an overdose and was taken to St Stephen's Hospital and then admitted to an asylum on the edge of London, a grim institution where patients were locked in wards and heavily sedated. It was a horrific experience.

Christine Hill was dismayed when she went to visit Madeleine at the asylum. 'They were injecting her with sedatives and she could hardly move...They would come around and give her pills and I would say, don't take them...People were in there for twenty years.' Christine visited several times and recalled that Madeleine was lucid but in despair and 'just terribly sad about Chris'.[2] Some years later, Madeleine told Felicity Baker that she had meant to kill herself, but that the aftermath had been so ghastly that she was determined she would never do it again.[3]

The Hellers were back in London after their time at overseas universities. Florence was alarmed when she saw Madeleine: the glorious, if unhappy, young woman she had seen in San Francisco was huddled on her bed, clutching an antique doll called Cloud, childlike and vulnerable.

Some weeks later, Madeleine wrote to her aunt and asked whether she could stay with her after her discharge. Frank had always been very hospitable to the St Johns but he ruled this out. Madeleine was expressing very negative feelings towards Ted, and Frank did not want his three young children to be exposed to her hostility. He offered to pay for a bedsit, but Madeleine did not take up the offer.[4] She went to stay with friends. It would be a long, slow road back to mental stability.

Early in 1970, she sent a handmade card to her aunt and uncle, Margaret and John Minchin, congratulating them on their thirtieth wedding anniversary. She decorated the card with a drawing of daffodils and wrote:

> I'm sorry this comes a little late, but the daffodils have only just begun to bloom...I wish you many congratulations on your 30th wedding anniversary. Please forgive the paper—all I have with me at this moment! & the general amateurishness (I borrowed a 4 year old's messy paints)—I have just come out of hospital & this is almost the first thing I have done. I am being cared for very beautifully by some kind friends & I feel very reborn; a bit shaky but very eager. I hope to go away to the country on Sunday; meanwhile, London is very sweet—the sun is just shining through mist like a pearl & birds can be heard singing...[5]

Madeleine was still fragile, but she was determined to recover her health.

Her father believed she had inherited her mother's mental instability and that little could be done to help her, but Madeleine was a survivor and she began the painful task of rehabilitation. She felt unable to hold down a professional or office job and instead became a cleaning lady. Among her clients were filmmaker Clive Donner and his wife. They were so taken with their rather unusual cleaner that they invited her to stay with them at their house in the south of France—an invitation she did not take up.[6] Madeleine was a meticulous housekeeper and kept her own rooms beautifully. She used this work to help her climb out of depression.

Colleen Olliffe, now married to Michael Chesterman, organised a cleaning job for Madeleine at their flat at Number 2 Regent Square. Madeleine was still carrying a torch for Michael: had wept at the wedding reception, pouring out her heart to others at the table.[7] She was an unorthodox employee at Regent Square. She was friends with everyone in the flat, which was also shared by Winton Higgins, his wife Sue Young and another Australian, Ronny Matthews. Madeleine often stayed on for dinner, enjoying the joke of being such an upmarket charlady. She smoked copious amounts of marijuana, and her friends were amused that while she never seemed to have much cash, she always had enough for dope.[8]

Regent Square was a cerebral household, host to a floating population of academics, artists and political activists. Among those who often stayed was the young Czech photographer Josef Koudelka, whose clandestine photographs of the Soviet invasion of Prague in August 1968 had made him an underground hero.

Madeleine's friends knew she was often unhappy. Her relationship with her father remained problematic and she told Sue she was distressed about a forthcoming visit from Ted.[9] But she did not talk of her suicide attempt or her hospitalisation. Mixing with the people she had known at university a decade earlier, Madeleine presented as lively, clever and acerbic. She told friends of her efforts to find jobs, including as an assistant to the stage director Kenneth Tynan.[10]

She revealed more about her mental state in this period to her friends on the other side of town in Ladbroke Grove.[11] Here, everyone was openly searching for something—sex, drugs, transcendence, the perfect song—and there was acceptance of a drifting person like Madeleine. Christine Hill, who had been so loving to Madeleine during her depression and her time in the asylum, shared a flat in the Grove with the Australian artist Colin Lanceley. Sue Hill and her husband Phil Jones lived across the road. Phil had been a big rock blues singer in Sydney before he and Sue travelled to London. He worked in a picture-framing business at first but soon joined the band Quintessence, set up by Melbourne musician Ronald Rothfield. Rothfield began following an Indian-Mauritian mystic, Swami Ambikananda, or Swami-ji, as he was known. So too did Christine and Sue, and Madeleine.

Swami-ji gave his followers Indian-based names—Sue became Vidya; Phil was Shiva Shankar; Rothfield was Raja Ram. He did not give Madeleine a new name—perhaps because her name was already close to Mary Magdalene: Swami-ji was interested in Christianity and his teachings melded Hindu and Christian beliefs. He urged his followers to love God and warned them off the drugs that were so readily available.

Quintessence and its music became the focus of the ashram set up by Swami-ji, and the group was present at the regular religious gatherings, or *kirtans*, in the huge mansion blocks in the area. Quintessence was named London's underground sensation for 1970 and it headlined at the Glastonbury Festival that summer and again in 1971. Twice its concerts sold out the Royal Albert Hall. The band recorded five albums between 1969 and 1972. And all the time, Quintessence was driven by its devotion to Swami-ji. At concerts, the band tried to 'raise up the vibrations of the audience and ourselves to a more God-intoxicated state', Raja Ram told the BBC in 1970.[12]

At first Madeleine held back from Swami-ji. But the ashram's warmth and its effort to operate like a family were irresistible and soon she was a regular at the *kirtans*, where fifty or so people jammed into a single room to hear Swami-ji speak. There was food and music, and Madeleine danced enthusiastically to the fusion of progressive rock, jazz and Indian chants. Her spirit was healing. At the ashram Madeleine was invited to strip herself back to the basics and to find a truth about herself and her life. She grasped the opportunity.

News of the Hill sisters 'discovering' a guru down in Ladbroke Grove filtered back to the 'rather militantly secular' group at Regent Square.[13] A number of other Australians, including actors Janice Dinnen and Deidre Rubenstein, joined the ashram, but Madeleine kept her friends in separate silos, although soon she was signing letters and postcards to family and friends in Australia with *Hari Om Tat Sat*—the Sanskrit mantra, meaning 'The Lord, that is the truth'. The ashram had become a way for Madeleine to make sense of the world:

> Life can really mash you up…But we have our Lord and our Swami Ji & each other & must believe in the healing power of Love. And in any work which is a form of Love. Jai Guru Dev! Love ever.[14]

Madeleine was also looking for answers in therapy. One day in March 1971, she arrived at Regent Square, excited to announce she was being treated by a psychiatrist who followed the ideas of the radical R. D. Laing, a Scottish born medico who worked at the Tavistock Clinic in the 1950s and early 1960s where he had carried out extensive research on family relations.[15] Ted paid for Madeleine's therapy sessions.[16] He had turned to business after losing his parliamentary seat and was now making more money, thanks to the resources boom.

How much the therapy helped Madeleine is unclear, but Laingians saw mental illness as a product of social and cultural events, rather than determined by biology—something which would have allowed Madeleine to separate herself from the Sylvette narrative and to believe she was not at the mercy of her genes. In 1965, Laing had launched a controversial psychiatric community practice in London's Kingsley Hall, where patients and therapists lived together. He used techniques such as rebirthing, and he questioned the use of antipsychotic drugs, arguing that mental illness was part of a journey, which people could pass through to greater wisdom.[17]

Despite Madeleine's optimism the therapy sessions did not last. Laing was a controversial practitioner and many of his followers were dismissive of convention and rules. Even so, Madeleine was surely unprepared for her therapist's suggestion that they have sex. But she agreed. In the event, the sex came to nothing when her therapist could not achieve an erection. The sessions ended. Madeleine was not particularly distressed. She pitied the doctor and said later that the incident had helped salvage her self-esteem because there was now someone she could pity more than herself.[18]

Madeleine wanted to stay in London and she made attempts to find employment. She was perfecting the hand-to-mouth existence that she would endure for decades. She was still in touch with the extended St John network: her cousin Annabel Minchin was living in London in 1971. Annabel wrote to her father John, 'I had lunch with Madeleine on Sunday. It was really superb. She is really sweet. I like her much better than I ever did before.' Madeleine introduced Annabel to Cloud, the doll she had clutched in despair in the asylum. She treated the porcelain French-style doll like a person. Annabel reported that Madeleine 'looks like a card. She had on maroon boots, blue and white striped stockings and a long blue woollen dress with no sleeves and a jumper underneath (pale green) and a leather jerkin on top. People stare at her but she takes it in her stride.'[19] In May the following year, Madeleine sent a postcard to the Chestermans in Nairobi, where Michael was teaching. 'I am very crazy at the present time, but it is all necessary. I can't write,' she told them.[20]

In June 1972, the New South Wales Supreme Court granted Madeleine's divorce and awarded her one third of Chris's inheritance. It was more than four years since she and Chris had separated, but the news may have contributed to a new low point. In September, when she wrote to Margaret Minchin, thanking her for some gifts, she sounded almost paralysed: 'Forgive a short letter...writing has become formidable, almost impossible...'[21] The letter marked a significant shift. Madeleine's letters home from the US had presented a happiness that did not exist and she had concealed her growing despair behind a cheerful, contented tone. Now she made no secret of her anxieties and did not try to hide her fragile psychological state.

That openness was present when she wrote to Margaret again a few months later. Her aunt had been diagnosed with cancer, and Madeleine suggested Margaret read a book—'there's a Pelican [edition]; *alors ce n'est pas cher—Zen Flesh, Zen Bones*.[22] It's got these beautiful little stories in it. I'm sure it would appeal to you.' Then she turned to her own state, telling Margaret that life seemed 'a very mysterious business to me & not at all what I expected'. She was trying to 'sort out a lot of stuff that ought to have been sorted out sooner', but was finding that the 'practical side of things is giving as much trouble as the other, but that too is all one'. Her life, she said, was 'a mixture of hot & cold, with very little peaceful lukewarm between—another inevitability, at least for the time being, until one learns more'.[23]

It is not known if Madeleine was in therapy at that point. It is likely that she was sorting out her life with the help of Swami-ji and the ashram, not a professional psychologist. She told Margaret that she loved London: 'I don't know whether Mother England is going to keep me in her bosom or not, it remains to be seen; as long as she does, I count it as a blessing—strange, grey, disorganised creature.'

She signed off: 'Forgive me if this letter seems short. Words seem dangerous to me these days especially written down.'[24]

CHAPTER THIRTEEN

A Room of Her Own

S winbrook Road in W10 is not the meanest street in London, but it is bleak and uninspiring. When Madeleine first moved there, in 1972, she told Margaret Minchin she was living in 'a funny little house in the slums of North Kensington'.[1] But there was nothing remotely charming about Number 6. A Castlecrag friend who visited found it 'seedy and dark', and there was little furniture.[2] Yet Number 6 and Number 75, where Madeleine moved later, represented precious terrain for the young Australian. Her time in Swinbrook Road was not without sadness and she struggled to find a career direction. But, slowly and surely, she pieced together a life for herself and moved from despair to control.

The shift to Swinbrook Road, just a few minutes walk from Ladbroke Grove, was part of Madeleine's strategy for survival in the city she loved. She knew she would be on the breadline if she stayed in London and that she needed subsidised accommodation. Squats and shared households and council flats were part of the scene, but Madeleine proved better at working the system than some of her contemporaries. She became an expert in housing politics and subsistence living. Local councils required a tenant to live in an area for some time before qualifying for public housing, and Madeleine, intent on living close to the Portobello markets with their cheap produce, started renting Number 6 as the first step. Sometimes she was 'signed up' for unemployment benefits; sometimes she worked in bookshops and antique shops or in clerical jobs.

In 1972 Madeleine shared Number 6 with two other ashram followers, one of them Australian Ann Herbert, renamed Miriam by Swami-ji. Miriam was working in an office and also at Cranks, the first health-food store in London. Her older sister Diana, known as Lakshmi Mata, was also a devotee.

Madeleine was not easy to live with, even for other ashram members. She was working at Collet's bookshop, but when she was at home she was reclusive, shutting herself in her bedroom with her Grateful Dead album. Sometimes she emerged to smoke and drink cups of tea in the shared kitchen. She was researching the life of Helena Blavatsky, the founder of theosophy, and Miriam was fascinated as Madeleine talked about the nineteenth-century Russian woman who had claimed to be a medium and had been widely criticised for her teachings on the occult. Madeleine leafed through a folio of photographs and cuttings and the two women went around the corner to walk past the house where Blavatsky had lived before her death in 1891.

The project added to Madeleine's exotic image at Number 6, but the residents were often forced to more pragmatic pursuits. They were impossibly short of money. They scavenged the broken vegetable crates from the nearby Golborne Road markets for firewood and picked up anything useful, including discarded food. The *kirtans* were their main social life.

Madeleine was clean and tidy to the point of being obsessive, but her moods fluctuated: she was friendly one day and cold the next. Eventually Miriam had had enough and moved out to live with Janice Dinnen, now known as Parvati, and her two young children in Ladbroke Grove.[3]

Miriam and Madeleine were estranged, but Diana Herbert saw a lot of Madeleine that year. They spent the Easter weekend together, attended a *kirtan*, and meditated. On Easter Saturday night Madeleine lit a candle and put up a picture of Jesus. The next morning the women walked Swami-ji's dog, Sunrise, and Madeleine picked bluebells. In June Madeleine went with Diana to see a Betty Boop film at the Electric Cinema Club. In July Diana borrowed Madeleine's Steely Dan LP, and a few days later Madeleine went along to a party at Diana's workplace.[4] It was all entirely unremarkable but the gentle rhythm of life suited Madeleine. Unlike some others at the ashram, Madeleine still smoked marijuana and spent a lot of time doing very little. Existence seemed an exhausting undertaking for the thirty-year-old.

She was being left behind by so many of her contemporaries. Clive James had arrived in London in 1962. He shared a flat with Bruce Beresford for three years and studied at Cambridge. By 1972 he was a television critic for the *Observer*, and in 1979 he published the first volume of his autobiography, *Unreliable Memoirs*. Robert Hughes had hit his straps. He, Danne and baby Danton left London in 1970 for New York, where Robert had been appointed art critic for *Time* magazine.[5] They were Australians shaping cultures not their own.

By rights, Madeleine should have been part of that group. Later, Clive James would regard her as the most brilliant of the expatriates in London in the 1960s. In 2006, he wrote: 'Sometimes, when I'm reading one of the marvellous little novels of Madeleine St John, part of whose genius was for avoiding all publicity, I think the only lasting fame for any of the rest of us will reside in the fact that we once knew her.'[6]

Madeleine was not without ambition. She had embarked on the Blavatsky book, but she struggled with the project. And she failed to find even the most lowly jobs in publishing or the arts or journalism, the kind of jobs that other expats were using as their entrée to London. She was a sharp observer, a sparkling mind, but life was a constant challenge.

She felt at home with the English but she had always dreamed of visiting her mother's birthplace and now began taking lessons to improve her schoolgirl French. It is not known when she made her first trip to France but she told her cousin Felicity Baker, who was a French scholar, that on that first trip, her brain seemed to click into gear and she spoke French readily and well.[7] In September 1973, she wrote to Margaret Minchin about her visit to a spa in the south of France, which she described as a 'watering place very fashionable in Victorian times [espec.] with the British—but it is very French—lovely pastries & espadrilles in all colours eg. mauve, pistachio, gauloise bleu blue. I had a lovely time.'[8] Madeleine loved the country. In her novel *A Pure Clear Light*, a summer holiday in France for Flora and her children represents a time of harmony before the turmoil of her husband's affair: 'and they had all agreed, to a tiny child, that this was the life all right, in *la Douce France*, and they were bloody *fools* not to pack it in and move down here for good.'[9] In conversation and letters, as in her books, Madeleine loved to sprinkle French phrases, but she often spelled them incorrectly and sometimes did not quite get the idiom right.

In December 1973, Margaret Minchin died from cancer. She was just fifty-four. Madeleine wrote to her cousin Annabel, now married and expecting her first child:

> Dear little Annabel, All my love & sympathy & all God's blessings on your head. If it is of any comfort to your sadness please think of my sharing it with you; even though I'm far away in space I'm very close to you in time & my feelings are all for you; I am thinking of you all; & believing that the grace of God is as infinite as incomprehensible, I know you are safe in his care...[10]

She reminded Antony, Annabel's brother, of the letter he sent her after Sylvette died:

> You were my only cousin to write to me—I have always loved you for that. It was a sweet letter & as we're not children any more I have

little hope of writing one to you as sweet. But I hope I may try to tell you how much I feel your loss, how much & gratefully I loved your mother, & how I am thinking of you now...[11]

When Sylvette was alive, Ted's sisters had not been particularly close to Madeleine and Colette. But after Sylvette's death, the St John aunts had gradually become closer to their nieces. Margaret had always been fond of Madeleine, and Madeleine's letters suggest a depth of feeling towards her aunt.

Soon there was another death to contend with. Parvati (Janice Dinnen) was killed in a freak accident that horrified the ashram members and the wider expat community in London. The young actor was on the bus home to Ladbroke Grove, riding on the back stairs as people often did, when she slipped and was thrown onto the road. She was taken to hospital badly injured, and she died a few days later. Her body was brought back to her house in Ladbroke Grove and laid out in the front room. Swami-ji led the ashram followers in chants and songs in a long vigil.[12]

In 1976, Madeleine's London survival strategy paid off when she was granted a council house at Number 75 Swinbrook Road and given permission to sublet rooms in the terrace. She took to the role of landlady. She was expert at 'shabby chic' long before the term was invented, scouring the streets for cast-off furniture and objects. She collected the disused and discarded and gave them a new life on her kitchen shelves or in a corner of the living room. She was increasingly happy, too, thanks to what she would undoubtedly have called an *affaire du coeur*.

Dave Codling was a guitarist in the original Quintessence band. His ashram name was Maha Dev, and his wife and young children were also part of the ashram group. In 1972, Dave and singer Phil Jones (Shiva Shankar) had been sacked by the bandleader Raja Ram over musical and other differences. The ruptures had distressed many in the close-knit

Feiga and Jean Cargher, Paris, 1916.

Frederick de Porte St John, with wife Hannah and children. Front, from left: Florence, Pamela and Margaret. Back, from left: Roland and Ted.

A pregnant
Sylvette St John,
Sydney, 1941.

Building a life in
Castlecrag, circa 195
from left, John and
Margaret Minchin,
Sylvette and Ted.

First encounters: Ted, home from the front in 1943, with Madeleine, fifteen months.

All to myself: Madeleine, aged four, with Sylvette and Ted, Sydney, circa 1945.

Happy families: the St Johns at Castlecrag, 1953.

Madeleine and Colette in 1955, the year after Sylvette's death. 'Smiling for the camera', Madeleine wrote in her photograph album.

'The Octopus' at work on *Honi Soit*, 1960.
From left, Marilyn Taylor, Jane Iliff, Madeleine St John, Susan McGowan.
At typewriter, Clive James. In the background, David Ferraro and Helen Goldstein.

**Chris Tillam and
Madeleine in
their apartment
in Cambridge,
Mass, 1967.**

Madeleine in her room at 75 Swinbrook Road in the late 1970s.

Madeleine at a _kirtan_, with Swami-ji.

Madeleine in London, 1969.
Clockwise from top left: Colette, Felicity Baker, Florence Heller,
Madeleine holding Claire Heller, Michael and Juliet Heller.

Madeleine with Puck, Colville Gardens, 1990s.

Madeleine, 1998.

ashram family. Phil and his wife Vidya and their two baby sons went back to Australia in search of work.[13]

Dave and Madeleine had known each other from the *kirtans* but had not been close. They were in many ways an unlikely pair. Dave was a talented painter who had taught art before joining Quintessence, but he was not an intellectual and his Yorkshire working-class background was very different from Madeleine's privileged St John pedigree. But now his marriage was over, and he and Madeleine became lovers. Madeleine was secretive about the relationship; friends believed she loved Dave but was a little ashamed about it.[14] Madeleine told Florence Heller she had a northerner boyfriend who was not of her own social class.[15]

Madeleine was a snob. She relished her entries in *Debrett's Peerage & Baronetage* and *Burke's Peerage* and she was a pushover for a certain kind of upper-class Brit from public school.[16] Dave was hard to fit into the frame. But, in her own way, so was Madeleine. She was interesting rather than beautiful and not a typical bird for a seventies muso.

Dave never lived at Number 75 and recalled that he never saw the affair as long-term, although it lasted more than two years. He liked Madeleine enormously and was impressed by her competence and intelligence. They shared a search for meaning: 'We had endless discussions about spiritual stuff, where we came from and where we were going...She was very funny, she could take the micky out of people.' Dave's life was still a bit of a mess after the collapse of his marriage and his Quintessence career. To him, Madeleine seemed to be 'positive and getting on with her life. I envied her because she was so together, she had the ability to get a house together, things like that.'[17]

Madeleine's affair with Dave was an affirmation of her sexual appeal and her ability to have a man of her own. Her divorce had left her feeling desolate and abandoned, and she had wasted emotion in her infatuation with Michael Chesterman, but now she found a measure of security with Dave, at least for a time.

The affair had been an on-again, off-again relationship, but Dave was shocked when it ended. One minute they were getting along famously, the next they were standing on the stairs at 75 Swinbrook Road deep in an argument that had come out of nowhere. Dave recalled, 'We had a big bust-up and I left. That was it.'[18] Madeleine may well have brought the argument on—as she so often did when intimacy became too much for her—but she was desperately unhappy at the end of the relationship, telling friends that Dave had left her and that she was still in love with him.[19] Years later, she opened her third novel, *The Essence of the Thing*, with a rejection that comes out of the blue, as sudden as the rupture between herself and Dave.

Madeleine had long wanted a child, but when she became pregnant she had an abortion. She and Dave had just broken up and perhaps she couldn't face a child alone. Dave didn't know she was pregnant—he would find out from others some years later.[20] Madeleine told Colette that Swami-ji told her to have the abortion. She was not upset when she told her sister the story, but Madeleine wrote a poignant letter to Vidya Jones noting that Dave's sister-in-law 'had a baby boy at 4 a.m. on Thursday, Virgo/Libra cusp, very, very beautiful—you may imagine one's feelings'.[21] And on several occasions later in her life, she expressed regret about 'the child she should have had'.[22]

During her time in Swinbrook Road, Madeleine met Judith McCue, an Australian studying at the London School of Economics. They were introduced by Francis James, a mutual friend who had been a defendant in the *Oz* obscenity trial in 1964. He was charged with printing the offending edition and was defended by Ted at the trial. The eccentric James hit the headlines again when he was jailed by the Chinese in 1969 as an alleged spy.[23] When he was released in 1973, he spent extended periods in London, staying mainly at his club and treating Judith and Madeleine to meals there. But when his money ran out, he landed on his friends, including Madeleine. His war injuries and his time in jail had ruined his health and it is likely Madeleine nursed the maverick, who was old enough to be her father. Not that she seemed to mind. They were both complex personalities who loved to spar and were a match for each other.[24] Madeleine and Judith soon formed a strong friendship, which endured after Judith married and moved with her astronomer husband, Edward Kibblewhite, to the US.

As she made new connections in the seventies, Madeleine lost touch with some of her old friends. She saw the Chestermans, who were back home after a year in Africa. But they were now living near the University of Warwick, where Michael was teaching, and contact was limited. At the same time, Australia was being transformed by the Whitlam Labor government, and many expats were heading home. Bruce Beresford returned to Australia in 1970 and was busy defining the national character in films such as *The Adventures of Barry McKenzie* and the classics *Don's Party* and *Breaker Morant*.

Australia was changing and Madeleine was curious. In 1976 she made her first trip home after a decade away. It is likely that Ted paid her airfare. The teenage St John boys scarcely knew their half-sister. When Madeleine arrived at Vino del Mar, taking up residence in the maid's quarters, it was as if they were meeting her for the first time. Ed, now sixteen, had just started writing record reviews for *Rolling Stone*, which was, coincidentally, co-owned and co-edited by Octopus member Jane Iliff. To Ed, Madeleine was exotic: she nonchalantly smoked dope in the kitchen and introduced him to the American rock band Little Feat, who became one of his favourites.

Madeleine rose late, drank endless cups of tea, then, draped in scarves, whiled away the afternoon inside the house, rarely venturing out till late. She maintained a glacial pace and an indifference to work. And Patrick St John, at thirteen, noted how much Madeleine upset his mother.[25]

Colette had returned to Sydney in 1970 and travelled around Australia. She spent a year at the radical arts space, the Yellow House, near Kings Cross. But at the end of 1974 she suffered a severe nervous breakdown and was admitted to the North Ryde psychiatric hospital. She recalled:

> Suicide was always with me, it was my escape route, it was my comfort, it was my God, it was my religion. I was saving my money to go to India, everyone had been to the east. I said to myself, if things don't work out for me, there are opiates [there] and I could just die. My fantasy was to go overland to the Himalayas and just die.

She too was trying to sort out her relationship with Ted, repeatedly trying to win his approval: 'After we both left home I ran after that man, whenever I had the guts to come back and reconnect myself with the St John family.'[26]

Ted was back at the bar after his stints in politics and business. He had not grown rich from his mining and property interests but had done quite well.[27] Madeleine enjoyed an extended stay in Sydney, courtesy of Ted and Val. She visited the family's weekender in the high country at Mt Elliot just inland from Avoca Beach. Ted and Val had bought the old corrugated iron and timber farmhouse on a few acres in 1967. Ted loved the bush and it was a haven, especially for Oliver, who could roam freely and safely over the property. By the time Madeleine saw it in the seventies, Mt Elliot had become the centre of family gatherings for the extended St John clan.

In Sydney, Madeleine telephoned Chris and reminded him he still owed her money from the divorce settlement. 'Send me an invoice,' he told her. 'I don't do bills,' she retorted.[28] The wounds of their marriage were still raw.

Madeleine was not tempted to remain in Australia. She and Chris had left Sydney as bright young things, but their dreams had collapsed in Boston, and Madeleine scaled back her expectations. In London she had created a space of her own. Her life, no matter how reduced, was in London, not Sydney. She thought of Australia as 'an accident of birth rather than as her homeland'. She had been 'brought up on the idea that England was where I came from, in a deep sense where I belonged. Australia was a deviation of one's essence.'[29]

CHAPTER FOURTEEN

Madame Blavatsky

The decade or so that Madeleine spent at Number 75 Swinbrook Road was dominated by efforts to research and write a biography of Helena Blavatsky. The project dragged on and on, becoming a metaphor for Madeleine's own lack of direction. It was Madeleine's excuse for not pursuing an orthodox career. Ted held the Blavatsky biography up to his sons as an example of Madeleine's inability to complete projects, and he warned them against following in her footsteps.

No one is sure why Madeleine chose to write about the extraordinary Russian woman who moved from dabbling in the occult, holding séances in Cairo, to founding the Theosophical Society in 1875. One reason may have been that the fusion of the east and west inherent in theosophy matched Madeleine's interest in both eastern religion and Christianity. But perhaps Madeleine was simply intrigued by this controversial woman, who had a complicated childhood. The facts of Blavatsky's early life are scant but it is known she was only eleven when her mother died. Madeleine may have been drawn to explore a life she saw as parallel to her own.

Quite how long Madeleine worked on Blavatsky is unclear, but she talked about it to Miriam Herbert as early as 1972, told people in 1980 that it was finished, rewrote it and announced it finally finished in 1987, and was still trying to get it published in the early 1990s. The project defined her middle-age. The material was complicated but Madeleine embraced the act of writing. It was through Blavatsky that she became convinced that it was her role in life to be a writer. She began to see writing almost as a calling, reporting to Vidya Jones in Australia:

> I must tell you that there is nothing I know more destructive of the dreaded ego [than writing]. I really believe that to be fully engaged on a creative endeavour is a righteous spiritual path...[1]

Madeleine supported herself in this period with a succession of small jobs, as well as rent from subletting rooms at Number 75. She also signed up for unemployment benefits. There was money from the divorce settlement, although she had to wait for some time for the funds to come through. It is not clear how much money, if any, Ted sent to her in these years, but in 1980 he paid for her to travel to Australia again. He had taken a number of high-profile, but not lucrative, legal cases, but thanks to his earlier success in business, he and Val were more comfortably off than they had been earlier in their marriage. Val was not in paid work, but she spent a lot of time involved in fundraising and supporting Inala, a Rudolf Steiner–based institution for the disabled in Sydney's northern suburbs, where Oliver lived.

Madeleine's leisurely lifestyle and failure to get a 'real job' in London worried her father and stepmother, but their frustration increased when Madeleine visited Sydney and they saw her operating at close quarters. She was brittle and ready to take offence. Feiga, who had moved to Adelaide to live with Josette and her family, was terminally ill with lung cancer, and no one, it seems, had told Madeleine. When she found out, she was incensed, convinced her family was treating her with disrespect.[2] Madeleine visited Feiga just before she died on 26 April. Back in Sydney, she wrote to Judith McCue to say she was 'having a perfectly awful time'. She said of her grandmother's death:

> I would like it to be known (!)—the family is ignoring this fact studiously—that I am very disturbed & freaked out, one way & another & can handle nothing, let alone all the junk I seem to be attracting. This evening am working on trying to see the ludicrous side—as a means of surviving—&, so far, failing...We'll have to trust in a benevolent Deity—what else do we have?[3]

Madeleine was undoubtedly grieving for Feiga, but she was self-absorbed and could interpret the event and the reactions of her family only as an assault on her well being.

Val and Ted had planned a family holiday with Ed and Patrick to a beach resort in Fiji. It was to be a celebration of the end of Ted's work on the high-profile Barton case, in which he successfully defended the business magnate Alexander Barton and his son Thomas on corporate charges. But Ted was again busy in the Supreme Court, pursuing action against the Chelmsford Private Hospital in Sydney over the notorious deep-sleep therapy used on depressed patients in the 1970s. Ted had taken the case *pro bono*. The hearings continued for months, and Ted could not go to Fiji with the family. Val invited Madeleine in his place.

At the resort, Ed and Patrick enjoyed themselves windsurfing and drinking beers. They rather liked their half-sister, but the holiday was a strain for Val. Madeleine stayed in bed till noon then emerged swathed in layers of clothing to protect her fair skin and retreated to read a book under a palm tree. There was so much history between the two women that every conversation was a minefield. One day, seeing a family on the beach with an adopted Vietnamese child, Val remarked that she and Ted had thought of adopting but had decided they could not give a child enough access to his or her own culture. Madeleine was angry. 'Fuck you, you bitch,' she thought. 'How can you say that to me, who you prevented from doing French honours, who you never encouraged to have anything to do with French language, or people, or anything.'[4] Madeleine always considered her mother to be French. Indeed, she believed at this stage that her grandfather, Jean Meer Cargher, was French—she discovered only towards the end of her life that both Jean and Feiga were born in Romania.

On her 1980 trip to Australia, Madeleine also spent time with Vidya Jones and her sister Christine Hill. Christine was married to another ashram follower, Ralph Magid, an exuberant member of a well-known Melbourne Jewish family. The couple had returned to Australia and opened a bookshop in the outer Melbourne suburb of Mulgrave. At Mulgravia, as the group called it, Ralph and Christine were optimistic about their business and Vidya, separated from her husband Phil and with two little boys to rear, had moved to Melbourne to help them run the shop. The three of them welcomed Madeleine and the visit went well. Madeleine felt she was with her real family. She excelled herself with her 'party pieces' about far-from-glamorous Mulgrave, performing skits on 'the topography & Climate of Mulgravia' and 'the True Inwardness of a Modern Australian Shopping Complex'. In Mulgrave she felt she had space to 'talk'. Later, back in England, she wrote to Vidya about how much she missed:

> all the fun of being with youse & always will…Vidya my sweet it really is very very heartwarming to me to have your love & friendship & your dear relations as, let's face it, I really have no other 'family'. So I hope you lot never cast me out not that you would…[5]

The fear of being abandoned was never far from Madeleine's mind.

Madeleine met up with her old university and London friend Winton Higgins in Sydney—but only after they met by accident on a bus. They had lost touch in the seventies. Winton recalled that Madeleine seemed to be happy with the direction of her life.[6] The lives of those who had met through SUDS and *Honi Soit* had changed considerably in the last two decades. Many of the Octopus women were divorced or separated from their first partners; some had found their hopes of careers interrupted by children at a time when child care was hard to find; some had put aside their dreams. Suicide had touched them. One of the group, Helen Goldstein, haunted by depression, had died in her twenties after several suicide attempts. Tragedy struck another of their contemporaries when Diane Horler, sister of the theatre director Ken Horler, died after an illegal abortion.[7]

In June 1980, Chris's mother died. Madeleine had continued to write to Joan long after her divorce from Chris and it is likely they remained in touch until she died. It was another break with the past: Joan had been Madeleine's only link with Chris and her only source of any news about his life in Australia with Martha. Over time, Madeleine would create a new narrative about her American years. Her London friends would be told only that she had been married for a brief time. Few people knew the name of her former husband, or any other details. Madeleine held tight to her belief that Chris had had an affair, but he faded from her story.

Not so Sylvette. In Australia, Madeleine salvaged several photographs of her mother from the boxes of pictures that Ted had kept. She was convinced her father wanted to cut Sylvette from the family record. She believed Ted had enforced a silence after her mother's death and that taking possession of the photographs was a way to reclaim that past. In the end it was Madeleine who excised her mother from the family collection, but she felt she had 'rescued' Sylvette.[8]

Back in London in the middle of 1980, Madeleine was flush with funds after receiving part of the divorce settlement. Madeleine knew Chris needed the money and some of her friends chided her for taking it, but she was unperturbed. She considered it rightfully hers. She used the money to go to court and get rid of a difficult tenant, and then splurged on several pairs of expensive Charles Jourdan designer shoes.[9] In November she wrote to Vidya: 'I am not doing anything very responsible let alone

difficult, until the money's gone. I'm just doing a bit of this, a bit of that
& it is, of course, rather nice.'[10]

Her bond with Vidya was strong. When Vidya went through a
difficult period, Madeleine wrote to say she felt:

> powerless to offer any practical assistance…At this distance there are
> only words: & who needs those, especially mine. So I am just thinking
> of you sorrowfully in a void. So I beg you to write even a few words
> just as soon as ever you can & tell me how you are, exactly. The veil
> of myah (the darkness of the universe) gets thicker by the minute, one
> seeks ever the enormous joke at the bottom of the pile. So to speak.
> 'Some laugh, some weep some dance for joy.'[11]

The letter was tender and honest. Madeleine understood now, at some deep
level, that human existence was fundamentally absurd. Her emotional
security, imperfect as it was, was linked to Number 75, where she was
in control. Back in London after a few years away, Miriam was relieved
to find Madeleine had a room for rent. Both women were still attending
the ashram *kirtans* and Miriam, who had retrained as a nurse and was
working at the Royal Masonic Hospital, was happy to give Madeleine
another chance. Miriam paid twelve pounds a week for a room at the front
of the house; Madeleine had the beautiful large space on the mezzanine
with deep windows, over which she had grown a geranium creeper; and
another lodger, John Simmonds, a British cameraman, lived on the top
floor.

Miriam described the house as set up 'like a museum' with Madeleine's
second-hand goods given pride of place. Madeleine had an old Elizabeth
David cookbook and French cookware bought at the markets and she
imbued the objects with a value only she could see. Her cat, Darling
Point, named after the Sydney suburb, ate everything from boiled eggs
to bread and butter.[12] Madeleine doted on her cat. She wrote to Vidya:
'The puss is, as ever, the ever-sweet Darling precious.'[13]

Initially, Miriam was happy at Number 75. 'Madeleine has been ever so sweet to me and in 2 weeks I'll have a good (bigger) room here. I really feel at home back here in Swinbrook Road,' she wrote to her brother, Tim.[14] But Madeleine proved to be tricky. She had always been quick to judge and before long Miriam found her overly critical and set in her ways and her ideas. She was still using a lot of dope, despite Swami-ji's entreaties to his followers to stay away from drugs, and now had a smoker's cough.

In December that year, nineteen-year-old Tim, backpacking his way around Europe, came to stay with his older sister at Swinbrook Road for a short time. It was the first time he had met Madeleine. She was welcoming, but Tim quickly realised that he must not cross her. He remembered her as a control freak, crusty and 'snooty' at times. She was 'vivid, brittle, contrary, but never an ingénue'. Tim thought she was very observant, that she was always mentally taking notes. Madeleine invited Tim to her room and instructed him in the virtues of Schubert chamber music and its superiority to his symphonies. On New Year's Day, Tim and Miriam went to a *kirtan* at Islington. Tim recalled that everyone had waited for Swami-ji to arrive 'like the Messiah'. Madeleine did not attend, but when Miriam and Tim returned she asked: 'So, what was the message of the day?' Though still connected to the ashram, she had perhaps grown a little cynical.

When Tim decided to leave freezing London and chase the sun to Greece, Madeleine asked him to bring back some duty-free Bisquit cognac. She may have been down-at-heel, but she knew quality. Tim recalled that 'she was giving me a life lesson, she seemed like a woman of the world'.[15]

When he came back a few months later, Madeleine was a little less welcoming, although she sometimes included him when friends came round for long talking and smoking sessions in her room. As the dope kicked in, Madeleine relaxed. 'She was quite brassy, quite open about sex and sexuality,' Tim recalled.[16]

One day, a thin, long-haired man who lived close by drove Madeleine and Tim out of London to see horse chestnut trees in bloom. Madeleine insisted they were her favourite English tree and said Tim simply must see them. She produced a spliff and they started smoking. It was quite a trip, Madeleine, with her 'pinched, nervous' face, looking back from the front seat and gently mocking the young Australian as they rocketed, stoned, through the English countryside.[17]

By mid-1981, Miriam was again fed up with Madeleine. Tim had dropped in for a few days after travelling in Egypt and the visit had not gone over well with Madeleine. Miriam wrote to her parents in Sydney that she was looking for somewhere else to live:

> Being near Madeleine has become too heavy. She is always finding fault and accused both Tim and me of being ungrateful, taking things for granted etc. I don't know what she expects—flowers from Harrods or should we kiss her feet. She has a neurosis, where she needs to find fault continually. She has been lucky to have me around who minds my own business, is tidy, unobtrusive + coughs up the rent punctually. She always wants to play the landlady—she can't have things on an equal basis. As far as I can see the best thing for me is to find somewhere else where I can feel part of the household and have some friendly, open-minded people about, not one who is locked in her own head and can't (won't) get out.[18]

In August, Miriam left the household.

Unemployment in the UK was high, and Madeleine struggled to find even a part-time job. In many ways, she seemed to her friends to be living the life of a student. When Peter Grose and his wife, Roslyn Owen, bumped into Madeleine in the street near the Portobello markets one day, she invited them around for a meal. Peter, who had been part of the *Honi Soit* set, was now a literary agent, and Roslyn, who knew Madeleine from their school days at Queenwood, worked on a newspaper in Fleet Street. They were delighted to see Madeleine after almost twenty years, but were surprised when they were expected to sit on the floor at Swinbrook Road, eat spaghetti bolognaise and listen to a heavy metal band.[19]

When Ed St John visited his half-sister, he found Number 75

unprepossessing rather than charming. In Australia, brazenly smoking dope at Vino del Mar, Madeleine had seemed sophisticated. In a sparsely furnished house off the Portobello Road, the image was a little harder to sustain.[20]

CHAPTER FIFTEEN

Colville Gardens

Madeleine was delighted when Number 75 Swinbrook Road was demolished in the early 1980s and she was rehoused in a larger block of mansion flats at 55 Colville Gardens, Notting Hill. Colville Gardens was several steps up from Swinbrook Road, and her new home had a beautiful outlook across an open square to the spare and elegant All Saints Church. From her spacious flat on the fourth and fifth floors, Madeleine looked through trees to the belltower. The light was lovely, the air seemed fresh, and she had a home all her own, free of other tenants, in the heart of one of the world's great cities.

Her mansion block had been built in the mid-1800s as part of a large development centred on All Saints. The construction was funded by a wealthy vicar with a social conscience, but he ran out of money before the project was completed and the church was derelict for years. It became known as All Sinners in the Mud, because it had a disreputable congregation and was surrounded by half-built houses on farmland. The church was eventually completed in 1861, and property speculators continued to build houses in the area. Notting Hill was a new London address for upwardly mobile Victorians. But over the years, it became less appealing. The houses were too grand for city workers, but too small for the rich folk who preferred the more fashionable Kensington.[1] Between the first and second world wars, the area became more decrepit and it was not until the 1960s and 1970s that the Notting Hill Housing Trust began to improve conditions. In 1999, Madeleine wrote about those earlier decades when Notting Hill was home to:

> long-exploited Afro-Caribbean immigrants and their British-born offspring, and west Londoners who'd been through the war and the bombs and the rationing. They had never quite managed to find the cash to flee, like all their better-off neighbours, from the sad and seedy old post-war Hill, where the hundred-year leases were falling in and everything else was falling down, gradually, around their ears... [it] was the place the hippies colonised. One could still find a cheap room or a tenement flat—two rooms with a shared bathroom: and a key to the communal gardens (sure, you can use my key—peace and love!). The communal gardens were full of hippies smoking weed and playing guitars.[2]

When Madeleine arrived, in the early 1980s, Notting Hill was still edgy. Prostitutes used the porch at All Saints as their pick-up point, while their pimps took over the nearby phone box as an office.[3] Madeleine loved the surrounding streets with their nineteenth-century 'wedding-cake architecture' and the 'columns, balustrades, Roman arches and balconies with cast-iron trimmings', along with communal gardens, and the trees.[4] She relished the bohemian feel. With her roll-your-own cigarettes and her wild hair she merged happily into the scene. And she was even closer to her favourite market stalls on Portobello Road. At Colville Gardens she nested once again. She installed some of her beloved possessions from Swinbrook Road, including a huge yellow and blue canvas painted by Dave Codling.[5] She rescued cast-off objects from the street stalls and dumps, including the metal frame of a chaise longue which she hauled up the stairs, positioning it to create a unique sculpture. In her attic she hung net curtains around the bed and had a *trompe l'oeil* painted on the wall. The drawing room had pale grey walls and painted floorboards, with much of the area covered in seagrass matting. The curtains on the tall windows were antique linen, with thin blue braid sewn on a few inches in from the edges.[6] And she had Darling Point, her beloved cat, for company.

Madeleine was still trying to get a job, but had little success. She was thinner than ever, living on vegetables and cheese from the Portobello Road stalls, and she was smoking heavily. But she found Colville Gardens blissful. Up among the trees it was decidedly heavenly, with the rhythm of each leisurely day marked by the All Saints bells. Madeleine had begun attending Church of England services before the move to Notting Hill, but now, with a church so close that she could almost touch it from her kitchen window, she became a regular attendant.

Madeleine was a cultural Anglican: the vicarage was in her blood. But, increasingly, the church became embedded in Madeleine's life. She loved the music. She had not played the piano for many years, but she had a deep interest in music of all sorts, from traditional hymns to jazz. All Saints was a High-Church parish and some elements of its practice—such as the use of the Catholic mass books rather than the *Book of Common Prayer*—irritated her. But it was a beautiful building and she was prepared to overlook the 'bells and smells' copied from Rome.

Her years at St Catherine's had given her 'a very solid grounding in the C of E texts'. But Madeleine had rejected religion as a teenager. Now she was drawn to the idea of transcendence through religion as well as all its rituals. In 2004, she said:

> I am the sort of person who needs to be in a nice church or I don't want to be in any church. If it is some dreary little evangelical church with bad music and a dreary little vicar with an Australian accent, then I don't want to be there. If the service is not a nicely conducted one with the right stuff, the right atmosphere, I don't want to go.[7]

All Saints passed the test. It was a fine building with broad, well-proportioned aisles. It had been badly bombed during World War II, but when it reopened in 1951 it had new shrines, painted gold-leaf altarpieces and all the trappings of a High-Church place of worship. For Madeleine, the Church of England was also appealing because it was so much a part of the English landscape. As the official established church, it was woven into public life in a way she had never experienced in Australia. She loved walking across the square on Sunday mornings and chatting in the church porch after the service.

Religion was important to Madeleine. One of the relationships she consistently explored in her novels was between her characters and God. She was interested in living a moral life in a secular age. In *A Pure Clear Light*, published in 1996, one of her characters stands in the kitchen praying to the Blessed Virgin Mary and drags her family off to Communion on Christmas Eve. Faith is applauded, not denigrated, in her novels.

But Madeleine had eclectic tastes. In the early years at Notting Hill she still attended *kirtans*. Swami-ji did not ask his followers to reject Christianity, and Madeleine continued to look to both the church and the ashram for enlightenment. Friends who had scoffed at her attachment to an Indian guru were similarly surprised by her Anglican faith. Neither belief system seemed to gel with the acerbic Madeleine they had known in the 1960s.[8] Nor with the woman immersed in a project on Madame Blavatsky.

Madeleine was struggling with the biography after a decade of work, but it was clear to Felicity Baker that she was a gifted writer. She recalled that the manuscript was a critical look at Blavatsky. She felt her cousin was past her 'ashram phase' and was sceptical of theosophy and deeply committed to Anglican theology. But she did not think the biography was coherent. Little was known of Blavatsky's childhood, and Madeleine had opted to write a 'creative' version of her early years. She had written a 'tremendously sensitive picture of what it was like to emerge as a little girl in such a world, at such a time'. But merging that story with factual narrative was difficult, and Madeleine had not managed to tie the threads of the book together.[9]

Madeleine made friends with a small group of people in the All Saints congregation, among them, a young artist named Celia Irvine. The two women met at a religious retreat, which comprised a series of weekly meetings.[10] Madeleine and Celia were close to two other people at that point: David Bambridge, a primary school teacher, and Frances Barrett, who had attended All Saints since she was a small child. Frances organised the coffee after the Sunday services and sang in the choir. Celia, a talented artist, decorated the paschal candle and organised a carpet of flowers in the church on Corpus Christi Sunday.

Madeleine hovered at the edges. She loved the cut and thrust of debate outside the church after the Sunday service and was at times involved in the choir, but when Frances asked her to visit a sick parishioner, Madeleine said, 'I go to church in order to worship God, not to do social work.'[11]

More interesting to Madeleine were the arguments with the vicar, Father John Brownsell. Madeleine, David and Celia were a little gang of dissenters. They saw themselves as the 'naughty background kids' who challenged the vicar's decisions.[12] He had created an atmosphere that was so High-Church, Frances recalled, that 'Catholics didn't even know they were not in a Catholic church'.[13]

The Church of England was the 'FUN church', Madeleine told Judith McCue.[14] But she was serious about religion. She believed 'that we are all equally sinners and that we are all equally redeemed by the death and resurrection of Jesus Christ and we have to work out our salvation on the ground day to day'.[15] She said that her belief in God was her only way of managing a life that she often felt was 'a chaos of failure and futility'.[16]

As always, Madeleine kept aspects of her life and her friendship circles separate, although she once took Celia along to a *kirtan* held in a big house in Kilburn. There were about forty people, and copious amounts of tea were served. Everyone took off their shoes and danced. She was grateful to God, she told Deidre Rubenstein, who had spent five years at the ashram before returning to her life as an actor in Melbourne:

> God has been wonderfully good & I am wonderfully nervous—won-
> dering what game I am *meant* to be playing—for it can't really be
> this nice, so enjoyable—when is that monster going to leap out from
> the wings?[17]

Celia and the rest of the little gang sometimes gathered at Madeleine's
flat, where their hostess appeared to live on air. Invited for a meal once,
the friends were presented with half a lettuce leaf each with tomatoes and
sour cream.[18] And although the flat was simply furnished, Madeleine was
houseproud. She changed the curtains from summer to winter, and the
flat was almost always filled with music from the BBC. The Blavatsky
research was in evidence, with books out on the dining table. One day
Madeleine talked Frances into helping her proof the manuscript and
they spent hours sitting on the floor, wading through the punctuation.[19]

Madeleine was an engaging but complicated friend. Frances wondered
at times whether this expatriate Australian was striking a calculated
pose for effect. One day she telephoned Madeleine before lunch, only
to get a blast: 'Christ, Frances, I don't know how to tell you, but one
does not usually ring before 10 o'clock!' One Christmas morning after
church, Frances popped over to Colville Gardens but could not stay long.
Madeleine was livid. She had organised nothing but had assumed a few
of the gang would be around to celebrate—she worked on a very loose
timetable and was often oblivious to the pressures on people with regular
jobs and families. Frances was appalled, and she took a step back from
her demanding friend.

Frances had often lent Madeleine money to tide her over a financial
crisis. Madeleine was scrupulous about repaying the money quickly, always
with a small gift and loving notes. Once she wrote:

> Dear Frances, £100 with my most grateful thanks. You must have
> pulled me out of more financial black holes than you've had hot

dinners, at least lately—so here's a cold pudding to make up the difference. Hope it's OK! As I've never made it before & as you see it has not been tasted. Lots of Love, Madeleine.[20]

Other friends bailed her out too. Judith McCue sent money from Chicago. In February 1989, Madeleine wrote to Judith to say that her cheque to Judith had not been cashed and so she therefore proposed to repay her by buying 'frocks' for her young daughter, Jessica.[21] But survival in these years was often cobbled together. Madeleine's flat was distinctive, thanks to her talent at putting the pieces together, but it was freezing, and her friends wondered what she lived on.[22]

Frances saw how vulnerable Madeleine was. When Darling Point died, Madeleine told Frances that life without her cat was 'quite incredibly lonely'.[23] But soon Madeleine had another cat, a prized Turkish Vann called Puck, brilliantly white with different-coloured eyes—one blue, one brown. The All Saint's curate, Father David Clues, conducted a blessing ceremony, and Frances stood as godmother.[24]

Madeleine had always been quick to judge and lecture her friends, but this character trait was becoming even more pronounced. When Vidya Jones and her two young sons returned to London in 1985, the friends saw each other rarely and Vidya found Madeleine difficult:

> She was very sweet, she had a very sweet blithe quality, charming and *je ne sais quoi*; she really was one of those people who had an extra little thing. But she had another side to her, the side that was quite sharp and bitter. She couldn't help herself. It was not that *you* went on or off, *she* went on or off. You wouldn't know why. You could be having a lovely day with her and then she would get sick of you. She didn't have the capacity to keep something going. There's always a lull in friendship but you sustain it because you like the person. She would just destroy everything, destroy a relationship.[25]

Vidya had known Madeleine well for many years and loved her, and she understood her shortcomings. Madeleine was outgoing and sociable but often attacked those closest to her. The most common complaint about Madeleine, voiced by many of her friends over the decades, was that when there was a rupture, it was inexplicable. They would rack their brains but could never identify what they had done to cause offence.

Madeleine often looked for ways to control her friends. She wanted them to be better, and to fit them into the picture she had created of them and of her life. She set about remodelling David Bambridge. He recalled that Madeleine was 'quite cutting and prickly...rather grand at times, but also kind, generous and funny'. She was forever trying to improve him, once presenting him with a tweed jacket she had bought in a charity shop, with the implied message that it was suitable attire for a true English gentleman. On another occasion, it was an old copy of Fowler's *Modern English Usage*. Some of her gifts had a fustier value, like the GPO Bakelite telephone she found on a skip.[26]

Sometimes Madeleine met Felicity Baker for long walks around Kensington. Their relationship was complicated. Felicity was an academic at University College in London, and she felt that Madeleine was contemptuous of her success—Madeleine, not having followed the usual career paths in pursuit of a more creative life, and with little to show for her choice, protected herself by denigrating those who had. Felicity knew, too, that her cousin needed to control every situation. On the rare occasions when Felicity telephoned her, Madeleine immediately said she would call her back in a few minutes. It was clear that she needed time to get herself together and decide how to manage the conversation.[27]

Madeleine's relationship with her friend Judith McCue, who was now living in the US, was also complex. Her letters to Judith were lively, honest and intimate. But on the phone Madeleine was often scornful and attacked Judith's domestic happiness. Madeleine had wanted marriage and children, but now she could only survive her disappointment by dismissing the lifestyle she had not achieved.[28]

The patterns of Madeleine's interactions were becoming entrenched. Over and over, she would draw people in with her loving charm, intelligence, creativity and high values. But before long she would create a crisis or an argument, driving away friends who were left bewildered by her behaviour. Then, after a break, a card or phone call would signal a desire to resume relations. All her life, Madeleine made sure she rejected others before they could abandon her, then hauled them back on her terms.

At Colville Gardens, Madeleine was more isolated than she had been at her other London addresses. Her street in Notting Hill was quiet and there were several flights of stairs between her home and the world outside. The temptation to bed down on the couch and watch old movies in the afternoons on her old black-and-white television was strong. On the positive side, the distance from the world helped Madeleine focus on her writing, and she began to devote more time to the Blavatsky biography. In a letter to Judith in November 1986, she wrote:

> A dark November day, about 5 leaves left to fall, opera on R3, cat licking his lips, clock ticking & me at an impasse or a mini-impasse having written about 1¾ chapters of MY BOOK (which took about 1 ½ months—clock that!) & in a state of the can'ts about the next bit due to having just read over typescript...[29]

Writing was now a part of Madeleine's daily life, even if it was a cause of anxiety. She had a purpose. She told Judith that writing was:

> guaranteed to make pretty well everything else in life seem easy- calm- & problem-free. I find myself worrying about it all the time that I am not actually writing & that is most of the time so you could say that it has changed my life really & whether or not a publishable MS emerges from the experience seems to me at the moment the merest detail.[30]

The following year when her half-brother Patrick and his future wife Karen visited during a tour of Europe, Madeleine announced herself as a writer.[31] Blavatsky dominated her world. In June 1987 she told Judith that she was still so deeply involved in:

WRITING MY BOOK that altho' other things sometimes loom or impinge, I know & feel them to be trivial: and I really think that, even if I never succeed, trying to become a writer, is what I am here to do...All any of us needs is a role and mine seems after all to be to scribble, & doing that as well as I possibly can is the only thing of real importance...Of course, I should love to succeed, crash through, earn my keep, even contribute to others', but at this stage it is the doing which possesses my thoughts and energies.[32]

Madeleine was living on social services. Prime minister Margaret Thatcher, Mrs Hacksaw as Madeleine called her, was cutting a swathe through welfare but the 'Other England' continued behind the scenes. Madeleine wrote to Judith that the government had tightened the rules on benefits, but that at the unemployment office, staff were sympathetic and happy to keep the payments going to people like her who were 'grooving away on their little enterprises, books, painting, perpetual motion machines, God knows what'.[33] But the Thatcher cutbacks were changing the England that Madeleine knew and loved. In May 1990, she told Judith that the country was 'going to the Rottweilers, everyone here hates Maggie now but it's too late: her work is effectively done. Sans divine intervention (& we know how disobliging that can be) I fear that English civilisation as we have known & loved it is kaput.'[34] It was becoming clear to Madeleine that she would need to earn some money if she wanted to remain in London.

Madeleine and Colette had last seen each other in Sydney in 1980. Not long after, Colette set off for the US. In Santa Fe, she met Steve Lippincott, a student fourteen years her junior. He fell for Colette with her charm and ability to fill the room with her gypsy spirit and laughter. They married six months later, and by 1981 they were back in Sydney, at first living with Ted and Val at Vino del Mare. Steve found work in publishing and Colette worked as a couturier. For a time she was involved in the Coo-ee Emporium, which was set up as a showcase for indigenous art and crafts by her friend Louise Ferrier.

By the mid-1980s the Lippincotts were living in Melbourne. But once again Colette was on the edge. She found help in a radical psychotherapy program, which required patients to commit to live in at a facility all week for up to two years and to take part in intensive therapy. Colette felt she had found people who took her problems seriously, and she began to make progress. She and Steve spent weekends together and soon Colette was pregnant. Aaron was born in 1985, and sixteen months later, the Lippincotts returned to the US.

In London, Madeleine finally completed the Blavatsky biography. She wrote the last sentence on Guy Fawkes Day 1987, 'while rockets zoomed through the skies of Notting Hill'. It was the week before her forty-sixth birthday and she immediately began to think about her next book.[35] She was truly hooked on writing. In March, she wrote to Colleen Chesterman in Sydney:

> Whether it will eventually find a publisher is *very* problematical, but: it was the most fantastic fun to do. After writing, everything else is rather boring…PS Writing a book is nothing like writing an essay…i.e. it is not a drag, *On s'amuse bien*![36]

Madeleine gave the manuscript to Christine Hill, who had worked in publishing, to read for comment and criticisms. The first hundred pages had been read by 'horribly clever (New Coll. Oxford philosophy) person who was fairly complimentary'. So was Christine. 'Madeleine was not capable of being a bad writer,' she said. It was not a simplistic demolition job on theosophy. The manuscript was 'dispassionate and funny', although, Christine thought, it needed more work.[37]

But Madeleine's efforts to find a publisher went nowhere, and in the following year she gave part of the manuscript to an agent. She was worried the book was 'too eccentric for serious consideration' with 'awkward & complicated material *fairly* well put together'. She gave herself a B+. The style, she told Judith, was 'flashy & vulgar'.[38]

Her assessment may have been an attempt to protect herself from disappointment. She told Judith that she thought she had better try to write a novel, that 'the business of a writer must be, to write & go on writing until she scores a hit: and after that too'. She professed a motive beyond success, saying: 'It would be divine to score of course: but that, as my beloved music teacher would say, is not IT.'[39]

This period was a relatively happy one for Madeleine. There were visits from Australian friends and family. Colleen and Michael Chesterman were in London in the autumn of 1988 and Madeleine urged them to stay with her. The following year she saw Ted and Val when they spent time in the UK. The visit went well enough.[40] Ted was now immersed in research of his own. He had been out of politics for twenty years but was active in the nuclear and peace movements. In 1984 he was part of an unsuccessful campaign to elect Midnight Oil lead singer Peter Garrett as a Nuclear Disarmament Party senator. That same year he worked with poet Les Murray to compose 'The Universal Prayer for Peace: a Prayer for the Nuclear Age'. And he supported the World Court Project, which petitioned the International Court of Justice to outlaw nuclear weapons.[41] Now he was researching his anti-nuclear book, *Judgment at Hiroshima*, a work some in his family felt to be a magnificent folly, not unlike Madeleine's Blavatsky biography.[42]

Back in Sydney after their visit to London, Val and Ted were delighted to receive a 'loving card' from Madeleine.[43] The tension between Madeleine and her father and stepmother was never far below the surface, but Madeleine was capable of great sweetness.

By May 1990, Madeleine was lamenting she had lost a recent 'jobette' and was surviving on freelance copy-editing for James Hughes, a publisher she knew through the ashram. He had been given the name Jai Narain by Swami-ji. Madeleine was still hoping the Blavatsky book would earn her some money. She told Judith that the biography had been assessed by three publishers and a new agent, all of whom had pronounced it to be 'fascinating, definitely, but there's really no market for this sort of thing'. Madeleine felt she would have to think of a fresh angle, but had put the topic on the 'back burner whence it may in due course simply boil away: such a pity'. She told Judith that 'I somehow feel (not for quite the first time) that life is beyond my capacities...meanwhile am trying to write some fiction, which is abominably difficult & therefore terrific—but horrifying'.[44]

Six months later she was clinging to hope but told Judith that she would have to 'think up some Gee Whiz selling-point' for the biography which had now 'failed to excite 5 or 6 assorted agents & publishers'.[45] James Hughes felt the book was not well researched and was a 'bit of a rant' rather than a coherent challenge to theosophy. He thought Madeleine was distinctly unimpressed by Blavatsky and could not disguise her dislike of her subject, and he told Madeleine that her book was not working.[46] She had not developed the discipline to focus her material: she was smart and had a keen imagination, but she was not yet the writer she yearned to be.

Madeleine was still vulnerable to emotional low points. On 8 May 1990, she talked openly in a letter to Judith about her continuing battle to understand existence. Judith's mother had recently died, and Madeleine consoled her:

> this life really is a pig, there's just no 2 ways about it, and what we have to cling on to is so frail. Apart from God, of course: who can be very, very difficult—I at present tend to feel that He is not only an Englishman (this was always pretty obvious) but also educ at a Great Public School & Oxbridge (not Sandhurst): adorable, of course, & clever, my goodness, and good & courteous & charming, but temperamental not to say perfectly neurotic...& downright confused not to say deeply illogical attitude to women—!!! The poor thing tends to conceal (if not to deny) his feelings, until they break out in a great storm which frightens the cattle for miles in every direction...By which you will deduce that I have formed yet another ill-advised attachment to as

fine a specimen of English Social Class 2 manhood as a wee colonial could hope to see—never mind feel—which latter I have little realistic hope of doing, actually. [I want to] experience the liaisonette as an educational experience & and not simply yet another draught of bliss & pain. (But ah, such pain! Such bliss! Such idiocy!)[47]

Madeleine did not reveal the name of her new lover and adopted an ironic tone in comparing a contrary God with the repressed Englishmen to whom she was so often attracted. But, despite her humour, she could not hide her disappointment and pain. Her 'liaisonette' was probably already on the skids, she told Judith.

In the early 1990s, Madeleine saw Felicity Baker regularly. They met for lunch and afternoon tea, and Felicity shouted Madeleine to a performance of a new play, *The Singer*, at the Barbican, with Anthony Sher in the lead. The outing began well but Madeleine was bored by the play and at interval she screamed at her cousin: 'Why did you bring me to this?', before stalking out, leaving Felicity shocked at such a public display of bad manners. A few months later, in typical style, Madeleine telephoned her cousin as if nothing had happened, and their contact resumed.[48]

In October 1990, it was all 'madness & melancholy' at Colville Gardens. A fire in Madeleine's flat had destroyed her kitchen and she had builders in. Madeleine told Judith the year had been 'truly astounding in a small domestic way' and she was now 'thin (actually scrawny) sleepless, chain-smoking and in a word mad or at any rate more evidently incompetent than ever & all dare say my own fault'.[49] Still, Madeleine had seen the 'amusing side' of events. She had just spent ten days in the south of France with Tonia Date, who had rescued her from the mayhem in her flat. It was six months after her first mention of her 'liaisonette', and Madeleine referred obliquely to the affair. She told Judith she was not really worried yet about her finances:

because the sensation grows on me increasingly, that this life really is a ridiculous & absurd game which it is fatal to take too seriously—although of course one does when one's affections are aroused. I suppose it really is true in some deep way that love is the only permanent actuality. Or art, or something. Not just a fire & builders.[50]

By December, Madeleine had a job filing documents for a freelance investment banker. Her wage was not enough to live on and her financial situation was even more dire than usual. Ted sent her a combined birthday and Christmas cheque of $150. Madeleine was so insulted that she sent it back with what she described as a 'cool, calm, collected letter' telling her father he owed her money.[51]

Over the next few years, this claim would become a huge issue between Madeleine and her father and stepmother. More than forty years earlier, in 1948, Ted and Sylvette had been given a sum of money by the Carghers to help them build their house in Castlecrag. A decade later, Ted sold the house and used the funds to buy the mansion at Clifton Gardens. It appears Ted did not repay Jean and Feiga; indeed it is not clear whether they expected him to. But Madeleine believed this money belonged now to her and Colette, that it was part of the Cargher, not the St John, estate.[52] Madeleine wrote to Judith:

> I can't tell you how very grown up it makes me feel to have pronounced these words to the ghastly old ratbag at last but frankly darling I am not greatly looking forward to his apoplectic reply…At least I won't have to be grateful for any more 50–60 pound annual offerings from this retired QC MP fraud.[53]

Ted was indeed livid and wrote in scathing terms to his daughter. He felt he did not have a legal or a moral duty to send any money to Madeleine. In any case, he did not have the money.[54]

Madeleine described 1990 as 'wonderful, ghastly, I wouldn't have missed it for anything'.[55] She had turned the corner with her writing and by May 1991, she had completed her first novel. She had found writing fiction much easier than writing biography, indeed *The Women in Black* had been 'disgracefully easy'.[56] She had written it in about six months.

And now she finally gave up 'the struggle on behalf of Madame Blavatsky'.[57] The biography had beaten her. She hung on to the manuscript for a while, and then she tore it up. There was 'something rather grand about throwing away so many years of work'. Women never knew when to leave, she felt. They always clung on. It was a great day, Madeleine would say later, the day she took hold of the Blavatsky book and 'chucked it out'.[58]

CHAPTER SIXTEEN

The Women in Black

Madeleine had been writing plots in her head for years and she had a certain confidence in her ability. 'I could do better than that,' she announced to Florence Heller, while listening to a book reading on Radio 4.[1] She had an ear for dialogue. Years of sitting on London buses and walking the streets had honed her facility with the vernacular. She understood tone and distinctions of class. These skills hadn't helped her much with Madame Blavatsky, but they were superb for fiction. Madeleine wrote quickly, on her typewriter or longhand on the back of council notices and flyers thrust through the letterbox. She enjoyed making do with whatever was at hand.

Madeleine had lived outside of Australia for almost thirty years, but now she turned to the Sydney of her childhood and teenage years. *The Women in Black*, set largely in a department store called Goode's in the 1960s, sparkles with hope and humanity. Madeleine was still experiencing inner turmoil but she believed that there were enough sad novels in the world.[2] That she wrote a light-hearted novel set in Sydney is, however, extraordinary given what the city represented to her. Sydney was the 'gothic' city associated with the tragic death of Sylvette and the stepmother who had replaced her so quickly at Castlecrag. It was the city of the father who had rejected her and the location of her loss and abandonment. But she put her anger aside to write about the past with affection and forgiveness. Indeed, while *The Women in Black* is not autobiographical, writing it was likely therapeutic, allowing Madeleine to enjoy a more idealised version of her home city.

Madeleine drew on the people she knew for many of her characters. The most spectacular example of art imitating life is Magda, the saleswoman in charge of Model Gowns at Goode's. Magda is a Slovenian immigrant married to a Hungarian, Stefan. Husband and wife are exotic, glamorous and sophisticated. Magda's confident European sensibility sets her apart from the other 'women in black' who are good, solid types, but who cannot match Magda's style and exuberance. It is easy to see Madeleine crafting Magda as a blend of her French mother and Friedel Souhami, the German immigrant whom Madeleine knew in Castlecrag. In the 1930s, before her marriage to Ted, Sylvette sold cosmetics and, like all the Cargher women, she adored clothes and saw them as objects of beauty. Clothes mattered to Madeleine: she was always a 'considered' dresser, one friend recalled.[3]

The teenager in *The Women in Black*—the school-leaver Lesley, who adopts the more sophisticated name of Lisa when she goes to work at Goode's for the summer—shares Madeleine's sensibilities, though Lisa's family is lower middle-class, a few rungs down from the St Johns. Unlike Lisa, Madeleine did not face family resistance to her going to university, but she claimed that had she not won a Commonwealth scholarship Ted would not have allowed her to go. Some of Madeleine's university friends saw Colleen Olliffe and her family as the model for Lisa's family.[4] The Olliffes lived in the unfashionable southern suburb of Kingsford, and Colleen's father, Joe, was a proofreader. Colleen worked in the 'Christmas rush' at Sydney department stores.

The novel resonates with Madeleine's emotional experience. Lisa is offered a choice between the dominant but mundane world of Anglo-Australia and the vivid future promised by the migrants arriving in Sydney after the war. Madeleine's life as a child and teenager oscillated between these worlds, but *The Women in Black* rises beyond the divisions. There is acceptance as the newcomers show the Australians different ways to live and as the migrants are reshaped by their new country. It is a big idea, this clash of cultures, but lightly articulated by Madeleine. The novel is warm but not sentimental. Madeleine is amused by rather than judgmental of the society she describes. When Frank rushes away after a night of abandoned sex with his wife, Madeleine offers a telling commentary on the Australian male, but there is humour and compassion. In her fiction, Madeleine revealed a humanity she could not always summon in life.

She dedicated the novel to M & Mme J. M. Cargher. Her grandparents, with their different foods and accents, their menial jobs and marginal place in Australian life, were put centre stage. The dispossessed Europeans became the teachers who were ready to guide the Anglo-Australians to a more refined world. As Magda says, 'Ah, the people here know nothing.'[5]

Elements of Madeleine's early life appear in the novel. Lisa's fascination with a special party dress in Model Gowns recalls Madeleine's love of her mother's Dior copy, which she was wearing the last day Madeleine saw her. Sylvette's life resonated in the story of Rudi as he looks for an Australian wife. Madeleine was never sure why Sylvette married Ted.[6] The novel offers an explanation: Rudi and Fay—just like Sylvette and Ted—will both gain from their partnership. Fay looks forward to a bigger life when she weds the European, while Rudi will find a place in his new world, through his Australian spouse.

Madeleine showed the manuscript to James Hughes, who saw immediately that it was a very different proposition from the Blavatsky biography. He sent it to Esther Whitby, an old friend, with whom he had worked at Andre Deutsch.[7] The company published many great writers—John Updike, Norman Mailer, Philip Roth, V. S. Naipaul, Brian Moore, Jean Rhys and Gitta Sereny among others—and was one of London's most

THE WOMEN IN BLACK 169

respected houses. Esther Whitby was a talented editor and she thought Madeleine's novel was 'in every way a perfect little book'.[8] Her colleagues agreed that it was an exciting find, just the sort of writing the small publisher relished. And Madeleine was given a contract and paid an advance of £1000, a small but welcome sum.

In March 1992, she talked to James Hughes about a commission from his firm, Mitchell Beazley, to write a book on fairies. She was excited: it would pay 'seriouser money than novels do & it's the dole queue again for me if it doesn't come off!'[9] Hughes, her 'dear friend and mentor', wanted her to do the book, but the project came to nothing.

Thank God for her 'jobette' as a salesperson at an antique shop. Madeleine knew nothing about antiques, but she was good at sales, conversing brightly with clients. Every Saturday, she packed her minuscule lunch and headed to Stockspring in Kensington. She introduced herself to customers as a writer and often interrogated them about their lives. She was writing about the London professionals who lived and worked around her and her job was a time for empirical research. She even asked clients what cheeses they had in their fridges. Also working from the Stockspring space was Robert McPherson, a dealer who sold through the shop. He and Madeleine became friends, sometimes visiting each other's homes for drinks. An Englishman less than half her age, McPherson was a good match for this brittle Australian who was intent on presenting herself as more English than the English.

Madeleine wanted people to know where the St Johns slotted into society. Everyone was 'judged, ranked and organised in her mind', Robert recalled. She was fascinated by his girlfriend Georgina, who was from a French aristocratic family. But Robert thought Madeleine's politics were, 'like a lot of things in her life, somewhat confused. She had left leanings but she always wanted to support the upper class, and the two did not go together at all.'[10]

She still smoked heavily, retreating to the back office at Stockspring to roll her cigarettes. She often sat in the dark, and Robert assumed she felt more secure without the lights. There was 'a sadness about her', an aggression and vulnerability that suggested depression, he recalled. 'I always felt she was sort of on the outside, watching, like a commentator and not always getting involved.'[11] The antique shops on Kensington Church Street formed a lively community and Madeleine made friends with Jane Holdsworth, who also worked at Stockspring. Sometimes a small group would gather for supper at Costa's Grill, a nearby Greek restaurant. Madeleine revealed the story of Sylvette and Ted, and Val, but it was not a major discussion. She told Jane about Sylvette's death. 'She did not go on and on but dropped bits, and you were meant to take them up. They were like asides really.' Asides that had been honed over decades. Her friends were never in any doubt her childhood had scarred her. But Jane felt Madeleine had a strong sense of self: 'Hers wasn't the kind of character that shrank in on itself.'[12]

To some, Madeleine seemed quintessentially French. Even her pukka accent could easily have been the English acquired by a French speaker, according to one Stockspring client, Old Bailey judge and porcelain collector, Sir Stephen Mitchell. He was impressed by Madeleine, who seemed nothing like a regular 'shop girl'. For years, Sir Stephen had a Saturday morning routine, driving from his Hampstead home to trawl the Kensington Church Street shops for eighteenth-century Derby porcelain. He was a passionate and expert collector and he usually spent an hour or two at Stockspring, part of it in conversation with Madeleine. He picked her as a daughter of a lawyer from the way she reasoned. He found her an engaging conversationalist: observant and a clear thinker with an excellent vocabulary. She spoke English exceptionally well and had 'a marvellous strong voice'. She was dry and witty and tuned into popular culture and politics. He recalled that while some of her clothes looked as if they had come from Oxfam, Madeleine managed to seem French and elegant. He assumed she was short of cash, but she never complained about her circumstances.[13]

As the publication date for *The Women in Black* approached, publicist

Christobel Kent drummed up interest, pitching the book as 'a literary novel that reads with the ease of a soap opera...a sex-and-shopping novel as Muriel Spark might have written it'. The information sheet to booksellers and sales agents described Madeleine as 'an Australian of the same vintage as Clive James and Germaine Greer—need we say more'. The novel was set in 'the world of Jacques Fath [a post-war designer who was a contemporary of Christian Dior and Pierre Balmain] not Vivienne Westwood [the British designer who made punk fashionable]'. A brief biographical note said Madeleine had supported herself in London with a variety of menial jobs. 'Basically I was a *flaneuse* until I took up writing at—as you can see—the eleventh hour,' Madeleine quipped.[14]

The Woman's Hour on BBC Radio 4 serialised *The Women in Black* for its daily book reading in February and March. The reader for the ten episodes was Nicolette McKenzie, a New Zealand actor who had worked in London for many years. True to form, Madeleine found fault: the voice was 'ghastly...broad but ersatz BBC Australian'. The broadcast was 'very abridged, with a blunt instrument—but what the hell'.[15] She feigned indifference, but London friends felt that Madeleine was delighted with the fanfare, especially when she was interviewed by Michael Rosen for the BBC World Service book program.

On publication day, 25 February 1993, the publishers took their author to lunch, presented her with flowers and made a fuss.[16] She inscribed a copy of the novel to her editor: 'For Esther, undying gratitude and love. Madeleine.' Shena Mackay called *The Women in Black* a 'small masterpiece'. In her review she said: 'Apparently artlessly told, without condescension to its characters, it is actually a highly sophisticated work, full of funny, sharp and subtle observations of Australian life, and laconic, inconsequential and inarticulate dialogue which speaks volumes.' *The Times Literary Supplement* ran a review from Nicola Walker. She was not so kind. *The Women in Black* was a 'twee, not unenjoyable little tale, written in a whimsical style', but with 'stilted, vapid sentences'.

Walker criticised Madeleine for not engaging with her main subject directly: 'St John merely tickles the perpetual Australian dilemma of multiculturalism, [and offers only] fairy-tale resolutions'.[17] Abacus bought the paperback rights for what Madeleine called a 'derisory sum',[18] but her Kensington friends noticed the spring in her step. Robert McPherson recalled: 'She was suddenly given some validity, she felt she could do more than antiques on Saturday. There was an intellectual status, not the fame of being on telly, but the fame of books and writing.'[19]

The novel was not published in Australia, but the English edition was distributed here. Copies were hard to find and the St John clan heard about Madeleine's success via Florence and Felicity. Colette was disappointed that stores were not making a fuss. She was proud of her sister's achievement, even though it contrasted sharply with her own struggles at the time. Her marriage to Steve Lippincott had ended not long after the family had arrived in the US in 1987, and she had struggled to raise Aaron alone. In 1990 Ted paid for fares back home and Colette and Aaron moved to the northern beaches of Sydney.

Patrick St John was living in London with his wife Karen in a flat not far from Colville Gardens. The couple often walked past All Saints, directly below Madeleine's windows, and wondered if they would bump into her. Patrick assumed his half-sister knew that he was living in London, because she was still in touch with their aunt Florence. Madeleine could make the first move, he decided.[20]

In Sydney, Ted St John was privately thrilled that Madeleine was now a published author, but there was no reconciliation.

CHAPTER SEVENTEEN

Dear Ted

Ted's approval mattered to Madeleine, and she was drawn back time and again to the wounds of her childhood. The publication of *The Women in Black* was evidence, surely, to her father that she was worthy of his love. But Ted was almost grudging in his comments. He wrote to Josette in Adelaide and included a review of the book that had been sent by Florence Heller from London:

> This review isn't too flattering—but Florence says the reviewer was probably jealous! Being serialised on the BBC is no small thing. F says she can remember M saying years ago that she thought she could write a book which would be serialised on the BBC—and some years later, hey presto!

He added that 'Val has started to read M's book and likes it', but gave no sign that he intended to read it himself.[1]

A few months later, in October 1993, Ted drew up a new will, in effect cutting Madeleine out of his estate.[2] Madeleine's decision in 1990 to confront Ted over the Cargher money had done her little good. Ted was determined to ensure his oldest daughter had little claim on his assets. If Ted died first, Val would inherit everything, but each child would receive $10,000. If Val predeceased Ted, the will made different arrangements for what would happen upon his death: Madeleine would still receive $10,000, but the rest of the estate would be shared between Ed, Patrick and Colette, with special arrangements for the ongoing care of Oliver. It was a deliberate rejection of Madeleine in dramatic contrast to the way he intended to treat Colette. It is not known if Ted told Madeleine about the new will.

It was a tragic situation and perhaps inevitable. The mutual animosity between father and daughter was no secret within the extended St John family and some members took sides. But Madeleine had constructed enough emotional shields against the past to operate effectively, and her life was expanding, thanks to *The Women in Black*.

Madeleine and Esther Whitby grew closer in 1994 when Esther battled Andre Deutsch over her pension. Madeleine helped her through the difficult period, teaching her patchwork as therapy. The two spent hours sewing in the sunny kitchen of Esther's home in the northern London district of Chalk Farm. They gossiped and swapped life stories. Esther thought Madeleine was 'wonderful company'.[3]

She suggested to Madeleine that she needed a literary agent and put her in touch with Sarah Lutyens, who had also worked at Andre Deutsch before setting up her agency in 1993. Lutyens & Rubinstein, formed with Felicity Rubinstein, was located in Westbourne Park Road, a few minutes' walk from Colville Gardens. It was the proximity that tipped the balance for Madeleine. On 4 October 1994, she wrote to Sarah:

> My first novel, *The Women in Black*, was published by Andre Deutsch in February 1993 and in paper by Abacus in March 1994; I have written two more and am at present working on yet another, but none of these has yet been seen by anyone (including Andre Deutsch, who

have first option on my next as per contract). So I dare say it is time that one or other of them was.[4]

On 15 December, Madeleine wrote again to Sarah, this time in her sprawling hand: 'I am very glad that you have decided to represent me...'[5] She had embarked on one of the most important relationships of this period of her life.

Madeleine was not long back from a trip to France. In September, Robert McPherson, her friend from the antique trade, had married his partner Georgina. Madeleine was among the guests, travelling with friends to the wedding, which was in a chateau near Amiens that was owned by Georgina's family. The chateau had been used as a field hospital during World War I and was steeped in history. The poet Roland Leighton, fiancé of writer Vera Brittain, died in the house from war injuries and he was buried in the military cemetery just outside the village. Madeleine loved the heritage: there was a dining table with axe marks from the time the Russians tried to take Paris in the early nineteenth century and there were original wallpapers in some rooms. The McPherson nuptials took place over a couple of days and Madeleine was in her element, secure among friends. Faded grandeur, whether French or English, was her thing. 'Anything from the upper classes had to be okay—she had a deference to the English upper class in particular,' Robert remembered.[6]

In Sydney, Ted was desperately ill in hospital. Weeks earlier he had been diagnosed with a lung complaint, which neither he nor the family thought life-threatening.[7] Ted was seventy-eight and had always been very fit. He was still absorbed in writing his anti-nuclear book—a decade after he had begun. But he must have been a little concerned about his health because shortly before he entered hospital, he told his sons and Val that he was now giving all his possessions to Val. The plan was that his will would be rendered irrelevant, because he no longer had money or property to bestow.[8] It seemed he was taking out insurance against Madeleine.

Ted deteriorated rapidly and the family realised he was dying. When Florence Heller heard of it, she travelled across London to break the news to Madeleine. Madeleine was composed. She told her aunt that she had 'said goodbye to my father a long time ago'.[9] But the next day she phoned Florence to say she had had a strong reaction to the news. On 21 October 1994, Madeleine wrote a card to her father. She posted it to her cousin Annabel Minchin in Sydney, asking her to pass it on to Ted.

> Dear Ted, Florence came here all my way from Highgate & then up all the stairs to bring me the sad news. Think of it. What a shame that you could send no answer to my last letter of so many months ago—but life is like that, isn't it? The memory of happy times long ago is forever bright in my mind. God be with you & my love, Madeleine.[10]

The letter was conciliatory, but Madeleine could not avoid a sharp under-current, even as her father lay dying. Ted never saw the letter: Annabel had not received it when Ted died on 24 October. Madeleine never asked what happened to it, and Annabel, unsure what to do, put it in a drawer of her desk. Neither Ted nor Val nor her half-brothers nor Colette would know that Madeleine, estranged for so long, had made a last overture to her father.

A memorial service for Ted was held at St Luke's Anglican Church, Mosman, on 3 November. The eulogy was delivered by Justice Michael Kirby, who described Ted as a man with 'a restless, reforming spirit', who 'attracted calumny and praise in equal measure'. His admirers, Kirby said, saw Ted as a modern pilgrim.[11]

The *Sydney Morning Herald* reported that only one politician was there to mourn the man who had stood on principle, and had helped bring down a prime minister.[12] In federal parliament on 7 November, MPs made their formal condolence speeches. Labor's Barry Jones looked back at the Gorton incident in the 1960s when Ted had denounced his leader and noted there was a 'puritanical flavour going through Ted St John which made it very difficult for him to understand what it was that made John Gorton tick'. Jones said that Ted 'was a remarkable man' with 'a very fierce independence of mind in a variety of areas'. Don Dobie, the Liberal member for Cook, with whom Ted shared an office in Parliament House, said:

> We were very close friends for a period of three years…he was a man of real conviction. He was not scared by anybody in a senior position. He was not angered by Harold Holt's interjection during his maiden speech; he was annoyed by it—and so he should have been.

Then Dobie dropped a bombshell for the St John family. He told the House of Representatives that Ted had 'a lot of tragedy in his personal life. He had three disabled children, which is more than most people have to face. He faced that, particularly with his second wife, Val, with great courage and great strength.'[13]

When Madeleine heard about Dobie's comment she challenged him. He wrote back, saying that Ted 'disclosed to me that he had two daughters who suffered from disabilities. That is the sum total of my knowledge.'[14] Dobie's inadvertent insult to Madeleine and Colette reflected Ted's views of his daughters in the 1960s when both women suffered depression. If there had ever been hope of reconciliation between Madeleine and her immediate family, Dobie's statements surely put an end to them.

Madeleine had sounded compassionate in the card she sent to Ted. But on 29 December 1994, when she wrote to Colleen Chesterman in Sydney, she was brutal:

> Thank you so much of your letter in re. the ghastly Ted—it was extremely good of you to take this trouble—but as you will already have seen I hardly deserved it as I am just very sad at a wasted spirit & glad that he has gone where he can never hurt me or mine again: I mean the whole situation was a fuckup, & need not have been. *Waste.* Oh dear.[15]

Madeleine had spent much of her life swamped by negative emotions towards her father. At times, she had been circumspect in public; at times she hoped for Ted's approval; at times she had managed civility, even warmth towards him. But now, at fifty-three, Madeleine was, if not pleased, certainly relieved that Ted St John was dead.

CHAPTER EIGHTEEN

A Moment in the Sunshine

Madeleine was enjoying her new status as a published author. *The Women in Black* had sold few copies, but it represented a huge leap forward for Madeleine after decades scraping together an existence in council housing without a career and without a literary circle. Now, with agent Sarah Lutyens and her editor and friend Esther Whitby, she felt part of a wider world and was optimistic about building a life as a writer.

The Women in Black opened doors that had been closed since the sixties. Clive James had no difficulty remembering Madeleine when he read *The Women in Black* soon after it was published. He thought the book was a comic masterpiece[1] and recommended the novel to his old flatmate Bruce Beresford, now an established film director. Bruce was intrigued. He read it, loved it and bought the film rights—although a film was never made. Madeleine splashed out and bought several cashmere sweaters with the money.[2] Clive James recalled:

At least I can tell myself that I found the book, loved it and recommended it to Bruce, who at one stage had Monica Bellucci attached to the project [of the film].[3]

Bruce Beresford had not been particularly close to Madeleine at university although she recalled that 'unlike a lot of the blokes around that place [he was] a perfect poppet. He never teased you.'[4] Now they discovered they shared an interest in classical music and jazz as well as literature, and, over the next few years, Bruce visited Madeleine whenever he was in London. He enjoyed her company, but found her hostile towards Australia, a stance he felt was directly due to her feelings towards her father.[5]

Madeleine cut ties with Australia when she became a British citizen in 1995. But she was concerned about Colette and Aaron, and in September she embarked on her first trip home in fifteen years. Colette and Aaron met her at Sydney airport. Colette burst into tears, but Madeleine found the display of emotion difficult and backed away from her sister's embrace. Colette fretted that there were 'so many conversations' she could not have with Madeleine about their past.[6] Madeleine did not visit Val or her half-brothers. She saw Pom Jarvis, her daughter Jonette and her granddaughter Siobhan. She had the cachet of being a published author and she counselled Siobhan to wait till she was much older before she attempted to write and then to write something humorous because there were already too many serious books in the world.[7]

In Sydney, Madeleine had dinner with her cousins Antony and Annabel Minchin and Antony's wife, Eliza. It was an enjoyable evening, but Madeleine could not refrain from insulting some of their guests.[8] She had high expectations of others' behaviour, but could often be very rude herself. Colleen and Michael Chesterman, who regularly saw her when they visited London, held a dinner in her honour at their Paddington terrace house. Madeleine was rather grand, performing for her old university friends in the role of author.[9]

The visit to Australia rekindled Madeleine's interest in the St John family history. Back in London, she wrote to Antony to thank him for some family photographs:

> Many, many thanks for the photographs—it's super to have them. I'm
> entirely fascinated by the story-of-the-forebears (which I find utterly
> tragic & awful & romantic & ridiculous and whatever else you've
> got) so any snippet you come across, do tell me or if no appalling
> hassle—send me a copy.[10]

A few years earlier, Ted's brother Roland had written a memoir, *Memories
at Sunset*, which touched on his early life at school and in the vicarage.
Madeleine read the unpublished manuscript and was excited about
recovering the memories of Quirindi. She wrote to Antony:

> I've been thinking that we ought each to write down what we
> remember about it and its inhabitants...those recollections...might
> make quite a nice (amazing, bizarre, unique) record for all those other
> (zillion) descendants who are so much further from it.[11]

But Madeleine's focus was on the micro-world of Notting Hill and inner
London. She had been productive, given that she had turned to fiction only
four or five years earlier. The procrastination of the past had evaporated.
After Andre Deutsch accepted *The Women in Black* for publication she
wrote a second novel but discarded it. 'I knew I would have to write it
in order to get to the stage where I could write one that worked,' she
said later.[12] Then she wrote a novel that she felt was 'much too short',
and then another that was also 'too short'. But she was 'horribly pleased'
with that one. Both of the complete but unpublished novels were 'about
90s London...& extremely politically incorrect'.[13] They were written
as Madeleine experienced the rapture and despair of being in love. An
infatuation with a younger man, a neighbour who attended All Saints,
had ended in tears and Madeleine looked back in anger and amazement
at having allowed herself to be—in her terms, at least—badly treated.
She confided in Judith McCue, who recalled later:

He was a neighbour and they often exchanged pleasantries. She would watch him come and go from her window…Madeleine became hopelessly infatuated with him but, as much as she fantasised about him, she never indicated to me that there was any reason for her to expect more than a platonic friendship. She was, however, heartbroken when he seemed to cut her dead and turned up in church (after being away a while, I think) with young woman in tow. To her, this was a sort of betrayal or disloyalty.[14]

Sarah Lutyens began looking for a publisher for one of the two completed novels. Madeleine had originally called it *Little Lambs Eat Parsley*,[15] a version of 'liddle lamzy divey' (little lambs eat ivy) from the 1943 novelty song, 'Mairzy Doats'.[16] One of the characters in the novel sings the rhyme as a lullaby. Sarah felt the title was unappealing. She renamed it *Learning to Talk*, and she sent it to Andre Deutsch as required under Madeleine's earlier contract, although Madeleine made it clear she would not stay with the publisher; Esther Whitby had left the firm in unhappy circumstances and Madeleine probably felt some loyalty on that score. Tom Rosenthal, publisher at Andre Deutsch, rejected *Learning to Talk*, telling Sarah by letter that, while 'we have all read [the book] with much joy, we all also feel that it isn't a sufficient advance on the first book that we ought to offer blandishments to her to persuade her to stay with us against her declared will'.[17]

Other publishers were hesitant. Hodder and Stoughton rejected the manuscript, Carole Welch writing: 'It's well written and constructed and both marvellously and horribly true to life, but in the end I just felt it was too slight and not one I could get others excited about.'[18] Penguin UK's editorial director, Fanny Blake, wrote:

Nearly, but not quite I'm afraid. I like a lot of this but felt that it needed more tables and chairs. Too much dialogue and not enough narrative. As it stands, I think it is a little too slight for us to publish without it getting lost, so I am afraid I'm going to have to pass.[19]

Jonathan Burnham at Chatto & Windus found it 'well-paced and enter-taining, with some very nice descriptive touches, but...'[20] Doubleday's Joanna Goldsworthy deemed it 'very precise in its portrayal of relationships, and it's wonderfully witty too. But it's such a slender piece, a novella almost, that we feel it would get lost on our list.'[21]

With a clutch of rejections, Sarah changed her strategy and sent both novels into the market as a double act. Suddenly, two publishers were interested in *Learning to Talk* and *A Private View*. Robin Baird-Smith at Constable made an offer for both, but Sarah decided to go with Christopher Potter at Fourth Estate. In a fax to Sarah, Potter said:

> I'd be absolutely thrilled if I were to become Madeleine St John's publisher. I can see Fourth Estate publishing these novels particularly well alongside E. Annie Proulx, Carol Shields and my most recent acquisition, Mary McGarry Morris...Ours is a small list of novels; novels that we love passionately and which everyone in the company reads.[22]

He offered Madeleine an advance of £5000 for each book. She was delighted, and took Felicity Baker to a celebratory lunch at a restaurant near the British Museum. Madeleine was very formal, very well dressed and a little 'grand'. She was showing off. Felicity took flowers, which she knew Madeleine would appreciate. But over lunch, Madeleine revealed she had been diagnosed with emphysema. Her GP had told her that unless she gave up smoking she would be dead in two weeks.[23] Madeleine was prone to exaggerate and the prognosis was probably less extreme, but she was already struggling for breath at times. She continued to smoke, and her respiratory condition gradually worsened.

Being taken on by Fourth Estate was an important development for Madeleine. Potter had a reputation for discovering 'sleepers' that became bestsellers, and Fourth Estate, an independent house founded in 1984 by Victoria Barnsley, was a stylish and innovative company. Potter had success in the early 1990s with books such as *Longitude* by Dava Sobel,

Fermat's Last Theorem by Simon Singh, and *The Diving Bell and the Butterfly* by Jean-Dominique Bauby. Potter told Sarah that he would prefer to publish *A Private View* ahead of *Learning to Talk*, but that he was not particularly worried about the sequence.[24]

But the titles were still not right. Madeleine wrote to Sarah suggesting *Learning to Talk* be called *Real Tears* and *A Private View* become *A Pure Clear Light*.[25] The latter title is from 'Jesus Bids Us Shine', the nineteenth-century children's hymn written by Susan Warner:

> Jesus bids us shine
> With a pure, clear light
> Like a little candle
> Burning in the night.
> In this world of darkness
> So let us shine—
> You in your small corner
> And I in mine...[26]

The title crystallised the religious themes in the book and the notion that holding fast to an individual, even childlike, faith may be our only hope in a transitory and unknowable world.

Potter began work on publishing his new author. He held back *Learning to Talk*, the book rejected by Andre Deutsch and others, and published *A Pure Clear Light* early in 1996.

Set among the thrusting professional class of 1990s London, *A Pure Clear Light* is, at one level, a story of an affair that shakes a happy, if unexciting, marriage. Simon's sexual desire runs parallel to his wife Flora's search for meaning in religion. Both obsessions threaten the marriage, but Madeleine suggests that both sex and religion are central to the human need for permanence in an uncertain world.

Infidelity had been an issue for Madeleine since her fears that Chris had had an affair at Harvard. Three decades later she had a more nuanced view of fidelity—she had experienced broken relationships and intense infatuations—and *A Pure Clear Light* reflects that complexity.

Reviewer Peter Craven called *A Pure Clear Light* a 'book about the search for truth'. He thought the novel superior to *The Women in Black*, noting that Madeleine was 'swifter and neater…when she turned from the remembrance of a long-ago Australia to contemporary London'.[27] *The Times* gave the novel a good review, highlighting its big themes. Madeleine wrote to Antony Minchin: 'The only problem is that I don't like the review although other people seem to think it's a good one. I just think it is peculiar—it makes the book (poor little book!) sound so desperately serious…as if I would! People are just so odd.'[28]

Madeleine had told friends over the years that she never wanted to write serious books and she never drew on her personal grief in her writing. But *A Pure Clear Light* is no mere comedy of manners. The novel is filled with the world Madeleine knew in Notting Hill. Lydia decorates her flat almost as Madeleine decorated Colville Gardens:

> The walls were all painted a sort of greyish-lilac, with cream wood-work, and the floor was covered with some sort of seagrass matting. Cream calico curtains, hanging to the floor; a deck-chair with a white canvas seat; a glass coffee table—its legs seemed to be to be made of glass too; they must be perspex…[29]

The novel draws on Madeleine's religious practice and her need for faith in trying to make sense of her world. Flora's dalliance with religion reflects Madeleine's involvement at All Saints and her belief in a spiritual answer to life's problems. Sarah Lutyens recalled that Madeleine 'believed incredibly powerfully in the moral compass of Christianity', although she was 'so unchurchy and so worldly'. She had a strong belief, without the 'cant'.[30]

Madeleine dedicated *A Pure Clear Light* to Colette, perhaps to honour her, perhaps to send her younger sister a message about how to live. Madeleine may well have intended parallels between her sexually attractive sister and Gillian Selkirk, the mistress in the novel, and between herself and Lydia, the keeper of moral integrity. Madeleine was often highly critical of Colette. She had not approved of her behaviour in London and Ibiza in the 1960s, and later in life she described Colette as an 'Ibiza hustler [with] lots of drugs and lots of rich boyfriends'.[31] Throughout their adult life, Madeleine and Colette had had a rocky relationship, and it is possible to see Madeleine's view of those tensions in her second novel.

When *A Pure Clear Light* was published, Madeleine decided she could afford to leave her 'adorable' Saturday-morning job at Stockspring. She wrote to Antony that she was 'seen off with a magnificent dinner party, v. English with snowy white damask & antique wineglasses, flowing claret & etc—11 of us around the long thin table incl. une française, un espagnol 2 colonial (incl. me) and the rest Brits and all perfectly lovely'.[32] The group included Robert and Georgina McPherson and Jane Holdsworth and her partner, Bob Newman.

Madeleine organised a night at the English National Opera with six of her chums from Kensington Church Street. It was an avant-garde production of Wagner's *Tristan and Isolde* and Madeleine told Antony that it had been 'extraordinary! Espec sitting in the gods as we were—excruciatingly uncomfortable, but one must suffer for Art.'[33] She was enjoying her late-in-life success, truly happy in the glow of *A Pure Clear Light*. But Robert McPherson recalled that Madeleine had been difficult, determined to 'educate' her friends:

> [It] was all in black and white and no one liked it and it was three and a half hours and we were dying to go and she was enthralled… all we could do was think about food…She told us off for not liking Wagner, we were all peasants…I remember a brief interlude and we could stuff our little faces with ice-cream.[34]

Madeleine loved the opera and the farewell dinner and told Antony: 'So that is (v. untypically for me!) Life in London—dinner parties & operas & that sort of thing. In fact, Life as it ought to be, all the time, for all of us, I say.'[35]

When Father Alex Hill arrived at All Saints as a curate in 1997, parishioners told him Madeleine had written a novel about them.[36] Madeleine gave him a copy of *A Pure Clear Light* with the inscription, *Ecclesia Anglorum Mater Sanctorum*—Church of the English, Mother of the Saints.

Alex was far more High Church than Madeleine and the two of them debated theology. He felt that Madeleine was delighted when he married, seeing it as proof he could not have been quite so High Church given that he had chosen a wife rather than celibacy.[37] He saw her as an introvert who paraded as an extrovert. She was hard to put in a box. 'In her company you never noticed anything else but Madeleine, or perhaps her horrendous cat. She held court, and like a lot of small people she overcompensated.'[38] The cat was Puck. He was viciously protective of Madeleine, and visitors kept their distance.

Madeleine had a life she could not have imagined a decade earlier. She was more content than at any time, and had settled into a chatty correspondence with her St John cousins in Australia. In May 1997 she wrote to Annabel Minchin thanking her for a press cutting about the sale of the Souhami's Walter Burley Griffin house in Castlecrag after Friedel's death in October 1996. Madeleine wrote:

> Dear Annabel, Thank you so much for the cutting on the Souhami house—naturally I was fascinated & rather sad at Renate's selling it—you'd have thought they might have kept it in the family; she did have 2 sons, I suppose she still has. *Sic transit mundi*, as usual.

She said she was saddened by the marriage breakdown of another cousin. Annabel too was divorced, and Madeleine chided them gently: 'Please girls, be warned by me: *the single life has its sorrows*. It isn't all white pussycats & sleeping in as late as you like and eating chocolate biscuits instead of cooking proper meals. (As you may have found.)'[39]

For Madeleine, in fact, there was a good deal of sleeping in late. And in the afternoons she stretched out on the lounge with Puck and watched movies on television. She consumed popular culture and even enjoyed

Buffy the Vampire Slayer. Perhaps she identified with Buffy's desire to control her world and her statement, 'The hardest thing in his world is to live in it.'[40] Madeleine loved *Clueless*, the 1995 Hollywood teen comedy broadly based on Jane Austen's *Emma*. 'Laugh? We nearly died,' she wrote to Judith McCue.[41]

Madeleine spent a considerable amount of time alone, rolling her fags, eating like a bird, listening to talk on Radio 4 and music on Radio 5. She watched the tennis.[42] And she listened to news, though she was not greatly interested in politics. She found people intriguing—even if she found it hard to get along with them.

In these later years, her capacity both to charm and to wound her friends became even more apparent. Jane Holdsworth found Madeleine 'unforgettable' but also intense, with a habit of focusing so much emotional attention on you that it was difficult to remain impassive. But Jane grew wise to Madeleine's manipulation:

> She would slightly pick an argument with you and then would go on and on and on and she would turn it around and say that you had picked the fight and she would flounce off. She did that with me a couple of times and there would be no communication for weeks or maybe months and then a little postcard through the post saying, shall we meet up? After a while I got used to it so I knew the method.[43]

Unless her friends were prepared for a permanent breach, they had to allow Madeleine to control the rhythm of the relationship.

CHAPTER NINETEEN

The Essence and the Booker

Madeleine called her third novel, the 'Nicola book'. The title had changed from *Little Lambs Eat Parsley* to *Learning to Talk* to become *The Essence of the Thing* by the time Fourth Estate began work on its publication. Christopher Potter liked his new author a great deal and enjoyed their meetings to discuss the manuscript:

> It was really about the rhythm and I tried to be sensitive to the fact that with such short words, even minute editing is not insignificant because any slight change sends the wrong idea...She was very pernickety about punctuation and that made it quite interesting [but] I could never tell what she would be absolutely adamant about and what she didn't care about.

Potter respected her subtlety and her certainty. Madeleine never expressed doubt: her books were finished products when she handed them over. Potter saw her as a serious person with a strong spiritual centre. 'It seemed as if she was here to find something out.'[1]

Madeleine proved a demanding client for Lutyens & Rubinstein, but she was delighted by Sarah, who was so well read and prepared to give a great deal of attention to her newest client. Soon the professional relationship of agent and author became a friendship. The women met for coffee or lunch at Raoul's in Notting Hill, and Madeleine sent postcards almost daily to Sarah or dropped in at the office. They visited each other's homes and went together to the British Film Institute screenings at Southbank, Madeleine becoming angry if Sarah did not appreciate a film.

'She was incredibly powerful; she made you do things,' Sarah recalled.[2] When Sarah took a trip to Sydney, Madeleine insisted she ride the bus from the city to Watsons Bay, retracing a journey Madeleine knew well. She wanted to know what had happened along the route in the time she had been away. Sarah did the trip, but by car. Back in London, Madeleine was furious that her agent had not followed instructions: Sarah had had the wrong perspective and ruined the entire exercise.

But Madeleine's wit and unique way of looking at the world compensated for her prickliness. She was very fond of Sarah's young son and worried about whether he was receiving the correct musical education. 'Are you teaching him music? Has he got access to the right kind of music teachers? Are you doing singing with him, are you? How often?' Madeleine hunted down the best guitar teacher in London and insisted Sarah employ him.[3]

Sarah and Felicity Rubinstein worried about the precarious finances of their client and sought foreign language publishers for her books. Barry Humphries had written enthusiastically about *The Women in Black* in the *Spectator*. His endorsement would help create interest in the new novels. In May 1997, Felicity sent him a copy of *A Pure Clear Light* and a proof copy of *The Essence of the Thing*. Susannah Godman, a young assistant at Lutyens & Rubinstein, was sent around to Colville Gardens with the books for Madeleine to sign. Felicity wrote to Humphries:

> I do hope you will love them as much as you loved her first novel and it would be wonderful if you could mention her in your *Spectator*

column around publication time. I can't tell you how thrilled Sarah and I are to have found a fellow fan in you.[4]

Madeleine was anxious: 'What if Dame E doesn't like PCL or E of the T? Anything is possible…even life after death,' she wrote to Felicity.[5]

In August 1997, *The Essence of the Thing* was published. Madeleine dedicated it to Judith McCue. The novel covers an episode in the life of Nicola Gatling, a thirty-something-year-old Londoner working in publishing and living contentedly with Jonathan, a banker. Her life is turned upside down when on an ordinary weekday night, she comes back from a brief outing to buy cigarettes to Jonathan's announcement that their life together is over. The novel is a stand-alone piece but readers of *A Pure Clear Light* were reintroduced to some of the key characters, who play bit parts in the new novel. Madeleine was creating a micro-world in a London populated by members of her fictional 'family'. Friends and acquaintances in the two books overlap, joined by the thinnest of threads at times, but nonetheless connected. There's even a gentle joke at her own expense in *Essence*: Jonathan hears a radio book reading of 'some footling tale about some shop assistants in an antipodean department store, fretting about their wombs and their wardrobes and other empty spaces—ye gods!'[6]

The Essence of the Thing is perhaps the most autobiographical of Madeleine's novels.[7] Its cigarette-smoking heroine of limited financial means, but infinite style and goodness, almost by accident finds domestic happiness with a tall, handsome, phlegmatic man, who suddenly one day ends the thing without explanation.

Whether or not she is drawing on her own experience of men, Madeleine paints an unflattering portrait of her main male character. Jonathan is desirable, but also emotionally ill-equipped and ultimately rather weak, even pathetic. Madeleine may have called on her memories of the disappointing American years for the disjointed, prosaic exchanges that mark the collapse of love. She strikes a perfect note with her dialogue rendering the way people stumble through intimacy or the lack of it. Nicola's friends and family find it hard to empathise with her despair but offer what they can—loyalty, tolerance, love and acceptance.

But the most poignant autobiographical element is the pain—the confusion and agony of rejection, the dullness of life without the Loved One. Once again, Madeleine is interested in the transient, unknown elements of life. The need for religious belief is not as overt as it is in *A Pure Clear Light*, but the novel is about the need to trust and hope in life itself. It is a micro-canvas, what Christopher Potter, referencing Jane Austen, called a 'tiny little bit of ivory' pointing to the big moral dilemmas involved in being human. Even if their lives seem ridiculous, her protagonists have a sure, definite line to 'reckon against' as does every 'deeply religious person'.[8]

The Essence of the Thing attracted limited interest on publication, and Fourth Estate did not put it forward for the 1997 Booker Prize.[9] It was the judges who called it in as they assessed what they considered the best novel published in the Commonwealth. It was one of 106 novels read that year by the six-member panel chaired by Cambridge literature don Gillian Beer. The Booker was often controversial, but in 1997 it proved more so than usual. The panel was divided, arguing over whether or not Ian McEwan's *Enduring Love* should be on the shortlist.[10]

When the judges met on 15 September to determine their shortlist, Christopher Potter was on leave at home, keen to know whether Madeleine's book had made the cut. As the afternoon wore on without a phone call from the office, he assumed *Essence* had missed out. It was late in the day when he turned on the radio news to hear the list. He was thrilled. *The Essence of the Thing* was on the shortlist. It was up against Jim Crace's *Quarantine*, Mick Jackson's *The Underground Man*, Bernard MacLaverty's *Grace Notes*, Tim Parks's *Europa*, and Arundhati Roy's *The God of Small Things*. *Enduring Love* was not on the list.

Fifty-five-year-old Madeleine St John had become the first Australian woman to be shortlisted for the Booker. *Little Lambs Eat Parsley* a.k.a. *Learning to Talk* a.k.a. *The Essence of the Thing* had prevailed. The Booker

Prize was £20,000 that year but Potter knew it would be worth much more to Madeleine and Fourth Estate, delivering status as well as sales and transforming Madeleine's career. At her home in Chalk Farm, Esther Whitby took calls from former colleagues at Andre Deutsch, congratulating her for the part she had played in discovering the latest Booker candidate. Fourth Estate organised a reprint of 15,000 copies of *The Essence of the Thing*, and the press in London and Australia started asking questions about this unknown author with the plummy name.

In Sydney it was the middle of the night, too late for the news to make the morning papers, but perfect for radio. At the ABC, producers hurried to find people to reminisce about their old university contemporary. Actor John Bell hadn't seen Madeleine since their days in campus repertory, but he was called upon for comment, nonetheless.[11] In their homes across Sydney, the extended St John family found their phones running hot as friends and relatives called to exclaim upon Madeleine's news. A friend telephoned Colette's home on the northern beaches, but she had already left for work. Eleven-year-old Aaron took the call and scrawled a note for his mother before he dashed off to school: 'Mumma, my Aunt Madeleine has won a book prize.'[12] A day later the Australian papers carried stories about the expatriate who had started to write in middle age and was now shortlisted for one of the most prestigious prizes for literature in the English-speaking world. The *Australian* turned most of its features page over to the story, which included a phone interview with Madeleine by Luke Slattery. Madeleine gave him only five minutes, most of it filled with elliptical self-deprecation that must have left readers wondering what she was on about. 'It's mad. They'll all read it just because it's being talked about. Quite mad,' she announced as she sought to downplay her excitement. Slattery talked at length to Colleen Chesterman, who said her friend was unlikely to see herself as an Australian success story.[13]

The *Sydney Morning Herald* began its coverage on page one, with a large photograph of Madeleine. Christopher Henning, the paper's London correspondent, wrote that the author was 'gob smacked…stunned… appalled' by the Booker fuss. He quoted Madeleine: 'These lists, let's face it…there are squillions of books out there. Who knows what the best six are? With the best will in the world, with the best-chosen judges in the world, it all comes down to a personal taste thingy. It is to such a degree a matter of luck. It's not about me being brilliant. It's about me being lucky.' Even so, she told the *Herald,* she wished Miss Medway, her principal at Queenwood, 'could see this'. And what of the publicity whirl she had been thrust into? 'No, I hate it. I have not had my first cup of coffee, so I am probably going a bit barmy. I could get to enjoy it, but I don't want to. I know it isn't going to last.'[14] The *Herald* tracked down Chris Tillam but he said little about the woman who had divorced him thirty years earlier. The paper found Colette at Palm Beach and she was more expansive, claiming that a major contribution to Madeleine's writing was her dysfunctional relationship with Ted. Their father, she said, had inflicted an 'enormous amount of pain and suffering'. The paper convinced Ed St John to write a personal piece about his half-sister. Ed had worked as a music journalist and TV producer and was now the CEO of Warner Music Australia. He wrote a fair and honest account of Madeleine, pointing out that he did not really know her:

> I knew her once, but not now. It's hard to explain how familial rela-
> tionships can deteriorate to a point where people cannot or will not
> speak to each other, but that is what has occurred. Three years ago,
> the blood link that joined us was severed by the death of our father.
> Madeleine and Dad always had a very stormy relationship, one that
> came to a grinding impasse some time before he died, but it's ultimately
> for him that I am writing this.

Ed noted that his father loved writers and writing and would have been 'immensely proud' of Madeleine's Booker shortlisting. He told of her visit to Australia when he was a teenager:

To an impressionable teenager, the Madeleine of the late '70s was a hugely fascinating figure: exotic, mysterious, worldly. She didn't actually appear to do anything, but she did nothing with an immense amount of style and great humour. It was always said, at family dinners, that Madeleine wrote a brilliant letter (and she did). It was accepted as an article of faith that it was a Great Shame she had never put her talents to good use.

Now she had emerged as an author. 'As she would put it herself, it's a bizarre twist to a peculiar life,' the piece concluded.[15]

Ed's article was generous without avoiding the complexities of Madeleine's relationship with her family. Annabel Minchin rang Madeleine. The conversation began well but deteriorated when Annabel mentioned the piece. Madeleine fumed. 'She said something like, "Your complete insensitivity is breathtaking but only what I would expect from an Australian." It was incomprehensible to her that I would call her and tell her [about Ed's piece]', Annabel recalled.[16]

In London, Madeleine gave a series of interviews. Journalists trooped up to her flat for cups of tea and brief histories of the expat as novelist—not that she was easy to squeeze into the stereotype of the Australian abroad.

In the *Age,* Andrew Clark picked up on the theme of Madeleine's dysfunctional family in childhood and described Ted St John as 'a remote martinet' at home.[17]

In the *Herald*, Christopher Henning wrote a second, longer piece noting Madeleine's strenuous efforts to be fair to Ted. 'Problematical says it all. I can add nothing to that. It is a complete description,' she said. When Henning asked if the relationship had given her anything, Madeleine laughed and said:

> I've always been so conscious of what it took away. I've never actually thought of what it might have given me. No, before he got problem-atical—in my view—my father gave me lots of stuff. He really did adore books and turned me on to great books when I was very tiny.

After he got problematical...really I don't think one can know. My
assumption is that you learn more from being happy than being
unhappy, but I would say that, wouldn't I?[18]

Madeleine was good copy. Later in her life she said that she hated 'the
whole thing with reviewers and marketing and what's happened to the
novel and the way it's promoted and discussed'.[19] But she performed well
for journalists.

The local London media was as interested as the Australians.
Madeleine told the *Independent on Sunday* that the shortlisting had come
just in time: she had been thinking of becoming a tea lady or a check-out
chick to make ends meet. She had a crack at Australia as 'such a monotone
place'. Journalist Emma Cook noted the white sixties furniture and
white net curtains at Colville Gardens were yellowing from Madeleine's
smoking.[20] The *Guardian Weekly* reported that the flat was 'cheerfully
chaotic'; Madeleine's face was 'well-etched' and the author herself 'gob
smacked' by the attention. Madeleine talked briefly about her past and
her marriage, saying Chris had 'got distracted by *une autre femme*, so that
was that'. She had 'never managed to meet another Prince Charming to
rescue me from the awful responsibility of running my own life'.[21] In the
Evening Standard on 14 October—the day of the Booker announcement
dinner—Madeleine suggested the shortlisting had saved her from the job
centre. Neil Norman wrote that in her flat, 'frayed rush matting makes a
half-hearted attempt to conceal the flaking grey-painted floorboards...a
trio of plastic ducks lie stranded in the bath and the loo seat is broken...'
He noted that Madeleine 'lights a cigarette before putting the pack down
next to her asthma inhaler'.[22] After the profiles, the *Herald*'s literary pages
sat up and took notice. On 27 September, the chief book reviewer Andrew
Riemer looked at *The Essence of the Thing* and *A Pure Clear Light*:

St John ignores the great issues most British novelists agonise over
nowadays—racism, inequality, the sins of Empire, urban decay.
Instead her characters seem wholly preoccupied by the trivia of their

class; work, husbands, wives, children, holidays in France, clothes, the pecking order and sex...they are for the most past vapid and shallow and banal...At first blush there is something anachronistic about these short, ironic fables...yet within the confines of her little world, St John strikes me as an accomplished writer...her ear for the pretentious is acute. I found her pared down, minimalist style eminently suited to laying bare her characters' follies and delusions.[23]

The London press was less glowing. The *Daily Telegraph* called *The Essence of the Thing* 'the last word in banality...The writing is careless and clichéd. And Madeleine St John's cast have all the reality and depth of stick figures on a road sign.'[24] The *Sunday Times* said the novel was 'tripe...grotesquely inane'.[25] Not that the critics were enamoured of other Booker candidates either, with most suggesting that *The God of Small Things* was the only one worthy of the prize. The *Economist* noted that half the novels on the shortlist were 'questionable choices: novels which are generally well written but are somehow smaller and less satisfying than novels which did not make the shortlist'. It included *The Essence of the Thing* in that half. It was about 'smart London life and could have appeared any time in the past thirty years...Though cunningly plotted, the whole thing is inoffensive and forgettable.'[26]

The Booker judging panel may have been divided, but the chair, Professor Beer, felt that some of the critics were against *The Essence of the Thing* because it was:

> concentrated in bourgeois life. There was a sense that this was a kind of trivial world and therefore emotionally trivial...Those of us who liked the book thought it had extraordinary concision and depth. I thought it had paced itself so beautifully; she really has this extraordinary ear for dialogue. One of the other judges commented that he had not heard the language of thirtyish people in London picked up with such accuracy before.[27]

Few in Madeleine's camp seriously believed she could win, but they set off with excitement to the Guildhall dinner on 14 October. Madeleine, stylishly dressed and with her bobbed hair freshly coiffured, shared a table with Victoria Barnsley and Christopher Potter from Fourth Estate and her agents Sarah Lutyens and Felicity Rubinstein.[28] Also on the table was Alan Rusbridger, editor of the *Guardian*. The selection committee had met just an hour before the dinner to decide the winner, thus avoiding leaks.

Christopher fretted that Madeleine was not really being given her due by the literary glitterati that night. She had never been part of that crowd and now he thought she was being ignored even though she was in the top six. Somehow, the evening was to be endured. Part of the ceremony was the presentation to each candidate of a copy of his or her novel in a hand-tooled leather cover. Madeleine thrust her copy at Christopher. He could have it; she was not particularly impressed.[29]

At home, viewers of Channel 4 watched a special program anchored by arts presenter and writer Melvyn Bragg. Carmen Callil, A. S. Byatt and Will Self reviewed the shortlisted novels. They were divided on *The Essence of the Thing*. Callil thought it very well done but damned it with faint praise: 'If you like Joanna Trollope, you will love this novel.' Byatt said it was 'the one I got the most out of; the one that really excited me'. She said it had to be read not as if written by Joanna Trollope but as if by Kafka. 'It is a book about people living in a kind of smoke of thinness; they have nothing to say. It doesn't mean they don't suffer, but they have no concepts,' she said. Will Self did not agree. He was a thirty-something-year-old London professional, but the novel, ostensibly set in his world, did not resonate with him. Self said that he knew no one who resembled Madeleine's characters. But when Gillian Beer summarised each novel for the audience, she described *The Essence of the Thing* as:

> a serious comedy about grief. [St John] makes the reader know what splitting up can mean; we hear the people crack and split through her frugal, perfectly poised dialogue. She [has] children speak, rare in fiction. Taking a very narrow social group she uncovers profound differences of relationship within it.[30]

The summaries over, Beer announced *The God of Small Things* the winner. There was a whisper of disapproval around the Guildhall. The *Guardian's* Lisa Jardine wrote later that 'the critics seemed determined to trash Arundhati Roy before the words were out of Professor Beer's mouth'.[31] In the fallout, *The Essence of the Thing* scarcely rated a mention. The evening over, Christopher Potter accompanied Madeleine into the deserted streets to search for a taxi.

It was disappointing for Madeleine, but the Booker experience opened new doors as well as some old ones that had been closed for years. Friends in Australia wrote to Madeleine to congratulate her. Jane Holdsworth rounded up the gang from Kensington Church Street for a supper party for Madeleine. The guests watched the Channel 4 telecast on tape and agreed that Madeleine looked terrific.[32]

Madeleine was still churning through people, pulling them in and spitting them out. Celia Irvine and David Bambridge, her friends from All Saints, dropped away. Jacqueline Bateman, a friend of Celia's, continued to visit Madeleine, stopping by at Colville Gardens with a bottle of wine every few weeks. She enjoyed their chats about everything from grammar to the British aristocracy, but she knew Madeleine was 'capable of being very rude to people; she treated people as if she was the headmistress to five-year-old kids. She could be terribly autocratic.'[33] They agreed on their favourite book—Thomas Pynchon's *The Crying of Lot 49*—but decided his other works, *V* and *Gravity's Rainbow*, were 'as boring as batshit'. Then, one day in the autumn of 1997, home after a summer in Barbados and a side trip to Cuba, Jacqueline went to Colville Gardens with a copy of a fashion magazine from the 1930s that she had bought from a street market in Havana. It should have been the perfect gift for Madeleine. But, as often happened when one of her friends went out of their way to spoil her, Madeleine reacted badly. It was as if she was pre-empting the abandonment that she connected with intimacy. It was the last time Jacqueline saw her.

It was much the same with Colette and Aaron. With the royalties from her books, Madeleine flew them both to London for Christmas. But the visit went badly. 'It was monstrous to be there,' Colette recalled. 'Part of the problem was she was so terribly sick and she was pretending not to be.'[34] Aaron turned twelve that December. He was disappointed with the lack of family warmth from Madeleine. But when Colette was out of the flat, she would sit him down at the dining table and instruct him in etiquette. Aaron recalled: 'I saw it as a loving act, the first time anyone sat down and said—this is how you act.' It reminded him of visiting his grandparents, Ted and Val. He did not begrudge his aunt: 'She was trying to help me, better me.'[35]

In 1998 Madeleine welcomed Libby Smith, one of the Octopus gang from Sydney University days. She and Madeleine had lost touch when Libby joined the Sydney Push, married, had children and worked in New Guinea and Canberra. But they re-established contact after the Booker publicity. The plump young Madeleine of the 1960s was now fashionably thin. Libby thought that she had all but stopped eating. She found Madeleine still 'gentle and kind' on one level but also 'hypocritical and judgmental'. She seemed hostile to Australia, a terrible snob and much more conservative in her views than when she had been young. Madeleine bought tickets to the West End production of *Oklahoma!* starring Hugh Jackman, but was upset when she discovered Jackman, whom she admired, was Australian.

She was enjoying the fame of the Booker and had 'a sense of vanity' about living at a Notting Hill address. She was still keen to educate Libby in all sorts of things, including the correct form of manners to adopt if, by chance, they were invited to a country home for the weekend. It was a disappointing encounter for Libby. At university, she had looked up to Madeleine, but now her old friend seemed trapped in a past that no longer existed.[36]

Madeleine continue to let her friends down. Esther Whitby was working on a memoir of her days at Andre Deutsch and wrote with some feeling of her former client, 'Madeleine St John, whom I would go to see in her fifth-floor eyrie overlooking or, rather, confronting, the spire of the church to which she made frequent visits.' She was:

> clever and delightfully eccentric, she was one of the most amusing people I have known. She was also one of the most malicious. I wish I could remember what she said when over a cup of tea at the Chelsea Flower Show, after a particularly savage remark I told her this, with something like admiration…At this time her star had not yet risen. It was only a year or so later when the first of her god-laced-with-adulterous-upper-class-sex novels was shortlisted for the Booker that among the flurry of excited phone calls from friends who still worked at Deutsch and thought of her as 'my author' her voice was absent.[37]

In Sydney, in the aftermath of the Booker publicity, Chris Tillam went in search of 'relics' from their marriage. He sent Madeleine a bundle of letters she had written to Joan and the book of photographs that she had compiled in her last days in Boston. He apologised for waiting so long to return a couple of family mementoes. 'As for the little book, Joan had it for thirty years, you should have it for the next thirty,' Chris wrote. He told his ex-wife that he had 'tried to read your novels, but they're not my cup of tea'.[38] Madeleine did not reply.

She had always found 'The World' to be a 'very funny place, which we never quite get used to'.[39] As she got older, and her world narrowed to Colville Gardens, she began to focus more than ever on her childhood. She spent hours talking to Sarah Lutyens about the road from the centre of Sydney to the house she lived in in Watsons Bay as a child. Images of the past were seared in her memory, but she was a British citizen now and she was angry at the Australian press for claiming her as an Australian.

CHAPTER TWENTY

A Sense of Betrayal

Four years after Ted's death, Madeleine was still owed $5000 of the $10,000 allocated to her in his will. She wrote to Val asking for the money and for Colette's bequest to be paid. Madeleine had few compunctions about the demands. She had always felt Ted owed her money from her Cargher grandparents and that he had not supported her when she needed help in London. To Madeleine, scraping by in London, her father and Val looked well off.

In fact, Ted valued influence as much as money and had often pursued cases, causes and projects that did not deliver high fees. And he was 'hopeless with money'.[1] He had left Val asset rich but cash poor and she struggled to pay his bequest to Madeleine. Ted and Val had thought the Clifton Gardens house would fund their later years, but they were caught by the property slump at the end of the 1980s and sold Vino del Mar for a relatively low price. They bought a less expensive property at Bayview on the northern beaches, with the aim of living on the money left over. But they were soon running out of cash, and in 1994 Ted tried unsuccessfully to sell their Mt Elliot holiday house. When Ted died, Val

202

converted the downstairs area at Bayview into a self-contained flat to rent and kept the Mt Elliot property on the market. She sent Madeleine $5000 and gave Colette $3200 over the next three or four years, but it was not until mid-1998 that she sold part of the Mt Elliot land, for well below the anticipated price.[2] Patrick bought one of the blocks to help his mother.

When Val received Madeleine's letter asking for the remaining $5000, she wrote back that she was 'saddened that you have so little trust in me as to write as you did. However I do understand your frustration at the delay.'[3] She outlined her financial situation and said that the 'boys have received nothing and in fact Patrick has been helping me'. Val explained that contracts had been exchanged on the Mt Elliot block and that the settlement would take place at the end of July:

> You may be sure that all sums will be sent off as soon as possible after that. Also, after the payment of my debts, I hope to be able to do something to help Colette with Aaron. I haven't had a chance to tell you how pleased we were to hear of your Booker Prize nomination and also how much I have enjoyed your novels. With love, Val.[4]

Madeleine was astounded. She did not believe there was so little money in Ted's estate. She wrote back, demanding an explanation of how Ted had managed to die 'virtually penniless':

> That my late father should have made bequests totalling $50,000 which he hadn't the assets to cover, plus the simple fact itself of his being unable to leave even $50,000 behind, is so entirely out of character and beyond all probability that one is left in a state of total confusion; and that you yourself should at a stroke have been abandoned to the state of penury you describe after having enjoyed, while he lived, a more than adequate income, only compounds the confusion.[5]

Two weeks later, Val wrote to say the money would be deposited forthwith. She tried to explain:

As I have said, I have had to live frugally in the past four years but I was never living in penury. The loss of Ted is still an aching void but nonetheless I live a very good life with a loving family and a large circle of friends who include me in their activities…Yes, we lived comfortably. We were never rich; we always seemed to have a big overdraft. I am proud of the fact that throughout his career T gave so much time and effort to the causes of justice, the underprivileged, international peace and the environment. He often worked without fee and if you remember at the time we brought you to Sydney for a holiday he worked for 6 months on the infamous Chelmsford case for 'legal aid', which scarcely covered his overheads. To be sure, living in that lovely house at Clifton Gardens was perhaps beyond our means, especially in the lean parliamentary years and before he returned to the bar but it gave us great pleasure and as we paid off the mortgage over 25 years we knew that we would sell it to pay for our retirement. We had no pension or superannuation but chose to invest in the real estate of our home instead. As you know, during his retirement, T worked tirelessly on the causes of world peace—his book and the World Court Project. A large amount of money was spent in the process (lobbying at the UN in New York, attending conferences, research books, etc). I was happy for this to happen as I was proud of what he was doing and I shared in all his undertakings. To be sure, we also had holidays, which we perhaps could not afford, but these were wonderful times and amongst our happiest memories. He had a very hard life with enormous pressures and I am so happy that he had these special interludes. Also I rejoice that I spent a lot of money on a slap-up 75th birthday party for him so that his friends and family could praise him to his face and that he could hear the things which we were not to hear again until his death.[6]

Val told Madeleine that if Ted had lived, they would have been forced to take a mortgage on Bayview till the Mt Elliot land sold, so short were they of cash. She had had a tough time with her stepdaughters, and Madeleine's demands brought back those old stresses. In that same 1998 letter she wrote:

Madeleine, I have recently been sorting family papers and came across a loving card from you in November 1989 to us both after we had visited you in London. That was the last time I saw you and I remember what a pleasant occasion it was and how I was conscious still of my affection for you. When Ted and I married in 1955, I did my best to care for you with love and sympathy. I, at 27, didn't try to take the place of your mother but wanted to care for you and make up for the difficult time that you had had…It appears that I did not meet your needs and I am sorry for that but I loved you and did my best for you. Your criticism of me at the time was that I tried too hard. Now I am afraid that your feelings towards me have turned to hostility and I am sorry. Wishing that things were different between us, with love, Val.[7]

On Val's instruction Ted's solicitors sent Madeleine a copy of her father's will. Madeleine knew now just how far he had gone to stop her getting an equal share with her sister and half-brothers.

It ought to have been the end of the matter, but there were more recriminations to come. In November 1998, *HQ* magazine published a long profile of Madeleine written by Jane Cornwell, an Australian freelance journalist in London. It was based on Cornwell's conversations with people in London and Australia, an interview with Madeleine and material provided by Ed and Val. Madeleine had initially refused an interview. Cornwell spoke to Bruce Beresford, who suggested to Madeleine the article was a good idea because it would help with his efforts to raise funds for the film of *The Women in Black*. Madeleine was greatly influenced by Bruce. She thought him 'a really cool guy, so unaffected, so untouched. Like somebody holy really.'[8]

In the end Madeleine granted the interview, believing it to be 'on the quite explicit undertaking that the family (evidently of some initial interest to the author of this piece) would not form any part of the inquiry—let alone constitute its reason for being'. She expected the article to deal 'wholly with *The Women in Black* plans for film of, friendship at Syd. Uni with

B. Beresford et al, etc. . .' and the interview would be confined to 'strictly anodyne, non-family non-private matters'.[9] Jane Cornwell interviewed Madeleine at Colville Gardens and Steve Pyke took photographs.

Cornwell liked her subject, and the article in the November/December issue of the magazine was largely sympathetic. Headed 'The Essence of an Expat', it ran over five pages. There was the usual Madeleine attack on an ignorant Australian audience, and Cornwell neatly captured a writer, defensive yet intelligent, acerbic and amusing. On the final page Madeleine was quoted describing Ted as 'around the bend' and her family as 'dickheads'.[10] Later, Madeleine claimed that she had made the comment about dickheads in the context of Ed St John's 1997 article in the *Sydney Morning Herald*. She had told Jane Cornwell that Ed's decision to 'publish his account of my private life and griefs was the action of a dickhead'.[11] Cornwell's article continued:

> Madeleine St John avoids listing specific grievances against her father but maintains that his whole goal in life was to upset her and her sister Colette as much as possible. 'Basically,' she asserts, 'he was around the bend.' She is equally scathing about other members of her estranged family: she loathes her stepmother Valerie and says it's impossible therefore, to have a relationship with her half-brothers Ed, Patrick and Oliver. 'Me and my sister are in one armed camp, they're in the other.'[12]

Invited to respond, Ed defended his parents and expressed pride in his half-sister. He and Val provided a handmade birthday card Madeleine had sent Ted, to show the relationship had not always been dysfunctional. Madeleine was appalled. She went through the article line by line, annotating the offending sentences, the 'gross misrepresentation' and 'serious falsehoods'.[13]

She engaged Sydney law firm Tress Cocks & Maddox for advice on a possible defamation action against ACP, the publishers of *HQ*. She was outraged at the reproduction of the birthday card and vowed to defend the copyright of her letters. Sarah Lutyens worried that Madeleine was obsessed with the case and was wasting her time and money.

Madeleine felt Cornwell had obtained the interview 'under false pretences'. She believed she had been duped.[14] She was adamant she had 'never spoken about, much less discussed or in any other way published, family matters—history of, relationships with, feelings about, or any other aspect whatsoever—with any journalist, freelance or other, anywhere, at any time'. She was angry at Val and Ed for 'collaborating' with Cornwell and she insisted that:

> none of the statements, feelings, attitudes or etc etc etc imputed to me concerning the family in the article originated with me. They are all, in other words, false, mendacious, fanciful and—in that they imply my having talked about these private matters in the press, if not for other reasons in addition—defamatory.[15]

Madeleine's reaction was extreme, but not surprising. She was pathological in her desire to control her environment and interactions. But she had been naïve about the processes of journalism and publicity. Cornwell had followed usual practice, using some material already published and comments that Madeleine considered throwaway lines. A more pragmatic person might have brushed the article aside. But Madeleine was not easily pacified: in a letter to her lawyers on 14 May 1999, she sought redress. She said that 'as injurious as any single item' in the article was the general implication that she had 'actually sat down one day' with a journalist and discussed intimate, private matters. She was upset at suggestions in the article that she was 'batty' and involved in an 'alleged' family feud.[16]

Jane Cornwell recalled in 2012 that Madeleine had 'been on the warpath' after the publication, and she was alarmed she had hurt the writer, whom she had liked.[17]

The lawyers advised against a defamation action. The chances of success were remote and it was not clear that the article was defamatory, but ACP could be asked to publish an apology or retraction.[18] They also advised against copyright action, but informed Madeleine that they could warn Cornwell and ACP that she held the copyright to her letters. Madeleine was astonished at the legal advice and argued that she needed protection against her own family. 'These people are capable, given the opportunity, of anything,' she told the lawyers.[19]

The *HQ* article reinforced a view of her life and her family that was now central to Madeleine's sense of herself. To see Val and Ed's behaviour as anything less than monstrous would be to admit her own failings. On 21 July, Madeleine's lawyers wrote to Val asking her to hand over all of Madeleine's letters within seven days.[20]

Val's lawyers declined on her behalf, arguing that the letters were part of Ted's personal estate.[21] ACP refused to run an apology or retraction but agreed it would not republish the article without Madeleine's written consent. The magazine denied there were any factual errors or misquotes and argued the reproduction of the birthday card was fair dealing under the Copyright Act.[22] Madeleine threw in the towel. She had spent $1386 and had to concede 'nothing further can reasonably be done'.[23]

The letters that Madeleine had sent Ted and Val over the years— sometimes grateful, sometimes cutting, always emotional—remained an issue of contention in the family. Madeleine wanted them back because she thought they might be used against her; Valerie held on to them because she thought they might be used against Ted. The tug of war over the letters embodied the bitterness Madeleine felt for her stepmother, a bitterness that did not fade with time.

CHAPTER TWENTY-ONE

A Stairway to Paradise

Madeleine was now more financially secure than she had ever been. After the Booker shortlisting, Sarah Lutyens negotiated a much higher advance, £30,000, from Fourth Estate for her next book, *A Stairway to Paradise*. Madeleine splashed out on travel and shoes, but she found it difficult to complete the novel:

> Once I know what I am doing, it's plain sailing, but I must confess I find it's very difficult to get to that point, to the point where one is really sure of where the thing is going...[I am] spending an awfully long time pussyfooting around, because it's getting to a stage now where it's too easy to repeat myself and do something that's pretty much like what I've done before. So I think it's starting to get more difficult.[1]

She was distracted: the isolation that had helped her to write had been broken by renewed attention from friends and family. But her success restored a confidence that had been battered over the years. She revelled in her new literary status and enjoyed reconnecting with friends. The Booker also brought her a New York publisher. Kent Carroll, a principal at the firm of Carroll & Graf which he co-founded in 1982, sought out her work on a trip to London.[2] The firm published Beryl Bainbridge and Jane Gardam, and Carroll was always on the lookout for new women writers of similar style. He found Madeleine 'quite wonderful, smart and interesting'. He enjoyed the way she told her stories: she established characters, gave the reader information and drove the narrative with 'authentic dialogue, pitch perfect'. It was as if you were overhearing the secret life of her characters, he said.[3] Kent and Madeleine began a trans-Atlantic friendship. Whenever he visited London, Kent took Madeleine and Sarah Lutyens to lunch. Madeleine was possessive of her publisher and sometimes ordered Sarah to depart so she could talk to him alone, tutoring him in the cultural offerings of the capital, telling him which concerts and plays to attend.[4]

Somehow, Madeleine finished *A Stairway to Paradise*. Once again, her characters worry their way through life in professional inner-London where a perfect salad can seem more vital than world peace. Madeleine was concerned not to repeat herself, but *Stairway* deals with the issues that dominate all her work: love, sex, rejection, moral choices.

Beautiful, desirable Barbara has no career and no direction. She has no trouble attracting men, but the one she wants, the married Alex, she cannot have, and the one who wants her, the divorced Andrew, she does not love. Barbara, living in a housekeeper's flat in Belsize Park—a suburb where Madeleine once lived—makes moral decisions about both men. She refuses to take advantage of Andrew by leading him on, and she refuses to pursue a clandestine affair with Alex.

Madeleine's religious faith is on display as the novel examines the struggle between desire and duty and the complicated connections between the carnal and spiritual sides of human nature. This is explicit in a scene in which Alex, in bed with Barbara, ponders the lines from the marriage ceremony in the *Book of Common Prayer*—With my body I thee worship. "'To think," he said, "that the best, the truest, the most literal description of sex that we have in the language is from the hand of some Tudor clergyman, Cranmer, I suppose…"'[5] The balancing act between body and soul is deliciously present in the title of the novel, which comes from the title of a George Gershwin song.[6]

Chris Tillam once wrote that the precision of Madeleine's writing 'had its origin in another practice', referring to her study of the piano.[7] But Madeleine had stopped playing the piano long ago. She indicated to Jane Holdsworth that it was too painful: music unleashed so many strong emotions. But music was important to Madeleine. An appreciation of a range of styles from classical to jazz to popular, along with literature and theatre, was part of what it was to be educated. There is every reason to believe that, like Barbara in *A Stairway to Paradise*, Madeleine could hum her way through the Gershwin songbook.

In *A Stairway to Paradise*, children are wise beyond their years and yet vulnerable to the passions and obtuseness of their parents. It contains what can be read as an explicit depiction of Madeleine's childhood memories of the Castlecrag years in the 1950s. Marguerite, aged eleven, and her brother Percy, nine, debate when and if their parents will divorce. The children are as anxious and knowing as the two little girls in Castlecrag in 1954. 'He was now standing still, thinking, he was considering his parents. "They're much *nicer*," he said at last, "when they're not together."'[8]

Christopher Potter was disappointed with the manuscript. He felt *Stairway* was not as crisp as Madeleine's earlier works.[9] And the book's production was marred by arguments over the cover. Madeleine had not been happy with the treatment Fourth Estate gave *A Pure Clear Light* or the paperback of *The Essence of the Thing*. Potter fretted that Fourth Estate had never published Madeleine quite as well as he would have liked. 'We never got the look of the thing right and I was always in a battle with marketing [who wanted] to make the books look more popular.' He wanted the covers to be 'more literary, cooler'.[10] The production of *Stairway* stretched everyone's patience as Madeleine complained endlessly through her agent. Sarah Lutyens faxed Madeleine's criticisms to Potter.[11] The agent and publisher were close but the exchange tested their friendship. Potter reminded Sarah that 'Madeleine's control of the jacket cannot stretch to the colour of the flaps and particularly not for the "reason" that yellow = fever + blue = bad luck. This isn't a book of feng shui.'[12] Madeleine, Sarah realised yet again, had the knack of putting one in a position where it was hard to maintain perspective. 'Her views were so black and white, so morally unbendable, so something that one thought was minor she thought of as major indeed,' Sarah recalled.[13]

Madeleine dedicated this fourth novel to Kathy Kettler, her friend from her San Francisco days. She was enormously grateful to Kathy for her support at a time when she felt herself to be on the edge of a nervous collapse, but the women had lost touch when Madeleine and Chris moved to Harvard. She had no way of telling Kathy about the dedication, but perhaps she thought that with the book due to be published in the US, her friend would discover the honour. But Kathy knew nothing of the novel, or the dedication, until long after Madeleine's death.[14]

A Stairway to Paradise was published in March 1999, and if Potter was a little disappointed with the manuscript and Madeleine anguished over the cover, the Booker shortlisting meant that literary London paid attention. In *The Times*, Helen Dunmore said the novel was a 'moral comedy as well as a social one'. The characters in the book 'grope forwards, propelled by the sense that their lives are not as they might be'. Dunmore praised Madeleine's strength as a 'sharp mimic and astute observer of the self-deceptions that mask life's sadness', but also noted that sometimes her 'moral rock' was too close to the surface 'and her points too thoroughly made'.[15]

In the *Sunday Times,* Stephen Amidon said Madeleine had once again proven herself to be an 'elegant, droll observer of modern erotic folly'. Alex was particularly well drawn as a character, an Englishman prevented from being a great lover by a surfeit of good manners. Amidon thought Barbara less successfully drawn, with her 'aimlessness bordering on vapidity'.[16] David Robson in the *Sunday Telegraph* found the novel far more substantial than *The Essence of the Thing*. 'Not since Mary Wesley has the literary scene been blessed with such an intriguing late developer.' The pleasure of the book, he wrote, was not its plot, but its dialogue: 'She not only has an ear for the cadences of daily speech but a nose for those terse, pregnant exchanges in which the whole course of a life can alter in a matter of seconds.'[17]

Felicity Baker sent copies of the reviews to Antony and Eliza Minchin with a note: 'I think M has reached a point where journalists will take seriously everything that comes from her—good!'[18]

But Madeleine was not easily satisfied. A few months later she argued with Potter about the cover for the paperback edition of the novel: 'Sorry to come back with so many objections: am not a happy bunny.'[19]

She was happier with American editions of her books. Her New York publishers presented the novels as sophisticated and stylish literary works. Carroll & Graf used a modern painterly look in the three covers designed by Christine van Bree for the 'London' novels—*Essence*, *Stairway*, and *A Pure Clear Light*. Kent Carroll would have published *The Women in Black* as well, but the rights were tied up with Deutsch.

Madeleine was now well known enough to be commissioned by newspapers for the occasional piece. On 27 April 1999, the *Guardian* ran a short article by her about Notting Hill. The film of the same name, starring Julia Roberts and Hugh Grant, was opening that night, and Madeleine reflected on the changes in her neighbourhood. But she was horrified with the editing of the article by the *Guardian* and she was anxious the same thing would not happen to another piece for the *Daily Telegraph*, part of a weekend feature called 'My Favourite Flower'. Madeleine chose gardenias, the flowers of her Aunt Josette's wedding bouquet. Sarah Lutyens wrote to the *Daily Telegraph*: 'Madeleine has just had an appalling experience with the *Guardian* when a piece of hers on Notting Hill was massacred and she has said that she doesn't want the piece used unless it is run as she has written it...'[20]

Gardenias were important to Madeleine. The flowers appear in

A Pure Clear Light when adulterer Simon sends them guiltily to his wife. They are very French, a favourite choice for buttonholes for French men in times past. Madeleine's untitled piece is filled with childhood memories, especially of her mother Sylvette—surely the person referred to as Solange—'trapped in the smallest possible cage' of her marriage.

> The gardenias arrived late in the afternoon in a fragile florist's box tied with white gauze ribbon; the very ribbon, even, had most supremely carefully to be untied. The slightest touch—my dear—the very slightest breath!—might damage them, when they would begin immediately to go yellow, and then—oh, horror!—brown: they would be as good as dead before you even left the house. They had to be put in a cool—the very coolest—place, altogether alone (preferably under guard, in fact) until the absolutely last moment, when they might at last be pinned on. And when, in the penultimate moment the box was opened, and their perfume was released—when one was at last permitted to drink in the divine odour—then, and only then, did one truly understand that this was to be, in its length and breadth, a gala occasion: and that was why there had been so much rushing about, and fearful fussing, and argument; such last-minute stitches in time, and cries of near despair, and anxious dartings here and there: and the infinitely frail and fragrant gardenia was the only proper pinnacle of it all. This truth was revealed to me, as a child, staying for a weekend with my maternal grandparents, with my twenty-year-old aunt preparing—or being prepared—to go to a dance: far away in a lost place where young girls went out with gardenias in their hair joyfully to meet their doom while the band played *Take the A Train*. Solange was someone I got to know only after her gardenia days were done: after they'd worked their awful magic, after she'd been trapped in the smallest possible cage. But she had gardenias in her mind: she managed one hopeful morning to acquire two infant gardenia plants. She looked at them solemnly and joyously, holding her children's hands while she explained the importance of never—never!—touching the flowers. They all looked solemnly, joyously at the twin infant gardenias: it was one of those lessons for life.

I saw some gardenia plants very like them being flogged off at a fiver a time in Portobello Road last summer. Why not? I thought—me with my flat, my flowerpots. But I remembered the look in the eyes of Solange, on the day when it had finally to be faced that one of her gardenia plants was definitely, irremediably dead. Never again that fathomless sorrow, I thought: never that awful night. I'll wait until I have the greenhouse, I thought, walking away up Portobello— the greenhouse expressly for gardenias—in the Chinese style, say. A *pavilion chinois* where one might drink gardenia-scented tea in the late afternoon. And a gardener expressly for the gardenias. He could wear a Chinese hat. One can just about hear the tiny bells ringing in the late afternoon breeze on the hipped roof of the Gardenia Pavilion. There is a very polite notice—possibly in Chinese—which says: Please Do Not Touch the Gardenias. Thank you.

The piece was not published. Perhaps it was deemed too elliptical for the paper, or perhaps they knew that it would be impossible to convince Madeleine that it needed editing. Madeleine was incandescent when it was dropped. She had laboured over it and now the press was trampling on her childhood.[21] Sarah carried the load. She realised Madeleine was so vulnerable that writing would only become more difficult for her.

Lutyens & Rubinstein now did everything possible to capitalise on Madeleine's Booker fame.[22] Sarah had already secured about 100,000 DM for German publications and about £7000 for publication in Israel and Denmark. And Madeleine earned US$24,000 from the US editions of her books between 1999 and 2001.

Susannah Godman tried to interest filmmakers in *Stairway*. 'We found Madeleine's writing rich and witty,' Angus Towler, script editor at London Weekend Television's drama unit, wrote to Susannah in April 1999. 'However, I'm afraid we weren't convinced that the plot was sufficiently well-layered to span three or four episodes of a television serial.'[23] Irena Meldris, script executive at Picture Palace Films Limited in London, said:

> I very much enjoyed Madeleine's perceptive, mesmerising writing that takes one on a journey of inner rather than outer landscape. And I found Barbara's character easy to identify with, her unfulfilled meanderings being one of the most distinctive features of the end of the 90s generation.[24]

But, she said, it would not work as a film.

In 2000 Madeleine put a stop to Sarah's efforts to sell her books to foreign language publishers and banned translation of her books, so agitated was she by some of the results. She sent a letter to Sarah:

> This is to confirm—or to reassure you that you were not dreaming when you heard me say—that I do not want any more translation rights in any of my novels to be sold. The fiasco of the French [translation incident] having demonstrated the futility (to say no worse) of the exercise. And I am more than sorry that I did not manage to make this entirely clear earlier and that you have been to the trouble of talking *l'oeuvre* up at Frankfurt & for all I know elsewhere...Again—sorry about all this but what can you do? As they say. If we don't speak again before then—A very, very happy Xmas. Madeleine.[25]

Sarah had been Madeleine's agent for seven years and the author had always been high maintenance. But her contrariness escalated as her health deteriorated. Increasingly, Sarah found it difficult to get anything right for her demanding client. As she said, 'The tragedy was that Madeleine could never wholly embrace the good things that came her way.'[26]

A Tourist in Athens

In the autumn of 1999, with four books published, Madeleine fulfilled a dream of travelling to Greece. Her emphysema was getting worse, but she had never before had the money to be a tourist and now she was determined to see more of the world.

On 2 October she left Susannah Godman to look after Puck and took an Olympic Airways flight from Heathrow to Athens for a two-week guided tour with the upmarket travel company Voyages Jules Verne. Madeleine cut a somewhat lonely figure as the 'Greece of the Classics' tour began, at times withdrawing from the group to smoke and often trailing behind as she struggled for breath.[1] But not for long.

The tour group included Robert Tooley, a Middlesex accountant, and his schoolteacher wife Kathy, Mike Ahern, a London civil servant, and his wife Teresa, a high-flying tax partner at PricewaterhouseCoopers. They were all younger than Madeleine, but they quickly became friendly, sharing dinners and conversations as they wound their way from Mycenae to Delphi. Madeleine enjoyed the tour enormously. At Epidaurus she stood with Teresa and sang 'Oh Breathe on Me, Oh Breath of God', and their voices echoed around the amphitheatre.[2] They drank too much over dinner and broke into song again. At the Acropolis, Madeleine grabbed Teresa's arm: 'You'll never guess, you'll never guess what I just heard!' A teenage girl walking with her father had climbed the steps to see the Parthenon loom into sight and exclaimed: 'Gee Dad, check it out!' Madeleine loved the juxtaposition.

In Greece Madeleine was interesting to be around and interested in everything around her. Teresa had a theology degree and Madeleine enjoyed debating the classic proofs of the existence of God with her. By the time they got back to London, the friends had exchanged numbers and soon began a semi-regular pattern of dinners and nights at the theatre.

Madeleine was fascinated by Teresa's experience of working in the city; she wanted to know about a typical day in an office. 'It was almost Proustian,' Teresa recalled:

> She was wanting to know what was a meeting like, did we stand, did we sit and who poured the tea? Sometimes she would ring me up—she might have heard an expression and she wanted to run it past me. If I came out with something like 'step up to the plate' she would check whether that was what we really said at PwC. She got the idiom, the vernacular, the culture and psyche.[3]

Teresa heard not a trace of an Australian accent and thought Madeleine was 'cut-glass English'. She noted how Madeleine immediately slotted everyone into a class. She was an expert on the nuances of language, dress and behaviour. But Teresa found her frightening at times, very passionate about a subject and overly intense.

Greece had been fun, and, in the summer of 2000, Madeleine decided to travel again—this time flying to Spain to spend time with her old childhood friend Tomas Kalmar and his second wife Bridget. Madeleine and Tom had not been in touch since the sixties, but Tom, visiting the UK in 1997, had seen one of her novels in a bookshop and contacted her.

The trip was not a success. Tom found Madeleine to be an 'incredible snob'. One day at the Alcazar Palace, she objected when Tom chatted to a couple of American tourists. He thought Madeleine now 'lived in a world where there were very few people that you were able to talk to, and the rest were beneath contempt'. Madeleine lectured Tom on his behaviour and was 'quite dense about some of the social graces'. Her emphysema was becoming severe, and even walking up the street for lunch was too much for her.[4]

Tom's brother Georg, who had also known Madeleine as a child, was in Seville. He recalled his disgust at this 'British snob' who was contemptuous of anyone who was not British. Madeleine chided Georg for speaking to the local kids in the street. 'She was the parody of an upper middle-class British person trying to be upper class,' Georg said. 'She was trying to be as Anglican as she could be; she perhaps had contempt for the Spanish because they were Catholic.'[5]

Back at Colville Gardens, Madeleine struggled to get up and down the stairs to her flat. But she was plucky. Towards the end of 2000, she corresponded with Antony Minchin's wife Eliza, who was professor of classics at the Australian National University and was spending a term at Oxford:

> I actually made a monster effort yesterday because it was Remembrance Sunday and went to church. I went to St Mary Abbots in Ken High Street and arrived by luck just in time for 1st stage of the service, outside by the Kensington War Memorial—'O God our help in ages past' sung *en plein air* acc. by military brass, lots of chaps and some chapesses in fancy dress, clergymen with a suffragan bishop cadet corps from local schools of all 3 services, some blokes in wigs and pin-stripe trousers, a bunch of people in royal blue gowns (who they?), military men in tricorn hats, brownies and masses (about 150) of Members of the Public. All traffic stopped for the entire service. All frightfully impressive and heartfelt & The Right Thing.[6]

CHAPTER TWENTY-THREE

Friendships Lost and Found

A fragile Madeleine turned sixty towards the end of 2001, knowing that her prognosis was not good. A hospital-sized oxygen bottle had been installed near her bed on the fifth floor at Colville Gardens, with a long tube snaking down the stairs and around the rest of the flat. Her emphysema was now severe and she relied increasingly on the kindness of friends and neighbours to run chores and entertain her. One day Mike and Teresa Ahern came to visit, and they all staggered downstairs, the oxygen apparatus in tow, and went for a slow walk around Notting Hill.[1]

Another day, Jane Holdsworth's partner, Bob Newman, carried a frail Madeleine down the stairs so they could visit a furniture shop nearby and buy a piece she had picked out.[2] Sarah Middleton and her husband lived downstairs. They helped with similar manoeuvres and ran errands and bought groceries.[3]

Madeleine's most regular visitor was Susannah Godman. She often did Madeleine's bidding, sourcing and delivering a perfect cashmere sweater or a particular book she wanted.[4] By now, there was little hope that

Madeleine would publish another novel, and Lutyens & Rubinstein began to look after their client's domestic needs rather than her literary career.[5]

Bruce Beresford and Kent Carroll took Madeleine out on occasion; the oxygen tank accompanied them when Madeleine and Bruce went to the Royal Albert Hall to hear pianist Mitsuko Uchida play Schumann's piano concerto. One day, they went to the Ivy restaurant for lunch to meet young American writer and filmmaker Whit Stillman, whom Madeleine admired. On another occasion Bruce took his son Adam, an Oxford literature student, to Madeleine's flat to talk Shakespeare with her.[6] Madeleine was well enough to go to the Serpentine Gallery in Hyde Park to see an exhibition with Kent, but she had to decline a ticket to the Proms.[7]

As her life closed in, Madeleine took to writing tiny poems in a little brown-covered book that she kept by her side. It was all she could manage some days. She was devastated by the death of Puck, the cat with odd-coloured eyes:

> Death, cheated of me
> Took my cat instead
> How can I be forgiven.

Three days later, she wrote:

> There is no corner
> You did not make your own
> Your absence is total.

And again:

> Puck in 17 Syllables:
> My Lillywhite boy
> My beloved boy
> My pride and my joy
> My Cat.

Her handwriting was thin. Everything was an effort.

The Little Brown Book, as she called it, was with her always. She wrote out prayers, and glued copies of hymns among the poems and haiku, hymns such as the fourteenth-century 'Anima Christi':

> Soul of my Saviour sanctify my breast,
> Body of Christ be thou my saving guest,
> Blood of my Saviour, bathe me in thy tide,
> Wash me with waters gushing from thy side.

And 'Salve Regina', the Mediaeval prayer to the Madonna:

> Hail, holy Queen, Mother of Mercy, our life, our sweetness and
>   our hope.
> To thee do we cry, poor banished children of Eve;
> To thee do we send up our sighs, mourning and weeping in this
>   valley of tears.

Madeleine had told Jane Cornwell in 1998 that 'being religious is like being a writer: either you've got it or you haven't'. She downplayed her faith saying she just loved singing 'those old Victorian hymns'.[8] But religion meant much more to Madeleine than that, and she found solace in it now. In the years after the Booker shortlisting, Madeleine was increasingly isolated. Judith McCue said: 'She was terribly let down about the Booker. She didn't realise [initially] that when it died down, nothing changed and everyone just went away.'[9]

She was ill, and she was testy. Her favourite curate, Alex Hill, had left All Saints, but the priests from the parish still brought her communion. She had little contact now with Florence Heller, in part because Florence's husband Frank was not particularly well, but also because Florence had felt torn between Madeleine and Val. Florence recalled later that she and Frank had taken their roles as aunt and uncle seriously over the years, but had felt constantly dragged into Madeleine 'stormy relationships' with Ted and Val. Madeleine had wanted Florence as an ally and advocate, and Ted and Val had wanted the same.[10]

Madeleine's long friendship with her cousin Felicity Baker came to a dramatic end. Felicity was finding Madeleine 'more fixed, more controlling'. One day when Felicity telephoned, Madeleine insisted on hanging up and ringing back. When she did, she launched into a tirade, and Felicity decided enough was enough.[11] Madeleine was estranged, too, from Josette, who was often in the UK with her husband Ron to visit their youngest daughter Nicole in Yorkshire. They had the impression from Colette that Madeleine did not want to see anyone from Australia and they never made contact with her.[12]

Colette and Madeleine closed down contact around 2001 after a difficult phone call. Madeleine wanted Colette to find the 1954 coroner's court report into Sylvette's death and she wanted Colette to photograph various spots in Watsons Bay. She suggested Colette not bother calling again until she had. Colette, struggling financially and caring for her teenage son, could not face the tasks.[13] Communication ceased.

Madeleine had also lost touch with friends from her days in the antique trade. Robert McPherson recalled: 'She became more and more difficult. The more she needed people, the more she drove them away. She was not able to get out, and if you went to her, you were attacked and assaulted and hurt.'[14]

Madeleine was working on a fifth novel. But it was hard work. When Kent Carroll came to visit, she would put the manuscript on the sofa, select a section and read it out to him. It was classic Madeleine—domesticity and romance wrapped in acute, sometimes tart, language—a story about a young man called Henry and an older woman called Honoria.[15] But Madeleine seemed to be writing about a generation she did not know. She had exhausted her own experiences in her four published books and was far less certain about this novel. The moral authority of the earlier works was proving elusive. Kent was encouraging, but he knew she had a long way to go.

Susannah Godman typed Madeleine's handwritten pages, and Kent noted how 'heroic' the young woman was.[16] Madeleine could be cutting and cruel and often chided Susannah for her behaviour or decisions. She so intimidated Susannah that the young woman was too frightened to eat in front of her.[17] Madeleine was, as always, free with her advice. 'You must get married in church,' she announced to Susannah only to change this to 'You must not get married in church', the next time she saw her. Madeleine's firm views extended even to how to run water from a tap, but she was also warm and irresistible at times, sending thank-you notes and small gifts for errands run. And if Susannah didn't visit for a while, Madeleine sent a 'summons' in the form of a postcard or note.[18]

Despite still holding court, Madeleine's life was reduced. She survived partly because she did so little. The radio was her lifeline and she jotted down in her Little Brown Book comments she heard. The condensed haiku was her métier now:

> Here is the white rose
> which I stole this morning
> on the way home from church.
>
> The stolen rose
> hangs her head in sorrow
> Grieving for her lost garden.
>
> The day has slipped
> through my fingers
> Like a stream which
> Rushes to the sea.

On the other side of the world, Val St John was moving house and she came across letters to Ted from Madeleine. She wrote to Madeleine, saying she had not been able to find any letters at the time of her earlier request but was now sending some of them:

> I have read them again and have kept for myself (mainly letters to

me) a few particularly loving, appreciative ones. It was good to be reminded that you did not always consider me 'the stepmother from hell'. The others I enclose. Madeleine dear, I did my very best and I am so sorry that was not enough. Love, Val.[19]

Val had been subjected to years of vitriol and anger from Madeleine, and the *HQ* episode had been particularly bitter. But she continued to try to heal the breach with her stepdaughter. Madeleine was unmoved. She did not trust Val's overtures. She did not reply immediately, but in January 2003 she wrote back. Time had healed nothing, and Madeleine gave Val chapter and verse about the *HQ* article:

> In reply to your letter of last August, I would be grateful if you would note with the greatest seriousness the following:
>
> 1. I have never spoken about, much less discussed or in any other way published, family matters—history of, relationships with, feelings about, or any other aspect whatsoever—with any journalist, freelance or other, anywhere, at any time.
> 2. The only persons whom I know to have done so are Edward in his *SMH* article & subsequently by collaborating with the author of the *HQ* article, and yourself.
> 3. It follows from 1. that I have never described you to a member of the press (or to anyone else for that matter) as 'the stepmother from hell'; is this quote from the *HQ* article? I'm afraid I haven't the stomach to look that out even once more—it has given me enough distress already.
> 4. And that none of the statements, feelings, attitudes or etc etc etc imputed to me concerning the family in that article originated with me. They are all, in other words, false, mendacious, fanciful and— in that they imply my having talked about these private matters in the press, if not for other reasons in addition—defamatory.

On it went, with Madeleine outlining her position and then accusing Val of being still in possession of:

    i. A remarkable proportion of my letters;

   ii. My turquoise & seed pearl locket which my father nicked from me & gave to you shortly after your marriage.

Madeleine gave no quarter:

> Let's just say that you and I live on 2 different planets, that we always have done & that it's just one of those mad accidents of fate (fatal accidents of madness) that we should ever have had any connection...as for your understanding where I'm coming from—or vice versa—not a hope. What you have done may be perfectly okay on your planet: on mine, it is completely out of order. And that goes double for the allusion to my mother and the alleged nature of her death. Inexcusable.[20]

Madeleine was angry beyond all reason, and she was determined to destroy any chance of a reconciliation with Val. The letter detailed old hurts. The claim that Ted had taken from her a piece of jewellery to give to Val refers to a locket that had been given to Madeleine by Ted's sister Pam. The circumstances are unclear, but it is likely it was a St John heirloom of sorts. Whatever the rights and wrongs of the event, Madeleine could not let it go even fifty years later. Val had become the focus of all her bitterness.

Madeleine was now confined to her flat. Susannah saw her regularly but Madeleine also had a succession of paid carers subsidised by public agencies. She found the helpers variously irritating.[21] One ruined a cashmere jumper by putting it through the washing machine and Madeleine found it hard to forgive the mistake. Towards the end of 2003, Peta Worth, a young Australian woman on a working holiday in Europe, was given the job through the agency, Care UK. Peta went to Colville Gardens every Tuesday about lunchtime. She vacuumed, cleaned the bathroom and lavatory and kitchen and went down to Portobello Road to shop and pay bills.[22] Peta found Madeleine eccentric, but a keen listener. She talked about her main job as the nanny to twin boys who lived not far away. 'She lived a lot through what I was doing,' Peta recalled. Madeleine spoke often of Paris, and Peta thought her 'very French'—she had lovely cotton lace nighties and French provincial furniture.

Madeleine was frustrated by her illness and talked a lot about the past. She had no regrets about leaving Australia, but she displayed some affection for the place. She survived on crackers and tomatoes and fruit, and occasionally Peta bought sardines from a Spanish shop on the Portobello Road and French bread. Peta had been in London since 1998, working for a few months at a time and then travelling in Europe. True to form, Madeleine gave her plenty of advice about where she should go and urged her to keep travelling.

One day, at Madeleine's request, Peta took pictures of Madeleine's new cat, Tiger Lily. Unlike her predecessor Puck, Tiger Lily was not very fierce and she slept a great deal of the time. Madeleine was concerned at her advanced age and worried she might die. She was 'very much her own cat', but she did allow you to pat her, now and then, Peta recalled.[23]

Towards the end of 2003, Madeleine had a long stay in hospital and friends worried that she would not recover. Once again, however, she was hypercritical of their efforts to help. Sarah and Felicity sent a hamper to the hospital, but Madeleine reacted angrily at what she felt was a waste. She loathed being pitied and was very alert to any hint of this in her friends' behaviour.[24]

That spell in hospital was truly terrible. 'So ill,' she told Antony Minchin in a letter sometime later. 'They give you steroids which have the most awful side effects even if they do keep you alive.'[25] She was trying to live long enough to finish her book.

Around the end of 2003, Madeleine broke off the long friendship with Sarah and also ended her contract with Lutyens & Rubinstein. Sarah found it 'very, very painful' and, like so many others in the past, she never really knew why Madeleine had dropped her. Sarah suspected it was something minor, like breaking an arrangement to visit or telephone. The rupture was classic Madeleine—a sudden rejection that was unexplained and irrational. Now Susannah Godman was Madeleine's last link with the agency. Sarah and Felicity were relieved that at least they could keep an eye on their former client through Susannah's daily visits.[26]

On 5 March, Madeleine asked Peta and Susannah to witness her will. She owned no property but she had about £25,000 to distribute. Bruce Beresford was to be her literary executor and Robert and Kathy Tooley her executors. They were happy to oblige the friend they had met in Greece a few years before. The will specified that her body be made available for 'therapeutic purposes (including corneal grafting and organ transplantation)' but not for medical education or research. Her estate was split between the Woodland Trust, a UK-based conservation charity, and the National Society for the Prevention of Cruelty to Children. And she left her jewellery to her cousin Nicole Richardson.

Madeleine made some specific orders about her life story: she wanted Judith McCue, her friend in Chicago, to 'receive all biographical material relating to my life and that she be permitted to write a biography of me should she choose to do so'.[27] In a 'memorandum of wishes' she told Bruce Beresford that no 'foreign publishing rights are [to be] granted to any of my works'. And she directed Bruce to 'seek the return of all my letters written to my father and currently held by my stepmother…and that any such letters returned are immediately destroyed'.[28]

She had arranged and paid for her funeral with John Nodes and Sons in Ladbroke Grove, and had asked Alex Hill to conduct her funeral. She drew up a letter detailing the ceremony: no music, no flowers and strict adherence to the *Book of Common Prayer*. She attached a copy of the letter to her will and noted there was another copy in the safe at All Saints. Madeleine was tying up the ends of her life. She squirrelled away a copy of the will in her flat and told Sarah Middleton where it was hidden. She left nothing to Colette or Aaron and nothing to any of the friends, not even Susannah, who had cared for her in recent years.

There was no mention of Chris Tillam: there was nothing from their shared years in the 1960s that Madeleine wanted to leave to her former husband.

CHAPTER TWENTY-FOUR

Her Own Story

In March 2004, Judith McCue went to an electronics shop in Chicago and bought a standard cassette recorder. She was on her way to London and she was on a mission, one she did not relish. Madeleine had asked her to record some interviews with her; she wanted to put her version of her life on the record.

Judith had lived in Chicago, with her husband Edward Kibblewhite, for the past twenty years. The couple had regularly visited Madeleine in London and there had been many letters and phone calls. Judith knew the details of Madeleine's life, having heard them over the decades since the women met in London in the mid-1970s. She was not looking forward to going over the events again.[1] Yet Madeleine prevailed, as she usually did, and on the afternoon of 23 March, Judith climbed the stairs at Colville Gardens, had a cup of tea with Madeleine, chatted about Judith's adult daughter Jessica, and tested the recorder.[2]

Madeleine was finding it hard to breathe. She was hooked up to her oxygen tank day and night, and used a special mask to drive the oxygen deep into her lungs. But she was determined to record the details of her childhood. She had never written about this time, but now it was the only story that mattered. It was a lifetime since Madeleine had lived at Watsons Bay and Ryde and Castlecrag and gone to school at St Catherine's and Queenwood. Yet those years were crystal clear in her mind. She could smell the harbour; she could hear Ms Medway; she could see her mother's Dior copy. Most of all, she could hear her father.

On the couch beside Madeleine were photographs of her grandmother as a young girl in Romania, of her grandfather dressed for the cameras in Paris, of her mother Sylvette lined up with the other little girls for gymnastics. As she showed Judith the pictures and the Cargher passports and other documents, Madeleine sketched the family history. Here was Sylvette on the boat to Australia in the 1930s; with friends in Sydney; in the Blue Mountains with Ted and Ian Sly and his family, the men in uniform, just before they were sent overseas in 1941. Madeleine's voice was deep, perhaps a little forced for the tape, and she battled for breath at times.

Sometimes Judith turned off the machine and Madeleine rested with a cup of tea and a little jazz in the background. Over several days, she took Judith through her early years. The longest they recorded without a break was about an hour. She was remorseless in her condemnation of her father and dismissive of her stepmother, ridiculing her beliefs and ambitions. She insisted that her mother's death was accidental, that it was not suicide. She was understanding of her sister as a child, but attacked the adult Colette mercilessly. But it was Ted St John who dominated her commentary as she recorded his sins of omission and commission. In a few brief sentences she recounted the beating Ted gave her fifty years earlier. Sometimes Judith challenged her statements or asked questions, but Madeleine gave her short shrift. She had a story to tell and she would tell it on her terms. She was not seeking clarification or answers; she had spent decades piecing the narrative together in her head. She knew this story backwards and she wanted others to hear it.

Judith had almost nine hours of tape when it was time for her to return to Chicago, yet only half the story was told. It ended in the late sixties: Madeleine talked about her life in the United States with Chris, but said nothing of her time in London. Yet she was content. She had recorded the story that really mattered, the story of how Ted St John—lawyer, politician, activist—had, to borrow from Philip Larkin, 'fucked her up'.

By the time she got back to Chicago, Judith was emotionally wrung out.[3] Busy with her own work as a publisher, she put the tape recorder, the tapes and the notes in a cardboard box and shoved them in a closet. The final tape was left in the recorder. Judith had no desire to listen to Madeleine's story again. What purpose would it serve to traverse the vitriolic commentary about Ted and Val and the St Catherine's headmistress with the unfortunate facial paralysis? She loved Madeleine, but she had little interest in writing her biography.[4]

The tapes were an insurance policy for Madeleine. Throughout her life, she had protected her privacy. She had torn up the Blavatsky manuscript, shredded letters, destroyed old addresses as well as friendships, and done a good job of warning people off. But she did not want to be forgotten. And she wanted her version of events to stand. In many ways, it was a version of the clash of cultures depicted in *The Women in Black*, but this time there was no happy ending, no resolution, no reconciliation. In this story, Ted remained the villain, Sylvette the wronged woman, and Madeleine and Colette the victims of a destructive marriage and their father's rejection.

Madeleine was intelligent and funny and she demonstrated her talent for wit and observation on the tapes. But she could not move beyond her obsessive need to prove that her mother had not suicided, that she had not deliberately abandoned her children that night at Castlecrag in 1954. For Madeleine, the tapes were proof of what had really happened in her childhood, proof too that the blame lay with 'the ghastly Ted' who had been the architect of the 'fuckup' that had been her life.[5]

As Madeleine approached the end of her life, the desire to secure her place in history became overwhelming. She created albums of family photographs using old brown paper and cardboard. She bundled them up with her personal papers, including the documents covering her divorce, her birth certificate, papers from her grandparents and material she had researched about the St John forebears, and she told Judith McCue that these were also part of the record. This was the biographical material she had listed in her will. Into the box went an annotated copy of the *HQ* article of 1998 and the legal letters that flowed from it, and correspondence about Ted's estate and the money she believed she was owed. There were no diaries, no fragments of earlier writing, no jottings about Madame Blavatsky. There were edited copies of the manuscripts of her published novels, returned to her by her publishers, but no correspondence with her agent or publishers and no letters from her longtime correspondents. There was nothing of her time with Chris, nothing of the Ladbroke Grove ashram, nothing of her trips to France and Greece and Spain. It was as if, looking back down the decades, nothing mattered beyond 'the Ted years'.

Madeleine had reconnected with Josette and was now saddened by her aunt's illness with cancer. She wrote to her in hospital:

> Dearest Josette, I thought I would just write a few words to you as it would probably be pretty tiring for you to talk on the phone even if possible while you are in hospital. Are they looking after you like a Princess! I should definitely hope so & after all suppose so—so that is okay. I suppose also that I needn't tell you how terribly I regret being all tied up here to an oxygen concentrator & totally unable to fly away and see you...hold your hand & tell you a funny story or two. So instead I shall just say that Spring is really definitely here—all the ornamental cherry trees are in blossom, my street is lined with them all the way down one side—enchanting—and each day is longer than the last...[6]

Madeleine had never met Josette's daughter Nicole, who was born in the 1960s in Papua New Guinea, but in the previous couple of years she had talked regularly to her by phone, keen to know about her children. Nicole enjoyed the conversations and realised how important they were to her cousin. One day Madeleine sent £50 to Nicole so she could take the children to high tea at Betty's teashop—an old-fashioned, very English thing to do.[7] She suggested Nicole needed a nanny to help with the children and offered advice from her own 'Australian nanny', presumably her carer Peta, about where to look for one.

With her will made, the tapes out of the way, and the biographical material collected, Madeleine decluttered her flat, giving away furniture, books and other possessions. She invited visitors to take something they wanted. A kitchen table went to Susannah, along with cookbooks. Madeleine put post-it notes on some objects specifying who should have them after her death. She purchased a new contact book and included only a handful of numbers, dumping a lifetime of friends and acquaintances. She kept only the numbers for local takeaway restaurants, for Tiger Lily's vet and a few friends—the chosen few.

Madeleine found 2005 a difficult year. In August, she wrote to Antony Minchin:

> Thank you so much for your letter & pix of so many months ago—sorry for the delay but everything is v v difficult & takes forever. I seem to have missed several chapters in the story—the last news I had of you was a message you left on my answering machine when I was in hospital at the end of—?2003? it must be…Which I was far too preoccupied to chase up at the time…In any case—congratulations on all your good news. Great to have a grandchild—especially a girl. Hope the hens are laying—can you get hold of a kind called Old Cotswold Legbar? They lay the most exquisite pale blue eggs.[8]

Madeleine was hospitalised twice, the doctors surprised each time that she rallied. Bruce Beresford visited her. He found her connected to all sorts of machines but uncomplaining and cheerfully lapping up the life stories of the nurses and other patients.[9]

Then on 26 March 2006, Josette died in Adelaide. At the funeral service, her eulogist noted how the little girl who had arrived in Sydney in the 1930s without a word of English had excelled at friendship and family despite times of great difficulty in her life.[10] Madeleine felt her aunt's death keenly. She began to telephone Josette's husband Ron Storer in Adelaide more frequently. Ron looked forward to the calls. Madeleine was entertaining and stimulating. She asked Ron to talk about his memories of Feiga and Jean Cargher, and she offered to send Ron her childhood impressions of Josette from when they both lived in Sydney. But she told him that she was having trouble completing the task: even writing exhausted her now.[11]

When Judith McCue visited again, Madeleine urged her to take the box of biographical material. Judith demurred. It seemed too final—a sign that her friend would soon die.[12] But Madeleine knew her time was running out. She wanted to die at home, high up in the eyrie, with the church bells marking out her days as they had done for twenty years. Ever the organiser, she put together a palliative care team. She still hoped to finish her novel, but writing was almost impossible.[13]

She had few visitors and only three people—Susannah Godman, Sarah Middleton and Jane Holdsworth—saw her regularly. Susannah took the load. As she put it later, she was the person who cut up the food for her. All three women drew on reserves of patience and generosity to help them manage their increasingly irascible friend. It was 'so very easy to do the wrong thing around Madeleine'. Her taste was perfect and her manners were sublime, but she felt no shame in making others feel ill at ease about their own behaviour.

Madeleine was keen to talk but she did not say much to Susannah about her old life, the life of the ashram and Swami-ji and the friends who had been so important back then. She did not mention her aunt Florence or her cousin Felicity; Susannah was unaware Madeleine had family in London. There was little said about the St Johns back in Sydney, but Susannah was left in no doubt that Madeleine thought Colette, with whom she had no contact now, was 'bonkers'. And Madeleine began telling Susannah that she wanted her, not Judith McCue, to look after her personal papers, contrary to the terms of her will.[14] Susannah resisted. She knew Madeleine was capable of suddenly changing her mind, lashing out against those close to her without reason.

On Thursday 15 June, around lunchtime, Madeleine had a serious respiratory attack and an ambulance was called. She refused to leave her flat until Susannah came to take care of Tiger Lily, but eventually she was admitted to St Mary's Hospital in Westminster.

When Susannah called in to see her that evening, Madeleine had perked up. Susannah saw her again on Friday evening. She was in a room of about six beds and was 'quite jolly'.[15] The friends talked about social class, Madeleine deciding that the man in the bed opposite was definitely 'lower middle'. Madeleine spoke again in negative terms about Judith McCue and reiterated her wish for Susannah to hold on to the biographical material. Susannah was convinced Madeleine would soon be out of hospital and that the question of the will could be deferred. She was on her way out of London for the weekend to join her husband, writer Louis Barfe, at their house in Suffolk, and she felt relaxed about leaving Madeleine, certain that her friend would soon be back home again at Colville Gardens.

Then, on Sunday 18 June, the hospital rang Susannah in Suffolk. Madeleine was dead.

Susannah was devastated. Madeleine had died alone, without family or friends, in hospital, far from her beloved Tiger Lily. It seemed the loneliest of deaths.

CHAPTER TWENTY-FIVE

After Madeleine

Madeleine was gone. The Gauloises and the Golden Virginia roll-your-owns had extracted their revenge. By the end of her life, her circle had shrunk, her family had all but disappeared from her life and her books were largely out of print. Yet Madeleine continued to exert power over those she had known. Her death opened old wounds, created difficulties for her friends and saddened many of those who had seen, up close, her complicated passage through life. Susannah Godman missed Madeleine terribly. For almost a decade, she had been a weekly, sometimes daily, visitor to Colville Gardens. She had loved this intelligent, intense and vulnerable woman. But she faced the dilemma of whether to honour her friend's deathbed wishes or follow the will Madeleine had made in 2004.[1]

Susannah went to St Mary's Hospital and, as Madeleine's designated next of kin, signed the death certificate. It stated that Madeleine had died of respiratory failure and chronic obstructive pulmonary disease. Jane Holdsworth made most of the calls to tell people the sad news, using the little address book that Madeleine had left. The calls were very difficult— Florence Heller and Felicity Baker had seen nothing of Madeleine in the final years. Family in Sydney were informed—they too had long been estranged.

Susannah contacted Alex Hill, whom Madeleine had asked to conduct the funeral service. He had moved to another parish and had various commitments so the funeral was delayed till 4 July.

In Sydney, journalist Tony Stephens wrote an obituary for the *Sydney Morning Herald*. It was published on 29 June and noted that Madeleine had been compared to Anton Chekhov, Muriel Spark and Anita Brookner.[2] On 1 July, at Val's request, Antony Minchin placed a death notice in the *Herald*:

> ST JOHN, Madeleine—
> Born Sydney November 12, 1941, died London June 18, 2006, daughter of Edward and Sylvette St John (both deceased), sister of Colette St John Lippincott and aunt of Aaron, fondly remembered by her aunts Florence Heller and Pamela St John, her friends, cousins and extended family. We were gladdened by her late career as a novelist. *The Women in Black, A Pure Clear Light, The Essence of the Thing* (shortlisted for the Booker Prize 1997) and *A Stairway to Paradise*. We were saddened by her long illness. Now she is at rest.[3]

Antony checked the notice with Val and Colette. Val later asked him to add her name, but by the time he got the message, it was too late. Colette, who had been rung by the *Herald* to confirm the death notice, asked for Josette's name to be included but that too missed the deadline.[4]

About thirty people gathered at All Saints for the funeral. Madeleine had decreed there be no eulogy, but Alex Hill decided she had set him a test. Life was a cat-and-mouse game to Madeleine and Alex believed she would have appreciated his outwitting her by speaking about her life before the service.

He told the congregation that the fact they were at the funeral meant they mattered to Madeleine—even though they may have been through hard times with her. He said she often withdrew from people. He would use the *Book of Common Prayer* as she had stipulated; the book had been indispensable to her, he told the mourners.

Florence Heller was comforted by his words. She had found Madeleine very trying at times and it helped that those difficulties were acknowledged by the priest.[5] Sarah Lutyens felt much the same: it was reassuring to realise there were so many others who had loved Madeleine but whom she had abandoned, without explanation, over the years.[6]

Madeleine's cousin, Nicole Richardson, came down from Yorkshire, but Felicity Baker did not attend the funeral. Bruce Beresford flew in from the States, and Christopher Potter was there, as were the Tooleys along with Teresa Ahern and Daniel Le Maire and his partner. Tina Date came dressed in leathers on a motorbike. Many of the mourners did not know each other because Madeleine had kept her friends so separate.

Judith McCue did not know Madeleine had died. This was not an oversight. Susannah and Jane had decided not to contact her. Their reasons were complicated: they were struggling to fulfil Madeleine's final wishes. Susannah felt burdened by the responsibility, and she 'put an enormous amount of thought' into what Madeleine said to her at the end of her life. It was a terrible decision to make. Judith's number was in Madeleine's address book. When Madeleine had included it, she had wanted Judith to be told of her death. But the message Madeleine had sent towards the end of her life was quite different.[7]

At the funeral, Madeleine's coffin was placed in the main aisle. Someone brought a wreath but was asked to remove it, in accordance with Madeleine's wish that there be no flowers. There was no music either, even though Madeleine loved hymns. It was as if she did not want her mourners to be comforted by music. Florence Heller and Ron Storer had asked for inclusions in the service but the requests were declined.[8]

A priest from the church read Psalm 39:

> I said, I will take heed to my ways, that I sin not with my tongue:

I will keep my mouth with a bridle, while the wicked is before me.

And Psalm 90:

> Lord, thou hast been our dwelling place in all generations.
>
> Before the mountains were brought forth, or ever thou hadst formed the earth and the world, even from everlasting to everlasting, thou art God.

Then Susannah read from St Paul's Letter to the Corinthians:

> But now is Christ risen from the dead, and become the first fruits of them that slept.
>
> For since by man came death, by man came also the resurrection of the dead.

The body was taken to Kensal Green Crematorium, accompanied by several mourners.[9] Madeleine had specified her body be donated for medical use but none of her organs were suitable for transplant.[10]

Later, Bruce Beresford and Nicole Richardson went with Susannah Godman to Colville Gardens. Susannah had shouldered the burden of arrangements after Madeleine's death and, with Jane's help, had cleared the flat. The question of what to do with Madeleine's photographs and the biographical material weighed heavily on Susannah.[11] She gave Nicole the photo albums, the Little Brown Book and a little wooden jewellery box with the initials MSJ carved on the lid. Inside the box were some inexpensive necklaces and other jewellery. Bruce admired a print on the wall—a sketch of the Sydney Conservatorium, where Madeleine had gone for piano lessons in the 1950s. When they looked behind it, there was a post-it note saying that Madeleine wanted him to have it.

Christopher Potter wrote a long obituary in the *Independent*. He had been commissioned to do a small piece and had wondered where he would find enough information. Madeleine had been so private, so discreet about her past. But he found there was a great deal to say about his author:

> Language and a questioning faith are the two poles of St John's created
> world, as may also have been true of her domestic world…Beneath
> the sly and witty veneer of her writing, she explores questions that
> are basically theological: we must do the right thing, but how can
> we tell what the right thing is? This question is at the heart of all
> her novels…She lived by a strict moral code, the rules of which were
> only truly clear to herself.[12]

Control and the desire for anonymity, he wrote, were her typical charac-
teristics. Potter enjoyed researching the obituary and felt, like Alex Hill,
that Madeleine had set him a test—follow the clues and see what you
can find.[13] Florence Heller typed a summary of the funeral and sent it to
Antony Minchin. In Sydney, Annabel organised the wake for Madeleine's
Sydney friends and family at the London Tavern in Paddington. Only a
handful of people attended—Antony and Eliza Minchin, Annabel and
her two daughters Cecilia and Angela and Pamela St John's daughter Jane.

Chris Tillam was there. It had been forty years since he had seen
Antony and Annabel, at his wedding in Clifton Gardens, and almost as
long since Madeleine had left him in New York. He had had no contact
with Madeleine since the unhappy phone call in 1976 when she had told
him he owed her money. He had read *The Women in Black*, but not the
'London novels'. But he was intrigued by Madeleine's repeated theme of
infidelity and betrayal.

Chris expected to see Colette at the wake and was disappointed when
she was not there. Neither were Madeleine's half-brothers; nor Val, who had
been upset to see Ted described as 'cold' in the *Herald* obituary.

There was still no closure for Val. She wrote to Florence and included
a copy of the 1998 *HQ* magazine article that had caused such trouble. She
wanted information from her sister-in-law. Florence replied, referring
to the difficulties that Val faced in taking Madeleine and Colette as
stepdaughters only a year after their mother's death:

> I am very sorry you are going through a bad time following Madeleine's

death. I suppose it is inevitable that one mulls things over after a
death in the family, especially when there are differences, and I trust
things will fall into place...I think it is important to set the record as
straight as possible about those early days, now shrouded in the mists
of time. Thinking about it makes one conscious once again of the
terribly difficult situation you encountered when you married Ted.[14]

Val wrote again, mentioning Sylvette's multiple attempts at suicide and
Ted's devastation after her death. 'I'm sorry to have dumped all this on
you but I think it is important for you to have the facts. It is a relief to
me to have put it away and I am no longer mulling over it. This letter is
the last of it.'[15]

Madeleine's death stirred memories for Chris, too. Shortly after her
funeral, he wrote a piece about his former wife and posted it as a tribute
on the internet. It was a brief, beautifully written account of their days
in California and the east coast of the US in the 1960s. The piece was
tinged with his regret, and included a passage in which he addressed
Madeleine directly:

> We were a match, we had made of each other a refuge in the shadows
> of the ruins of two families. We each brought our demons, and in the
> confined and fragile spaces of our marriage, you gave yours free rein.[16]

Jane Holdsworth took Madeleine's ashes home to Putney, and Susannah
took the biographical material to her flat at Brixton. Later, when she
moved permanently to Suffolk, Susannah took Madeleine's papers with
her and stashed them in the attic.[17]

In Sydney, Valerie St John agonised over the letters to Ted from
Madeleine that she still held. She talked to her sons and then destroyed
them. After all, that was what her stepdaughter had specified in her will.[18]

Jane Holdsworth worried about what to do with Madeleine's ashes.
Then one summer she and her partner decided to take them to France.
They scattered some in Paris and some near Amiens, not far from the

country house where Madeleine had spent a splendid weekend some years before at the wedding of Robert and Georgina McPherson.[19]

Madeleine St John, the Australian writer who had lived a lifetime in London grieving her French mother, was at rest, in the land that Sylvette had left seventy years before.

NOTES

ABBREVIATIONS

MSJ   Madeleine St John

CSJ   Colette St John Lippincott

TSJ   Ted St John (Edward)

VSJ   Val St John (Valerie Winslow)

CT   Chris Tillam

JT   Joan Tillam

HT   Helen Trinca

FH   Florence Heller (St John)

FB   Felicity Baker

JMcC   Judith McCue

Chapter 1: A WAR BABY

1   Madeleine St John, interview, recorded by Judith McCue, London, 23–29 March 2004 (MSJ Tapes, March 2004).

2   *Ibid.*

3   Her birth certificate registered Madeleine as Mireille. On 16 July 1963, when Madeleine was twenty-one, her father wrote a note: 'To Whom it May Concern, to certify that my daughter…is identical with the child, particulars of whose birth on the 12th November, 1941, was registered under the name Mireille St John.'

4   Edward (Ted) St John (TSJ) recorded by Veronica Keraitis, for the Oral History Project, National Library of Australia (TRC830), 29–30 September 1980.

5   *Ibid.*

6   *Ibid.*

7   FB, interview with HT, 16 October 2011.

8   Edward St John recorded by Vivienne Rae-Ellis for the Oral History Project, National Library of Australia (TRC4900/70), 5–7 July 1983.

9   *Ibid.*

10 Roland St John in *Memories at Sunset,* completed in 1991 and published by his son Nigel St John in 1994.

11 FH, interview with HT, 31 March 2011.

12 TSJ, Oral History Project, 1983.

13 Marriage certificate of Yancu Meer Cargher and Feica Avram, 30 September 1916.

14 MSJ Tapes, March 2004.

15 *Ibid.*

16 Medical records of Sylvette St John, Broughton Hall Psychiatric Clinic, 16 June 1954.

17 Passenger List—Incoming Passengers, S.S. *Orama,* 29 August 1929, NSW State Archives; Passenger Arrivals Index, National Archives of Australia.

18 Passenger List—Incoming Passengers, *Cephee,* 8 June 1934, NSW State Archives.

19 *Sydney Morning Herald,* 9 September 1936, p. 13.

20 Ron Storer, email to HT, 13 April 2011.

21 Sylvette Cargier, 'Girl Students in Paris', *Sydney Morning Herald,* 22 June 1937, p. 2.

22 FH, interview with HT, 31 March 2011.

23 Ria Murch (Counsell), interview with HT, 6 November 2012.

24 Gloria Skinner (Clarton), interview with HT, 9 April 2011.

25 TSJ, letter to Sylvette St John, 27 November 1939.

26 Certificate of Registration of Alien, of Feiga Cargher, 30 September 1939. Change of abode, registered 4 June 1940.

Chapter 2: 'PICKLED IN LOVE'

1   MSJ Tapes, March 2004.

2   Lorna Harvey, interview with HT, 19 October 2011.

3   Henriette Pile, interview with HT, 1 August 2012.

4   John Minchin, letter to Margaret Minchin (St John), 1942.

5   Margaret Minchin (St John), letter to John Minchin, 27 May 1942.

6   Margaret Minchin (St John), letter to John Minchin, May 1942.

7   *Ibid.*

8   Margaret Whitlam, interview with HT, 15 June 2011.

9 TSJ, Oral History Project, 1980.

10 MSJ Tapes, March 2004.

11 *Courier-Mail,* 31 March 1937, p. 9.

12 MSJ Tapes, March 2004.

13 FB, interview with HT, 29 September 2011.

14 FH, letter to VSJ, 6 August 2006

15 MSJ Tapes, March 2004.

16 'Donald Friend: Merioola and Friends', a paper delivered by Christine France at a conference at the National Library of Australia, 23–24 February 2001.

17 TSJ, Oral History Project, 1980.

18 MSJ Tapes, March 2004.

19 *Ibid.*

20 FB, interview with HT, 29 September 2011.

21 Margaret Whitlam, interview with HT, 15 June 2011.

22 CSJ, interview with HT, 15 July 2012.

23 MSJ report card, Edgeworth school, November 1948.

24 MSJ Tapes, March 2004.

Chapter 3: SYLVETTE'S DESPAIR

1 Ingrid Wilkins (Relf), interview with HT, August 2011.

2 MSJ Tapes, March 2004.

3 Medical records of Sylvette St John, Broughton Hall Psychiatric Clinic, 16 June 1954.

4 Jonette McDonnell (Jarvis), interview with HT, 26 June 2011.

5 Margaret Whitlam, interview with HT, 21 October 2011.

6 Lorna Harvey, interview with HT, 30 August 2011.

7 CSJ, interview with HT, 22 September 2012.

8 Medical records of Sylvette St John, Broughton Hall Psychiatric Clinic, 16 June 1954.

9 MSJ Tapes, March 2004.

10 *Ibid.*

11 *Ibid.*

12 FH, letter to VSJ, 6 August 2006.

13 VSJ, letter to FH, 4 September 2006.

14 Tina Micklethwait (Date), interview with HT, 13 June 2011.

15 MSJ Tapes, March 2004.

16 CSJ, interview with HT, 17 June 2012.

17 Antony Harvey, interview with HT, 6 September 2011.

18 TSJ, evidence at coroner's inquest, 27 October 1954.

19 FH, interview with HT, 21 March 2011.

20 MSJ Tapes, March 2004.

21 CSJ, interview with HT, 23 July 2012.

22 Medical records of Sylvette St John, Broughton Hall Psychiatric Clinic, 16 June 1954.

23 VSJ, letter to FH, 4 September 2006.

24 Medical records of Sylvette St John, Reception House, Darlinghurst, 15 March 1953.

25 MSJ Tapes, March 2004.

26 *Ibid.*

27 *Ibid.*

28 Medical records of Sylvette St John, Reception House, Darlinghurst, 1953.

Chapter 4: A MOTHER LOST

1 Details of the life of Margaret Michaelis are from an article first published in *World of Antiques and Art*, Edition 68, by Helen Ennis, associate professor at the Australian National University School of Art. Ennis has also published a biography, *Margaret Michaelis: Love, loss and photography*, National Gallery of Australia, Canberra, 2005.

2 MSJ Tapes, March 2004.

3 CSJ, interview with HT, 23 July 2012.

4 Medical records of Sylvette St John, Broughton Hall Psychiatric Clinic, 16 June 1954. The comments were recorded during an interview with TSJ.

5 MSJ Tapes, March 2004.

6 CSJ, interview with HT, 15 July 2012.

7 MSJ Tapes, March 2004.

8 *Ibid.*

9 *Ibid.*

10 Medical records of Sylvette St John, Reception House, Darlinghurst, 15 March 1953.

11 *Ibid.*

12 *Ibid.*

13 *Ibid.*

14 *Ibid.*

15 MSJ Tapes, March 2004.

16 CSJ, interview with HT, 23 July 2012.
17 Medical records of Sylvette St John, Broughton Hall Psychiatric Clinic, 16 June 1954.
18 *Ibid.*
19 Margaret Whitlam, interview with HT, 15 June 2011.
20 CSJ, interview with HT, 23 July 2012.
21 CSJ, interview with HT, 22 September 2012.
22 Deslys Hunter (Moody), interview with HT, 17 August 2012.
23 Medical records of Sylvette St John, Broughton Hall Psychiatric Clinic, 16 June 1954.
24 *Ibid.*
25 Dr Marie Illingworth, statutory declaration reported in 'Mental Health Charges Sent to Minister', in *Sydney Morning Herald*, 24 November 1954, p. 1.
26 MSJ Tapes, March 2004.
27 *Catherineian,* 1954.
28 Henriette Pile, interview with HT, 1 August 2012.
29 MSJ Tapes, March 2004.
30 CSJ, interview with HT, 22 September 2012.
31 TSJ, evidence at coroner's inquest, 27 October 1954.
32 Henriette Pile, interview with HT, 1 August 2012.
33 Friedel Souhami, evidence at Coroner's inquest, 27 October 1954.
34 MSJ Tapes, March 2004.
35 Tina Micklethwait (Date), interview with HT, 13 June 2011.
36 Dr J. F. N. Thomas, letter, 13 August 1954, lodged in evidence at the coroner's inquest, 27 October 1954.
37 MSJ Tapes, March 2004.
38 CSJ, interview with HT, 15 July 2012.
39 MSJ Tapes, March 2004.
40 *Ibid.*
41 FB, interview with HT, 29 September 2011.
42 'Medical report upon the examination of the dead body', signed by Dr Stratford Sheldon, 14 August 1954, and lodged in evidence at the coroner's inquest, 27 October 1954.
43 MSJ Tapes, March 2004.
44 Henriette Pile, interview with HT, 1 August 2012.
45 FH, interview with HT, 31 March 2012.
46 CSJ, interview with HT, 24 November 2012.

47 Felicity Baker disputes this account. In her account MSJ did not hear of the family's belief that Sylvette had suicided until FB mentioned it around 1972. FB, email to HT, 14 June 2012.

48 Finding by City Coroner, Mr Frank Leonard McNamara, 27 October 1954.

49 Dr Marie Illingworth, statutory declaration reported in 'Mental Health Charges Sent to Minister', in *Sydney Morning Herald*, 24 November 1954, p. 1.

50 FB, interview with HT, 29 September 2011.

51 MSJ Tapes, March 2004.

52 CSJ, interview with HT, 22 September 2012.

Chapter 5: FLOWER GIRLS FOR A STEPMOTHER

1 MSJ Tapes, March 2004.

2 Deslys Hunter (Moody), interview with HT, 17 August 2012.

3 MSJ Tapes, March 2004.

4 VSJ, letter to FH, 4 September 2006.

5 TSJ, Oral History Project, 1980.

6 *Ibid.*

7 MSJ Tapes, March 2004.

8 CSJ, interview with HT, 15 July 2012.

9 *Ibid.*

10 MSJ Tapes, March 2004.

11 *Ibid.*

12 *Ibid.*

13 *Ibid.*

14 CSJ, interview with HT, 22 September 2012.

15 MSJ Tapes, March 2004.

16 Deslys Hunter (Moody), interview with HT, 17 August 2012.

17 CSJ, interview with HT, 22 September 2012.

18 VSJ, letter to FH, 4 September 2006.

19 CSJ, interview with HT, 22 September 2012.

20 MSJ Tapes, March 2004.

21 Diana (Didy) Harvey, interview with HT, 26 August 2011.

22 Antony Harvey, interview with HT, 6 September 2011.

23 MSJ Tapes, March 2004.

24 *Ibid.*

25 Margaret Whitlam, interview with HT, 21 October 2011.

26 MSJ Tapes, March 2004.

27 VSJ, letter to FH, 4 September 2006.
28 MSJ Tapes, March 2004.
29 CSJ, interview with HT, 22 September 2012.
30 Deslys Hunter (Moody), interview with HT, 17 August 2012.
31 MSJ Tapes, March 2004.
32 CSJ, interview with HT, 23 July 2012.
33 MSJ Tapes, March 2004.
34 CSJ, interview with HT, 15 July 2012.
35 TSJ, Oral History Project, 1983.
36 MSJ Tapes, March 2004.
37 *Ibid.*
38 *Ibid.*
39 *Queenwood Gazette*, November 1957.
40 *Ibid.*
41 *Queenwood Gazette,* November 1958.
42 Former classmate, interview with HT, 2011.
43 MSJ Tapes, March 2004.
44 Susie Osmaston (Manion), interview with HT, 14 April 2011.
45 MSJ, letter to Susie Osmaston (Manion), 24 October 1997.
46 MSJ Tapes, March 2004.
47 FH, interview with HT, 12 May 2011.
48 MSJ Tapes, 2004.
49 FB email to HT, 4 January 2013.
50 TSJ Oral History Project, 1983.
51 MSJ Tapes, March 2004.
52 *Ibid.*
53 *Ibid.*

Chapter 6: SYDNEY UNI AND THE OCTOPUS GIRLS
1 Sue Clilverd (McGowan), interview with HT, 31 May 2012.
2 MSJ Tapes, March 2004.
3 VSJ, letter to FH, 4 September 2006.
4 MSJ Tapes, March 2004.
5 Clive James, email to HT, 22 February 2011.
6 Mungo MacCallum, interview with HT, 25 March 2011.
7 *Honi Soit*, 15 October 1959.
8 Colleen Chesterman (Olliffe), interviews with HT, 15 and 21 February 2011.

9 Jane Gardiner (Iliff), interview with HT, 15 March 2011.

10 Colleen Chesterman (Olliffe), interviews with HT, 15 and 21 February 2011.

11 Sue Clilverd (McGowan), interview with HT, 31 May 2012.

12 Mungo MacCallum, interview with HT, 25 March 2011.

13 Richard Walsh, interview with HT, 18 July 2011.

14 Jonette McDonnell (Jarvis), interview with HT, 26 June 2011.

15 Sue Clilverd (McGowan), interview with HT, 31 May 2012.

16 Angela McGrath (Wills), interview with HT, 11 April 2011.

17 Mungo MacCallum, interview with HT, 25 March 2011.

18 Winton Higgins, interview with HT, 28 February 2011.

19 Clive James, email to HT, 22 February 2011.

20 Bob Ellis, 'Out-takes', in *The Best Australian Essays 2003*, ed. Peter Craven, Black Inc, Melbourne, 2003.

21 Richard Walsh, interview with HT, 18 July 2011.

22 Sue Clilverd (McGowan), interview with HT, 31 May 2012.

23 Program for *Dead Centre*, collected by Dr Laura Ginters, Department of Performance Studies, University of Sydney, and Robyn Dalton, for their forthcoming book, *The Ripples Before the (New) Wave: Sydney University Dramatic Society (1959–64)*.

24 Libby Smith, interview with HT, 5 July 2011.

25 *Ibid*.

26 Colleen Chesterman (Olliffe), interviews with HT, 15 and 21 February 2011.

27 MSJ, letter to Antony Minchin, 23 July 1996.

28 Clive James, email to HT, 22 February 2011.

29 Carol Tattersfield, 'Young, Square and Angry', in supplement to the *Australian Women's Weekly*, 30 December 1959.

30 *Sydney Morning Herald*, 25 February 1960, p. 38.

31 MSJ, quoted by Christopher Henning, 'The Essence of Being a Writer', *Sydney Morning Herald*, 20 September 1997.

Chapter 7: ADRIFT IN CASTLECRAG

1 'Title Deeds', *Sydney Morning Herald,* 6 September 2008, p. D02.

2 MSJ Tapes, March 2004.

3 CSJ, interview with HT, 15 July 2012.

4 MSJ Tapes, March 2004.

5 CSJ, interview with HT, 23 July 2012.

6 Diana (Didy) Harvey, email to HT, 30 June 2011.

7   Libby Smith, interview with HT, 5 July 2011.

8   Winton Higgins, interview with HT, 28 February 2011.

9   CSJ, interview with HT, 24 July 2012.

10 Ed St John, interview with HT, 4 July 2011.

11 Libby Smith, interview with HT, 5 July 2011.

12 Program for *Dead Centre*, collected by Dr Laura Ginters and Robyn Dalton.

13 CT, interview with HT, June 2012.

14 Louis MacNeice, 'Bagpipe Music', *Collected Poems*, Faber & Faber, reproduced with permission, David Higham, London.

15 *Sydney Morning Herald*, 9 January 1959, p. 1.

16 CT, interview with HT, June 2012.

17 CT, tribute to MSJ, posted on the internet, July 2006.

18 CT, interview with HT, June 2012.

19 *Ibid.*

20 *Ibid.*

21 *Ibid.*

22 *Ibid.*

23 Annabel Ritchie (Minchin), interview with HT, 13 August 2011.

24 MSJ, letter to JT, 14 November 1961.

25 FB, email to HT, 1 June 2012.

26 MSJ Tapes, March 2004.

27 *Ibid.*

28 CT, email to HT, June 2012.

29 Deslys Hunter (Moody), interview with HT, 17 August 2012.

30 Denise Bradley (Haren), interview with HT, 6 June 2011.

31 CT, interview with HT, June 2012.

32 *Ibid.*

33 MSJ Tapes, March 2004.

34 Jonette McDonnell (Jarvis), interview with HT, 26 June 2011.

35 CT, tribute to MSJ, 2006.

36 MSJ Tapes, March 2004.

Chapter 8: TILL DEATH US DO PART

1   CT, interview with HT, June 2012.

2   MSJ Tapes, March 2004.

3   Jill Olson (Roehrig), interview with HT, 6 July 2011.

4   CSJ, interview with HT, 23 July 2012.

5   Jill Olson (Roehrig), interview with HT, 6 July 2011.

6   CT, email to HT, 16 June 2012.

7   CT, email to HT, 14 November 2012.

8   CT, interview with HT, 16 June 2012.

9   CSJ, interview with HT, 15 July 2012.

10 FB, letter to HT, 4 October 2011.

11 MSJ, letter to FB, 30 June 1967.

12 Winton Higgins, interview with HT, 28 February 2011.

13 CSJ, interview with HT, November 2012.

14 CT, email to HT, 14 November 2012.

15 *Oz* magazine was published in Sydney 1963–69 and remains one of the best-known products of the 1960s counter-culture. Neville, Walsh and Sharp (along with Peter Grose, for a time) edited the magazine. Neville and Sharp went to London in 1967 and co-edited (with Jim Anderson) the London version of *Oz*, which was published 1967–73. In 1964, Neville, Walsh and Sharp were convicted of publishing an obscene publication by a magistrate and sentenced to jail terms. But they won on appeal.

16 Colleen Chesterman (Olliffe), interviews with HT, 15 and 21 February 2011.

17 CT, interview with HT, 16 June 2012.

18 *Ibid.*

19 Colleen Chesterman (Olliffe), interviews with HT, 15 and 21 February 2011.

20 Antony Minchin, interview with HT, 14 June 2011.

21 Marilyn 'Mandy' Chapple (Taylor), interview with HT, 11 June 2011.

22 CSJ, interview with HT, October 2012.

23 CT, tribute to MSJ, July 2006. The Belvedere Private Hotel was at 81 Bayswater Road, Rushcutters Bay, and was run by Swiss hoteliers. It was demolished in 1969 to make way for the Kings Cross Tunnel and Expressway.

24 MSJ, letter to JT, 13 June 1965.

25 MSJ, letter to JT, 27 July 1965.

Chapter 9: AMERICAN DREAMS

1   MSJ, letters to JT, 27 July and 15 September 1965.

2   CT, letter to JT, 31 July 1965.

3   CT, letter to JT, 12 June 1965.

4   MSJ, letter to JT, 27 July 1965.

5   *Ibid.*

6   *Ibid.*

7   CT, letter to JT, 31 July 1965.

8   CT, interview with HT, June 2012.

9   MSJ, letter to JT, 15 September 1965.

10 *Ibid.*

11 CT, letter to JT, 26 September 1965.

12 Henry Breitrose, interview with HT, 10 July 2011.

13 CT, letter to JT, 26 September 1965.

14 *Ibid.*

15 *Ibid.*

16 CT, interview with HT, June 2012.

17 Tom Bell, interview with HT, 5 July 2011.

18 Jill Olson (Roehrig), interview with HT, 6 July 2011.

19 MSJ, letter to JT, 25 October 1965.

20 MSJ and CT, letter to JT, 14 December 1965. Henry Miller, *The Colossus of Maroussi,* Colt Press, San Francisco, 1941; Marianne Moore, 1887–1972, was an American modernist poet.

21 MSJ, letter to JT, 28 November 1965.

22 CT, letter to JT, 10 February 1966.

23 *Ibid.*

24 CSJ, interview with HT, 15 July 2012.

25 MSJ, letter to JT, 27 December 1965.

26 *Ibid.*

27 MSJ, letter to Antony Minchin, 25 February 1966.

28 CT, letter to JT, 25 January 1966.

29 MSJ, letter to JT, 10 November 1965.

30 CT, letter to JT, 25 January 1966.

31 MSJ, letter to JT, 25 February 1966.

32 MSJ, letter to Antony Minchin, 25 February 1966.

33 MSJ, letter to Annabel Ritchie (Minchin), 25 April 1966.

34 MSJ, letter to Antony Minchin, 30 March 1966.

35 MSJ Tapes, March 2004.

36 *Ibid.*

37 *Ibid.*

38 MSJ, letter to Antony Minchin, 25 February 1966.

39 Tom Bell, interview with HT, 5 July 2011.

40 *Ibid.*

41 MSJ, letter to JT, 30 March 1966.

42 MSJ Tapes, March 2004.
43 CT, letter to JT, 6 April 1966.
44 MSJ, letter to JT, 5 May 1966.
45 *Ibid.*
46 MSJ, letter to JT, 31 May 1966.
47 MSJ, letter to JT, 15 June 1966.
48 CT, letter to JT, 13 June 1966.
49 MSJ, letter to JT, 5 May 1966.
50 MSJ, letter to JT, 23 July 1966. (The Orchestra of French-speaking Switzerland was founded by Ernest Ansermet in 1918. He remained its music director till 1967.)
51 MSJ to JT, 18 September 1966.
52 CT, letter to JT, 10 September 1966.
53 Jill Olson (Roehrig), interview with HT, 6 July 2011.
54 *Ibid.*
55 MSJ, letter to Annabel Ritchie (Minchin), 9 October 1966.
56 *Ibid.*
57 FH, interview with HT, 31 March 2011.
58 MSJ Tapes, March 2004.
59 MSJ, letter to Annabel Ritchie (Minchin), 9 October 1966.
60 MSJ Tapes, March 2004.

Chapter 10: LETTERS HOME
1 MSJ Tapes, March 2004.
2 CT, letter to JT, 3 December 1966.
3 CT, interview with HT, June 2012; Allegra May, interview with HT, 6 July 2012.
4 CT, letter to JT, 3 December 1966.
5 MSJ, letter to JT, 5 December 1966.
6 CT, letter to JT, 8 February 1967.
7 MSJ, letter to Annabel Ritchie (Minchin), 26 April 1967.
8 Allegra May, interview with HT, 6 July 2012.
9 CT, interview with HT, June 2012.
10 *Ibid.*
11 CT, email to HT, 14 November 2012.
12 CT, interview with HT, June 2012.
13 MSJ, letter to FB, 30 June 1967.
14 TSJ Oral History Project, 1980.

15 MSJ, letter to Annabel Ritchie (Minchin), 26 April 1967.

16 MSJ, letter to FB, 30 June 1967.

17 CSJ, interview with HT, 23 July 2012.

18 MSJ, letter to FB, 30 June 1967.

19 *Ibid*.

20 *Ibid*.

21 *Ibid*.

22 *Ibid*.

23 *Ibid*.

24 CT, letter to JT, 6 June 1967.

25 Tomas Kalmar, interview with HT, 5 October 2011.

26 CT, letter to JT, 16 June 1967.

27 CT, interview with HT, June 2012.

28 MSJ, letter to FB, 12 September 1967.

29 FB, interview with HT, 16 October 2011.

30 MSJ, letter to JT, 9 October 1967.

31 CT, letter to JT, 2 October 1967.

32 CT, letter to JT, 9 October 1967.

33 CT, interview with HT, 10 June 2012.

34 MSJ, letter to JT, 9 October 1967.

35 CT, interview with HT, 10 June 2012.

36 Evan Whitton, 'Operation Cover-up', *Weekend Australian*, 18 January 1997, p. 27.

37 *Ibid*. I have also drawn on Evan Whitton's excellent summary in *Can of Worms 11*, Broadway, Fairfax Library, 1986; and Hansard of TSJ's maiden speech, and other newspaper accounts.

38 TSJ, Oral History Project, 1983.

39 CT, letter to JT, 28 December 1967.

40 *Ibid*.

41 *Ibid*.

42 CT, interview with HT, June 2012.

43 *Ibid*.

44 CT, letter to JT, 28 December 1967.

45 CT, letter to JT, 10 January 1967.

46 *Ibid*.

Chapter 11: AN EXPAT IN LONDON

1   Colleen Chesterman (Olliffe), interview with HT, 15 February 2011.

2   Winton Higgins, interview with HT, 28 February 2011.

3   CSJ, interview with HT, 15 July 2012.

4   CSJ, interview with HT, 23 July 2012.

5   Daniel Le Maire, interview with HT, 16 June 2011.

6   CSJ, interview with HT, 15 July 2012.

7   MSJ Tapes, March 2004.

8   *Ibid.*

9   *Ibid.*

10 CT, tribute to MSJ, July 2006.

11 Martha Ansara, interview with HT, 3 August 2012.

12 Diana 'Didy' Harvey, interview with HT, 26 August 2011.

13 Christine Magid (Hill), interview with HT, 14 June 2011.

14 *Ibid.*

15 Chrissie de Looze, interview with HT, 25 March 2011.

16 CT and Martha Ansara, interviews with HT, June and August 2012.

17 CT, letter to JT, 11 May 1968.

18 Chrissie de Looze, interview with HT, 25 March 2011.

19 Michael Chesterman, interview with HT, 10 February 2012.

20 MSJ, letter to FB, 15 February 1969.

21 *Ibid.*

22 CT, letter to JT, 10 February 1969.

23 *Ibid.*

24 MSJ, letter to FB, 15 February 1969.

25 CT, letter to JT, 5 March 1969.

26 TSJ, Oral History Project, 1983.

27 I have drawn on a number of newspaper and internet sources to describe these events. Ted St John covers the events in *A Time to Speak*, Sun Books, 1969, as does Alan Reid in *The Gorton Experiment*, Shakespeare Head Press, 1971.

28 Sir William Watson, *The Prince's Quest*, 1880.

29 Alan Reid, *The Gorton Experiment*, Shakespeare Head Press, 1971, p. 215.

30 TSJ, Oral History Project, 1983.

31 CT, letter to JT, 21 May 1969.

32 CT, letter to JT, 5 August 1969.

33 *Ibid.*

34 FB, interview with HT, 29 September 2012.

Chapter 12: TO THE EDGE AND BACK

1 CSJ, interview with HT, 23 July 2012.

2 Christine Magid (Hill), interview with HT, 14 June 2011.

3 FB, interview with HT, 16 October 2011.

4 FH, interview with HT, 12 May 2011.

5 MSJ, letter to Margaret and John Minchin, early 1970.

6 FB, interview with HT, 16 October 2011.

7 Chrissie de Looze, interview with HT, 25 March 2011.

8 Sue Sheridan (Young), interview with HT, 25 March 2011.

9 *Ibid.*

10 Colleen Chesterman (Olliffe), interviews with HT, 15 and 21 February 2011.

11 Christine Magid (Hill), interview with HT, 14 June 2011.

12 *New Horizons: The Alternative Society*, BBC TV, 1970.

13 Winton Higgins, email to HT, 2 November 2011.

14 MSJ, letter to Vidya Jones (Sue Hill), 20 May mid to late 1970s.

15 R. D. Laing argued that mental illness could be seen as a natural response to stress, especially in families.

16 FH, interview with HT, 12 May 2011.

17 In his book, *Wisdom, Madness and Folly: The Making of a Psychiatrist 1927–57*, Macmillan, London, 1985, R. D. Laing wrote: 'I have never said that parents or families or society "cause" mental illness, genetically or environmentally…I have never called myself an anti-psychiatrist…However I agree with the anti-psychiatric thesis that by and large psychiatry functions to exclude and repress those elements society wants excluded and repressed', pp. 8–9.

18 FB, interview with HT, 16 October 2011.

19 Annabel Ritchie (Minchin), letter to John Minchin, 21 September 1971.

20 MSJ, postcard to Michael and Colleen Chesterman, 21 May 1972.

21 MSJ, letter to Margaret Minchin, 4 September 1972.

22 A collection of Zen literature first published in Japan in 1957.

23 MSJ, letter to Margaret Minchin, early 1973.

24 *Ibid.*

Chapter 13: A ROOM OF HER OWN

1 MSJ, letter to Margaret Minchin, early 1972.

2 Ingrid Wilkins (Relf), interview with HT, August 2011.

3 Ann 'Miriam' Fenton (Herbert), interview with HT, 9 October 2011.

4 Diana Herbert's diaries, 1970–74.

5   Robert Hughes, *Things I Didn't Know*, 2006.

6   Clive James, *North Face of Soho,* Picador, London, 2006, Introduction.

7   FB, interview with HT, 16 October 2011.

8   MSJ, postcard to Margaret Minchin, 5 September 1973.

9   *A Pure Clear Light*, Text Publishing, Melbourne, 2010, Chapter 25.

10 MSJ, letter to Annabel Ritchie (Minchin), 28 December 1973.

11 MSJ, letter to Antony Minchin, 27 December 1973.

12 Diana Herbert, interview with HT, 19 October 2011.

13 Vidya Jones (Sue Hill), interview with HT, 24 July 2011.

14 Christine Magid (Hill), interview with HT, 14 June 2011.

15 FH, interview with HT, 12 May 2011.

16 Robert McPherson, interview with HT, 4 May 2011.

17 Dave Codling, interview with HT, 21 July 2011.

18 *Ibid.*

19 Ann 'Miriam' Fenton (Herbert), interview with HT, 9 October 2011.

20 Dave Codling, interview with HT, 10 January 2013.

21 MSJ, letter to Vidya Jones (Sue Hill), undated.

22 Frances Barrett, interview with HT, 5 December 2012.

23 Rod Tiffen, 'China Does Not Respond Positively to Humiliation', smh.com.au, 29 July 2009.

24 FB, letter to HT, 28 June 2011.

25 Patrick St John, interview with HT, 15 February 2011.

26 CSJ, interview with HT, 15 July 2012.

27 TSJ, Oral History Project, 1980.

28 CT, tribute to MSJ, July 2006.

29 MSJ, quoted in Neil Norman, 'How the Booker Saved Me from the Job Centre', *Evening Standard,* 14 October 1997, p. 25.

Chapter 14: MADAME BLAVATSKY

1   MSJ, letter to Vidya Jones (Sue Hill), 20 May, probably mid-1970s.

2   MSJ Tapes, March 2004.

3   MSJ, letter to JMcC, 4 May 1980.

4   MSJ Tapes, March 2004.

5   MSJ, letter to Vidya Jones (Sue Hill), 3 July 1980.

6   Winton Higgins, interview with HT, 28 February 2011.

7   *Daily Mirror*, 13 November 1964.

8   MSJ Tapes, March 2004.

9   FB, letter to HT, 28 June 2011.

10 MSJ, letter to Vidya Jones (Sue Hill), 25 November 1980.

11 MSJ, letter to Vidya Jones (Sue Hill), 3 July 1980.

12 Ann 'Miriam' Fenton (Herbert), letter to family, 7 July 1980.

13 MSJ, letter to Vidya Jones (Sue Hill), 25 November 1980.

14 Ann 'Miriam' Fenton (Herbert), letter to Tim Herbert, 21 June 1980.

15 Tim Herbert, interview with HT, 19 October 2012.

16 *Ibid.*

17 *Ibid.*

18 Ann 'Miriam' Fenton (Herbert), letter to parents, 3 June 1981.

19 Roslyn Grose (Owen), interview with HT, 15 April 2011.

20 Ed St John, interview with HT, 16 April 2011.

Chapter 15: COLVILLE GARDENS

1   F. H. W. Sheppard (general editor), *Survey of London: Volume 37, Northern Kensington*, 1973.

2   Madeleine St John, 'It's Not Just a Handy Carnival Location You Know', *Guardian,* 27 April 1999.

3   Alex Hill, interview with HT, May 2011.

4   Madeleine St John, 'It's Not Just a Handy Carnival Location You Know', 1999.

5   In 2011, Dave Codling denied he did the painting.

6   Jacqueline Bateman, email to HT, 10 June 2011.

7   MSJ Tapes, March 2004.

8   Libby Smith, interview with HT, 5 July 2011.

9   FB, interview with HT, 29 September 2011.

10 Celia Irvine, interview with HT, 16 May 2011.

11 Frances Barrett, interview with HT, 5 December 2011.

12 Celia Irvine, interview with HT, 16 May 2011.

13 Frances Barrett, interview with HT, 5 December 2011.

14 MSJ, letter to JMcC, 25 November 1986.

15 MSJ Tapes, March 2004.

16 MSJ, letter to JMcC, 2 May 1991.

17   MSJ, letter to Deidre Rubenstein, 16 July 1984.

18 Celia Irvine, interview with HT, 16 May 2011.

19 Frances Barrett, interview with HT, 5 December 2011.

20 MSJ, letter to Frances Barrett, undated.

21 MSJ, letter to JMcC, 20 February 1989.

22 Frances Barrett, interview with HT, 5 December 2011.

23 MSJ, letter to Frances Barrett, undated.

24 Frances Barrett, interview with HT, 5 December 2011.

25 Vidya Jones (Sue Hill), interview with HT, 24 July 2011.

26 David Bambridge, email to HT, 31 July 2011.

27 FB, interview with HT, 16 October 2011.

28 JMcC, interview with HT, May 2011.

29 MSJ, letter to JMcC, 25 November 1986.

30 *Ibid.*

31 Patrick St John, interview with HT, 30 August 2011.

32 MSJ, letter to JMcC, 22 June 1987.

33 *Ibid.*

34 MSJ, letter to JMcC, 8 May 1990.

35 MSJ, letter to JMcC, 16 February 1988.

36 MSJ, letter to Colleen Chesterman (Olliffe), 10 March 1988.

37 Christine Magid (Hill), interview with HT, 14 June 2011.

38 MSJ, letter to JMcC, 20 February 1989.

39 *Ibid.*

40 VSJ, letter to MSJ, 24 August 1998.

41 Edward St John papers, New South Wales State Library.

42 Ed St John, interview with HT, 4 July 2011.

43 VSJ, letter to MSJ, 24 August 1998.

44 MSJ, letter to JMcC, 8 May 1990.

45 MSJ, letter to JMcC, 10 December 1990.

46 James 'Jai Narain' Hughes, interview with HT, 16 May 2011.

47 MSJ, letter to JMcC, 8 May 1990.

48 FB, email to HT, 13 June 2012.

49 MSJ, letter to JMcC, 26 October 1990.

50 *Ibid.*

51 MSJ, letter to JMcC, 10 December 1990.

52 MSJ Tapes, March 2004.

53 MSJ, letter to JMcC, 10 December 1990.

54 Ed St John, interview with HT, 4 July 2011.

55 MSJ, letter to JMcC, 10 December 1990.

56 Madeleine quoted in Christopher Henning, 'The Essence of Being a Writer', *Sydney Morning Herald*, 20 September 1997.

57 MSJ, letter to JMcC, 2 May 1991.

58 Neil Norman, 'How the Booker Saved Me from the Job Centre', 1997.

Chapter 16: THE WOMEN IN BLACK

1 FB, interview with HT, 16 October 2011.

2 Jonette McDonnell (Jarvis), interview with HT, 26 June 2011.

3 Robert McPherson, interview with HT, 4 May 2011.

4 Colleen Chesterman (Olliffe), interviews with HT, 15 and 21 February 2011.

5 Madeleine St John, *The Women in Black*, Text Publishing, Melbourne, 2009.

6 MSJ Tapes, March 2004.

7 James 'Jai Narain' Hughes, interview with HT, 16 May 2011.

8 Esther Whitby, interview with HT, 17 May 2011.

9 MSJ, letter to JMcC, 19 March 1992.

10 Robert McPherson, interview with HT, 4 May 2011.

11 *Ibid.*

12 Jane Holdsworth, interview with HT, 16 May 2011.

13 Stephen Mitchell, interview with HT, 31 August 2011.

14 Andre Deutsch, Advance Information Sheet, No 562, 1993.

15 MSJ, letter to JMcC, 15 March 1993.

16 *Ibid.*

17 *Times Literary Supplement*, 5 March 1993.

18 MSJ, letter to JMcC, 15 March 1993.

19 Robert McPherson, interview with HT, 4 May 2011.

20 Patrick St John, interview with HT, 30 August 2011.

Chapter 17: DEAR TED

1 TSJ, letter to Ron and Josette Storer, 9 May 1993.

2 TSJ Will, 2 October 1993.

3 Esther Whitby, interview with HT, 17 May 2011.

4 MSJ, letter to Sarah Lutyens, 4 October 1994.

5 MSJ, letter to Sarah Lutyens, 15 December 1994.

6 Robert McPherson, interview with HT, 4 May 2012.

7 Ed St John, interview with HT, 4 July 2011.

8 Patrick St John, interview with HT, 30 August 2011.

9 FH, interview with HT, 12 May 2011.

10 MSJ, letter to TSJ, 21 October 1994.

11 Michael Kirby, eulogy delivered in St Luke's Anglican Church, Mosman, 3 November 1994.

12   Tony Stephens, 'They Came to Honour Edward St John: A Pilgrim of the Power of One', *Sydney Morning Herald*, 4 November 1994, p. 2.

13   Hansard, House of Representatives, 7 November 1994, pp. 2680–81.

14   Don Dobie, letter to MSJ, 12 July 1995.

15   MSJ, letter to Colleen Chesterman (Olliffe), 29 December 1994.

Chapter 18: A MOMENT IN THE SUNSHINE

1   Bruce Beresford, introduction to *The Women in Black*, Text Publishing, Melbourne, 2009.

2   FB, interview with HT, 16 October 2011.

3   Clive James, email to HT, 22 February 2011.

4   MSJ quoted in Christopher Henning, 'The Essence of Being a Writer', *Sydney Morning Herald*, 20 September 1997.

5   Bruce Beresford, interview with HT, 11 February 2012.

6   CSJ, interview with HT, 22 September 2012.

7   Jonette McDonnell (Jarvis) and Siobhan McDonnell, interview with HT, 26 June 2011.

8   Annabel Ritchie (Minchin), interview with HT, 13 August 2011.

9   Colleen Chesterman (Olliffe), interview with HT, February 2011.

10   MSJ, letter to Antony Minchin, 31 July 1995.

11   *Ibid*.

12   MSJ, quoted in Christopher Henning, 'The Essence of Being a Writer', *Sydney Morning Herald*, 20 September 1997.

13   MSJ, letter to JMcC, 26 September 1993.

14   JMcC, email to HT, 18 November 2012.

15   Sarah Lutyens, letter to Tom Rosenthal, 28 March 1995.

16   Milton Drake, Al Hoffman and Jerry Livingston, 'Mairzy Doats', composed in 1943.

17   Tom Rosenthal, letter to Sarah Lutyens, 24 March 1995.

18   Carole Welch, letter to Sarah Lutyens, 20 March 1995.

19   Fanny Blake, letter to Sarah Lutyens, 12 April 1995.

20   Jonathan Burnham, letter to Sarah Lutyens, 27 March 1995.

21   Joanna Goldsworthy, letter to Sarah Lutyens, 28 March 1995.

22   Christopher Potter, fax to Sarah Lutyens, 30 March 1995.

23   FB, interview with HT, 16 October 2011.

24   Christopher Potter, fax to Sarah Lutyens, 30 March 1995.

25   MSJ, letter to Sarah Lutyens, 16 May 1995.

26 'Jesus Bids Us Shine', words by Susan Bogert Warner, music by Edwin Othello Excell, first published in the children's magazine, *The Little Corporal*, in 1868.

27 Peter Craven, 'Light as Air, and Deep as the Darkening Sky', *Weekend Australian*, 27 November 2010, p. 22.

28 MSJ, letter to Antony Minchin, 2 March 1996.

29 Madeleine St John, *A Pure Clear Light*, Text Publishing, Melbourne, 2010.

30 Sarah Lutyens, interview with HT, 7 December 2011.

31 MSJ Tapes, March 2004. Colette rejects this comment.

32 MSJ, letter to Antony Minchin, 2 March 1996.

33 *Ibid.*

34 Robert McPherson, interview with HT, 4 May 2011.

35 MSJ, letter to Antony Minchin, 2 March 1996.

36 Alex Hill, interview with HT, May 2011.

37 *Ibid.*

38 *Ibid.*

39 MSJ, letter to Annabel Ritchie (Minchin), 6 May 1997.

40 CT, email to HT, 14 November 2012. Buffy quote from *Buffy the Vampire Slayer*, season five, episode 22, 22 May 2001.

41 MSJ, letter to JMcC, 14 November 1995.

42 Peta Worth, interview with HT, 10 October 2011.

43 Jane Holdsworth, interview with HT, 16 May 2011.

Chapter 19: THE ESSENCE AND THE BOOKER

1 Christopher Potter, interview with HT, 12 May 2011.

2 Sarah Lutyens, interview with HT, 7 December 2011.

3 *Ibid.*

4 Felicity Rubinstein, letter to Barry Humphries, 9 May 1997.

5 MSJ, postcard to Felicity Rubinstein, May 1997.

6 Madeleine St John, *The Essence of the Thing*, Text Publishing, Melbourne, 2009.

7 MSJ disagreed it was autobiographical. In Neil Norman, 'How the Booker Saved Me from the Job Centre', *Evening Standard*, 14 October 1997, p. 25, Madeleine said the novel owed nothing to her own experience: 'I am not paying off an old score…I know that there are writers who are heavily autobiographical, like Muriel Spark, but there is no way I could bring off a trick like that.'

8 Christopher Potter, interview with HT, 12 May 2011.

9 Melvyn Bragg in Channel 4 direct telecast of Booker dinner, 1997, Oxford Brookes University archive.

10 Jason Cowley, quoted in 'Tears, Tiffs and Triumphs', *Guardian,* 6 September 2008.

11 Luke Slattery, 'Mystery Writer', *Australian*, 17 September 1997.

12 CSJ, interview with HT, 24 November 2012.

13 Luke Slattery, 'Mystery Writer', *Australian*, 17 September 1997.

14 Christopher Henning, 'Booker Listing Sends Madeleine "a Bit Barmy"', *Sydney Morning Herald,* 17 September 1997.

15 Ed St John, 'Madeleine St John: a brother's story', *Sydney Morning Herald*, 17 September 1997.

16 Annabel Ritchie (Minchin) to HT, 13 August 2011.

17 Andrew Clark, 'Essence of St John', *Age,* 20 September 1997.

18 MSJ, quoted in Christopher Henning, 'The Essence of Being a Writer', *Sydney Morning Herald*, 20 September 1997.

19 MSJ Tapes, March 2004.

20 Emma Cook, 'Tea Lady, Check-out Girl? No, I'll Stick to Writing', *Independent on Sunday*, 21 September 1997.

21 Libby Brooks, 'Stranger than Fiction', *Guardian Weekly*, 5 October 1997.

22 Neil Norman, 'How the Booker Saved Me from the Job Centre', 1997.

23 Andrew Riemer, 'Shedding Light on British Prejudices', *Sydney Morning Herald,* 27 September 1997, p. 11.

24 *Ibid.*

25 *Ibid.*

26 'Judging the Booker Prize', *Economist*, 2 October 1997.

27 Gillian Beer, quoted in Jane Cornwell, 'The Essence of an Expat', *HQ*, November/December 1998.

28 Christopher Potter, interview with HT, 12 May 2011.

29 *Ibid.*

30 Gillian Beer in Channel 4 direct telecast of Booker dinner, 1997, Oxford Brookes University archive.

31 Lisa Jardine, 'The Brit Reaction to the Booker', *Guardian*, October 1997.

32 Jane Holdsworth, interview with HT, 16 May 2011.

33 Jacqueline Bateman, interview with HT, 10 June 2011.

34 CSJ, interview with HT, 22 September 2012.

35 Aaron Lippincott, interview with HT, 22 September 2012.

36 Libby Smith, interview with HT, 5 July 2011.

37 Esther Whitby's unpublished manuscript.

38 CT, email to HT, 14 November 2012.

39   MSJ, letter to Sue Manion (Susie Osmaston), 26 August 1998.

Chapter 20: A SENSE OF BETRAYAL
1   Ed St John, interview with HT, 4 July 2011.
2   VSJ, letter to MSJ, 24 August 1998.
3   VSJ, letter to MSJ, 12 July 1998.
4   *Ibid.*
5   MSJ, letter to VSJ, 11 August 1998.
6   VSJ, letter to MSJ, 24 August 1998.
7   *Ibid.*
8   Jane Cornwell, 'The Essence of an Expat', *HQ*, November/December 1998.
9   MSJ, letter to VSJ, 7 January 2003.
10   Jane Cornwell, 'The Essence of an Expat', 1998.
11   MSJ, letter to Tress Cocks & Maddox, 14 May 1999.
12   Jane Cornwell, 'The Essence of an Expat', 1998.
13   MSJ, letter to Tress Cocks & Maddox, 14 May 1999.
14   MSJ, letter to VSJ, 7 January 2003.
15   *Ibid.*
16   MSJ, letter to Tress Cocks & Maddox, 14 May 1999.
17   Jane Cornwell, email to HT, 6 April 2012.
18   Tress Cocks & Maddox, letter to MSJ, 27 May 1999.
19   MSJ, letter to Tress Cocks & Maddox, 1 June 1999.
20   Tress Cocks & Maddox, letter to VSJ, 21 July 1999.
21   Clayton Utz, letter to Tress Cocks & Maddox, 9 August 1999.
22   ACP Publishing Pty Ltd, letter to Tress Cocks & Maddox, 27 July 1999.
23   MSJ, letter to Tress Cocks & Maddox, 23 August 1999.

Chapter 21: A STAIRWAY TO PARADISE
1   MSJ, quoted in Christopher Henning, 'The Essence of Being a Writer,' *Sydney Morning Herald*, 20 September 1997.
2   Kent Carroll, interview with HT, 3 August 2011.
3   *Ibid.*
4   *Ibid.*
5   Thomas Cranmer, Archbishop of Canterbury, 1553–55.
6   'I'll Build a Stairway to Paradise' was written in 1922 by George Gershwin with lyrics by Bud De Sylva and Ira Gershwin.
7   CT, tribute to MSJ, July 2006.

8   Madeleine St John, *A Stairway to Paradise*, Text Publishing, Melbourne, 2010.

9   Christopher Potter, interview with HT, 12 May 2011.

10 *Ibid*.

11 Sarah Lutyens, fax to Christopher Potter, 30 November 1998.

12 Christopher Potter, fax to Sarah Lutyens, 7 December 1998.

13 Sarah Lutyens, interview with HT, 7 December 2011.

14 Kathy Kettler learnt of the novel and the dedication in a phone call from HT in 2011.

15 Helen Dunmore, 'Marital Arts Expert,' *The Times*, March 1999.

16 Stephen Amidon, 'Trying to Be Good in a Naughty World', *Sunday Times*, 1999.

17 David Robson, 'Under-achieving, Except in Love', *Sunday Telegraph*, 21 March 1999.

18 FB, note to Antony Minchin, 1999.

19 MSJ, note to Christopher Potter, 25 October 1999.

20 Sarah Lutyens, letter to Tiffany Daness at the *Daily Telegraph*, 30 April 1999.

21 Sarah Lutyens, interview with HT, 7 December 2011.

22 *Ibid*.

23 Angus Towler, letter to Susannah Godman, 15 April 1999.

24 Irena Meldris, letter to Susannah Godman, 25 March 1999.

25 MSJ, letter to Sarah Lutyens, 12 December 2000.

26 Sarah Lutyens, interview with HT, 14 May 2011.

Chapter 22: A TOURIST IN ATHENS

1   Robert Tooley, interview with HT, 10 February 2011.

2   Teresa Attlee (Ahern), interview with HT, 3 May 2011.

3   *Ibid*.

4   Tomas Kalmar, interview with HT, 11 October 2011.

5   Georg Kalmar, interview with HT, 7 October 2011.

6   MSJ, letter to Eliza Minchin, 13 November 2000.

Chapter 23: FRIENDSHIPS LOST AND FOUND

1   Teresa Attlee (Ahern), interview with HT, 3 May 2011.

2   Jane Holdsworth, interview with HT, 16 May 2011.

3   Sarah Middleton, interview with HT, February 2011.

4   Susannah Godman, interview with HT, 2 September 2011.

5   Sarah Lutyens, interview with HT, 7 December 2011.

6   Bruce Beresford, interview with HT, 11 February 2011.

7   Kent Carroll, interview with HT, 3 August 2011.

8   Jane Cornwell, 'The Essence of an Expat', 1998.

9   JMcC, interview with HT, January 2011.

10 FH, email to HT, 1 March 2012.

11 FB, interview with HT, 16 October 2011.

12 Ron Storer, interview with HT, 17 March 2011.

13 CSJ, interview with HT, 23 July 2012.

14 Robert McPherson, interview with HT, 4 May 2011.

15 Unpublished novel by Madeleine St John.

16 Kent Carroll, interview with HT, 3 August 2011.

17 Susannah Godman, interview with HT, 2 September 2011.

18 *Ibid.*

19 VSJ, letter to MSJ, 7 August 2002.

20 MSJ, letter to VSJ, 7 January 2003.

21 Susannah Godman, interview with HT, 2 September 2011.

22 Peta Worth, interview with HT, 10 October 2011.

23 *Ibid.*

24 Sarah Lutyens, interview with HT, 7 December 2011.

25 MSJ, letter to Antony Minchin, 19 August 2005.

26 Sarah Lutyens, interview with HT, 1 December 2011.

27 MSJ, Will, 5 March 2004.

28 Memorandum of wishes, in Will of Madeleine St John.

Chapter 24: HER OWN STORY

1   JMcC, interview with HT, 16 May 2011.

2   MSJ Tapes, March 2004.

3   JMcC, interview with HT, February 2011.

4   *Ibid.*

5   MSJ, letter to Colleen Chesterman (Olliffe), 29 December 1994.

6   MSJ, letter to Josette Storer, 22 April 2004.

7   Nicole Richardson, interview with HT, 30 April 2011.

8   MSJ, letter to Antony Minchin, 19 August 2005.

9   Bruce Beresford, 'Madeleine and Me', introduction to *The Women in Black*, Text Publishing, Melbourne, 2009.

10 Tape of funeral service for Josette Storer.

11 Ron Storer, letter to 'Madeleine's carer', 19 June 2006.

12 JMcC, interview with HT, 2011.

13 Susannah Godman, interview with HT, 2 September 2011.
14 *Ibid.*
15 *Ibid.*

Chapter 25: AFTER MADELEINE

1 Susannah Godman, interview with HT, 2 September 2011.
2 Tony Stephens, 'Writer Exposed British Mores', *Sydney Morning Herald*, 29 June 2006.
3 *Sydney Morning Herald*, 1 July 2006.
4 Antony Minchin, letter to FH, 7 July 2006.
5 Florence Heller, 'Madeleine's funeral', undated.
6 Sarah Lutyens, interview with HT, 14 May 2011.
7 Susannah Godman, interview with HT, 2 September, 2011.
8 Florence Heller, 'Madeleine's funeral', undated.
9 *Ibid.*
10 Susannah Godman, email to HT, 29 October 2012.
11 Susannah Godman, interview with HT, 2 September 2011.
12 Christopher Potter, Madeleine St John obituary, *Independent*, 6 July 2006.
13 Christopher Potter, interview with HT, 12 May 2011.
14 FH, letter to VSJ, 6 August 2006.
15 VSJ, letter to FH, 4 September 2006.
16 CT, tribute to MSJ, July 2006.
17 Susannah Godman, interview with HT, 2 September 2011.
18 Ed St John, interview with HT, 4 July 2011.
19 Jane Holdsworth, interview with HT, 16 May 2011.

ACKNOWLEDGMENTS

Madeleine St John destroyed most of her papers before she died, so piecing her life together was only possible with the help of her family and friends.

Colette St John Lippincott was open and generous and gave me access to a central part of Madeleine's story—Sylvette's psychiatric records.

Chris Tillam provided material and extensive correspondence between Madeleine and his mother Joan Tillam.

Judith McCue allowed me to use nine hours of interviews she recorded with Madeleine in London in 2004. Few biographers receive such a gift and I am grateful to Judith.

Florence Heller was a vital link to the Ted and Sylvette years. Felicity Baker spoke at length about the times she shared with her cousin in the US and London, and provided key letters and photographs. Annabel Ritchie and Antony Minchin offered childhood memories and precious adult correspondence.

Ed St John and Patrick St John supported the biography, knowing it would inevitably contain hurtful statements from Madeleine about their parents.

Nicole Richardson allowed me to see family photographs and records, and her father Ron Storer offered important documentation and memories of Jean and Feiga Cargher.

Henriette Pile, Lorna Harvey, Ria Murch and Gloria Skinner and, before her death, Margaret Whitlam recalled memories of the young Sylvette.

Deslys Hunter, Jennifer Palmer, Angela McGrath, Susie Osmaston, Roslyn Grose and Sue Schauer shared memories of St Catherine's and Queenwood. Thanks to Tina Micklethwait, Ingrid Wilkins, Roger Parkes, Jonette McDonnell, Renate Watkinson, Antony Harvey and Didy Harvey for memories of Castlecrag.

Madeleine's friends from Sydney University were keen to help record the life of their friend. Thanks to Colleen Chesterman, Jane Gardiner, Sue Clilverd, Libby Smith, Marilyn Chapple, Denise Bradley, Robbie Brentnall, Richard Walsh, Mungo MacCallum, Katherine Cummings, Peter Grose, Lee Cataldi and Winton Higgins.

Chrissie de Looze, Daniel Le Maire, Sue Sheridan and Michael Chesterman provided information about the early London years. American memories came from Tom Bell, Henry Breitrose, Mike Rubbo, Jill Roehrig Olson and Tomas Kalmar.

The Hill sisters—Vidya Jones, Chrissie Magid and Catherine Knoles—and the Herbert siblings—Ann Fenton, Diana Herbert and Tim Herbert—along with James Hughes and Deidre Rubenstein recalled the ashram period. Dave Codling didn't miss a beat when I tracked him down in Yorkshire to quiz him about an affair forty years ago. Madeleine's connection with All Saints was described by Frances Barrett, Alex Hill, Celia Irvine, David Bambridge and Jacqueline Bateman. Teresa Attlee, Rob Tooley and Kathy Tooley spoke warmly of the friend met in Greece. Thanks to Robert McPherson, Felicity Marno and Sir Stephen Mitchell for recollections of Madeleine as antique dealer and friend.

Madeleine's agent and publishers encouraged the project. Thanks to Esther Whitby, Christopher Potter, Sarah Lutyens and Kent Carroll. Susannah Godman and Jane Holdsworth, who were so close to Madeleine at the end, require special thanks. Bruce Beresford, Madeleine's literary executor, was an enthusiast from the start, and Clive James, an unabashed St John fan, helped via email.

Thanks also to Sarah Middleton, Peta Worth, Steve Lippincott, Aaron Lippincott , Priscilla and David Maxwell, Georg Kalmar, Jane Cornwell, Martha Ansara, Andy Costain, John McDonnell, Siobahn McDonnell and Phil Jones. Many people helped with documentation: Laura Ginters; staff at the National Library of Australia and the New South Wales State archives; Chris Fowler and staff at the Oxford Brookes University archives in the UK; Evangeline Galettis, school archivist at St Catherine's as well as Averil Condren and Beryl Cato; Donna Hughes, executive officer at the Queenwood Old Girls Association; and Chris Jenkins, who helped interpret Sylvette's medical records. Kathy Kettler was hard to find but the effort was worth it to hear her joy when told Madeleine had dedicated a novel to her. Angela and Darryl Miller, the current owners of Number 9 The Rampart, generously allowed me to view Madeleine's childhood home, and the residents of 53A Colville Gardens let me see inside her London flat.

Madeleine is a book thanks to the vision of Michael Heyward and the team at Text, especially senior editor Jane Pearson, who transformed my draft.

Thanks, as always, to my colleagues at the *Australian* for their conversation and interest.

I am grateful to all those who read chapters, provided feedback, or simply tolerated my Madeleine obsession over two years, especially Melinda Jamieson and Mathew Trinca (who also fed me during an Italian winter), Bruce Wood (ditto in London), Lyndall Crisp, Geraldine Doogue, Bob and Mathilde Swift, David Harman, Robin Trinca, Warren Scott, Jenny McPhee and Chris Ballantyne. Special thanks to my mother, Jo Trinca, for her unconditional support.

INDEX

Rothfield, Ronald (Raja Ram) 128, 136
Rubbo, Mike 80, 85
Rubenstein, Deidre 129, 154–5
Rubinstein, Felicity 174, 189, 190–1,
  198, 228
Rusbridger, Alan 198
Ryde, NSW 14–15, 16, 22, 231

S

San Francisco 85, 95, 96, 97, 119
Self, Will 198
Sharp, Martin 82
Sheldon, Stratford 38
'Shells' (MSJ) 51–2
Slattery, Luke 193
Sly, Ian 14, 231
Smith, Libby 61–2, 63, 67, 200
Souhami, Friedel 18, 19, 23, 36, 66–7,
  71, 167, 187
Souhami, Manfred 18
Souhami, Renate 18, 66, 187
Spain 218–19, 233
St Catherine's School, Waverley 8 32,
  43, 50, 152, 231, 232,
  MSJ and Colette Lippincott sent to
    board at 27–9, 31, 32, 35, 36–7, 38,
    41–2, 46
St John, Edward (Ed) (MSJ's
  half-brother)
  and HQ magazine's article about
    MSJ 206, 207, 208
  birth 65
  relationship with MSJ 76, 139, 143,
    149, 176
  Sydney Morning Herald article
    about MSJ 194–5, 206, 225
St John, Edward (Ted) (MSJ's father)
  and Sylvette St John's death 36–7,
    38, 39, 42, 242
  and Val St John 41, 42–3, 46, 47, 48,
    102, 174, 175
  birth and childhood 5, 54
  career 4, 14, 20, 30, 43, 57, 82, 97,
    102, 104, 109–10, 122–3, 129, 138,
    140, 142, 143, 176–7
  education 4, 6

fatherhood 12, 13, 50, 65
illness and death 175–6
involvement with Sylvette's
  psychiatric treatment 29–30,
  33–4
marriage 4, 8–9, 10, 11, 12–13, 15,
  19–21, 22, 23, 24, 31–2, 33, 35
military service 3, 4, 9, 10, 11, 12
relationship with MSJ 2, 44–5, 127,
  161, 177–8, 194, 195–6, 222–3, 233
will 173–4, 175, 202, 203, 205
St John, Florence *see* Heller, Florence
St John, Frederick de Porte (MSJ's
  grandfather) 4–5, 9, 49, 54
St John, Hannah Phoebe Mabel (née
  Pyrke) 5, 6, 9, 11
St John, Henry (MSJ's great
  grandfather) 4–5
St John, Karen 158, 172
St John, Madeleine
  abortion 138
  article on gardenias 213–15
  article on Notting Hill 151, 213
  ashram involvement 128, 131, 133,
    134, 146, 147, 153
  birth 3
  British citizenship 2, 180
  childhood 10, 11–12, 13–14, 15, 18,
    22, 23
  death and funeral 228, 236–42
  divorce 119–20, 123, 124, 130–1,
    140, 145–6, 196
  engagement and marriage 77, 80–3
  financial issues 72, 73, 74, 118, 129,
    142, 155–6, 164, 173
  French studies 54–5, 135, 144
  funeral 228, 238–40
  haiku poems 221, 224
  health problems 1, 101–2, 103–6,
    107, 111, 120–1, 125–8, 129–30,
    183, 200, 216, 217, 219, 220, 222,
    227, 230, 231, 234–5, 236
  Helena Blavatsky biography 133,
    134, 141–2, 153–4, 155, 158–9,
    160–2, 165, 166, 232, 233